Women Pilots of World War II

Women Pilots of World War II

Jean Hascall Cole

B-29

University of Utah Press
Salt Lake City

∞ The paper in this book meets the standards for permanence and durability
established by the Committee on Production Guidelines for Book Longevity of
the Council on Library Resources

Passage quoted on page 114 is reprinted with permission of Athaneum
Publishers, an imprint of Macmillan Publishing Co., from *The Secret Armies*
by Albert Marrin. Copyright © 1985 Albert Marrin.

Library of Congress Cataloging-in-Publication Data

Cole, Jean Hascall, 1922–
      Women pilots of World War II / Jean Hascall Cole.
         p.   cm.
      Includes index.
      ISBN 0–87480–374–8
      1. World War, 1939–1945—Aerial operations, American. 2. Women's
Air Service Pilots (U.S.)—History. 3. Women's Air Service Pilots
(U.S.)—Biography. 4. Women air pilots—United States—Biography.
I. Title. II. Title: Women Pilots of World War Two. III. Title:
Women Pilots of World War 2.
D790.C62 1992
940.54'4973'088042—dc20   91–29973
                                                                        CIP

Dedication

This book is dedicated to the memory of Betty Stine, Marie Michell Robinson, and Susan Clarke, of Class 44-W-2, and to the thirty-five other WASPs who gave their lives in service to their country.

P-51

Contents

Foreword

The first women military pilots in the history of our country helped to ease the pilot shortage in World War II and then stepped quietly into the pages of history.

Historians of military aviation, digging into many documents previously classified as confidential or secret, will find the remarkable record of these women.

The need for aviators and airplanes during the war years of 1941 to 1944 taxed the nation's resources. Thus, the decision was made by the Army Air Forces to try an experiment—to use women pilots. When the plea went out through newspapers and recruiters and into the ranks of civilian pilots that the AAF was recruiting women pilots, 25,000 young women volunteered. Of these, 1,830 were accepted and 1,074 completed flight training, having relearned flying "the Army way." They graduated, receiving their wings.

Known as WASPs, an acronym for Women Air Force Service Pilots, this group was formed into two segments in September 1942. The first was known as WAFS (Women's Auxiliary Ferrying Squadron), and the second as WFTD (Women's Flying Training Detachment).[1]

The WAFS, all exceptionally qualified pilots, were assigned directly to duties as civilian ferry pilots with the Ferrying Division, Second Ferrying Group, New Castle Army Air Base, Wilmington, Delaware.[2] They were given no flight training other than that required to check out on military airplanes. They were led by twenty-eight-year-old and Vassar-trained Nancy Love, a pilot with an extensive background who was already familiar with military protocol and with the Ferrying Division of the Air Transport Command (ATC) in particular. She had been employed in the Operations Office of the Domestic Wing, Air Corps Ferrying Command, Baltimore, Maryland. Her husband, Major Robert M. Love, was Administrative Executive of the Ferrying Command.[3]

The flight training program (WFTD), designated as the 319th Army Air Forces Flight Training Detachment, in Houston, Texas, was under the direction of Jacqueline Cochran, a world-renowned racing pilot. Graduates of this training school were to be assigned as ferry pilots within the Air Transport Command.[4]

From this school a total of eighteen classes of women pilots graduated. One class entered training each month between November 1942 and April 1944. The last class graduated in December 1944, the month the entire program was deactivated.[5]

In August 1943, or eleven months following the go-ahead for the WAFS and WFTDs, the two groups were merged into a single organization known as WASP (Women Air Force Service Pilots). Miss Cochran was appointed Director of Women Pilots with Mrs. Love as WASP Executive with the staff of the Ferrying Division of the Air Transport Command.[6]

The program for women pilots was initiated as a Civil Service program. The Commanding General of the Army Air Forces intended that it would eventually be militarized. This never happened, and the WASPs were disbanded as civilians.

This book, researched and written by Jean Hascall Cole, herself a WASP, documents the women of her class, the tenth class of women pilot trainees. The class entered training in August 1943 with 111 trainees. At graduation in March 1944, only forty-nine women received the coveted WASP wings. Sixty-one had been eliminated from the program or had resigned.[7] Mrs. Cole details the flight training accident in which one girl died and the deaths of two others while flying at their assigned duty stations.

Almost all living members of this class were contacted and interviewed by Mrs. Cole. It had been nearly fifty years between their WASP experiences and the time they reminisced with Mrs. Cole. This time period allowed the author and those interviewed to bring mature assessments and balance to their recollections.

Few books have documented WASP history. None has used the unusual treatment employed by Mrs. Cole. It allows her to make use of the opinions of many to broaden the understanding and assessment of WASP experiences.

When the program for women pilots was initiated in 1942, its objectives were these: (1) to see if women could serve as military pilots and, if so, to form the nucleus of an organization that could be rapidly expanded; (2) to release male pilots for combat; and (3) to decrease the Air Forces' total demands on the cream of the manpower pool. Of these objectives, Miss Cochran wrote in her final report:

The experimental purpose of the program ranked along with but subordinate to the purpose of releasing male pilots from routine and non-combat duties for combat service. In the fall of 1942, it seemed clear that every pilot released from home duty for front line duty was needed urgently.[8]

The WASP program went through many changes during its twenty-eight-month existence. The Army, never having dealt with women pilots, had much to learn (and much to unlearn) about their physical capabilities, their adaptability, their aptitude and psychological make-up, but primarily about their talents as pilots.

It is the aim of this introduction to discuss several aspects of the WASP program which were altered as the program progressed. It may then allow the reader to place Mrs. Cole's class, 44-W-2, within the context of the total program.

Probably one of the factors most affecting the changes in the program was the amount of previous flight experience each girl had before she entered the WASP. The WAFS and the early classes of the WFTD had a great deal of previous flight time. For example, of the original twenty-five women pilots in the WAFS, one had as many as 2,627 flight hours. Their average flight time was 1,162 hours.[9] This was a lot of flying time for someone who was no more than thirty-five years old. As the number of candidates with lots of flying time decreased, the requirements were slackened. Soon candidate cadets were required to have only a private pilot license, and eventually only a student pilot license with thirty-five hours of flight experience. Flight requirements never dropped below this level.

When the women pilots were first recruited for the WAFS they had to meet stiff requirements. They had to be between the ages of twenty-one and thirty-five, be American citizens and high school graduates, and pass the standard Army ''64'' physical examination administered by an Army flight surgeon. They had to have logged over five hundred hours of flight time and hold a commercial pilot license with a rating allowing them to fly aircraft of two hundred horsepower or more. They had to pass an Army flight check and each had to report at her own expense at Wilmington, Delaware, for the recruiting interview and flight test.

The women applying for the flight training school (WFTD) usually had less flight time than the WAFS. While they did not need to pass a pre-acceptance flight test or have a commercial license, they did have to meet all other criteria plus meet a height requirement of at least sixty inches.

As the flight experience requirement decreased, the height requirement was increased. In April 1943, it rose from sixty inches to sixty-two and a half inches. In the summer of 1944 it went to sixty-four inches.[10]

The age minimum changed as the Army gained experience with its women pilots. The age requirement was reduced in August 1943 (the month class 44-W-2 entered training) from twenty-one years to eighteen years and six months (the minimum age for male pilots was eighteen years).[11]

Other changes took place as the program progressed. A major one involved the location of the flight school. The training program started in Houston, Texas, at the Houston Municipal Airport, designated as the 319th AAFFTD (Army Air Forces Flying Training Detachment). With no military housing available, the trainees were billeted in local motels and bussed to the airport. This arrangement was totally unsatisfactory for a military flight training school.[12]

The school was moved to Avenger Field in the west Texas town of Sweetwater. This was to become the only flight school in the history of United States military flight training to be devoted exclusively to the training of women flight cadets. It was known as the 318th AAFFTD. Those training at Houston were moved to Sweetwater, along with the aircraft, as rapidly as possible. The move began in February 1943 and was complete in time for the graduation of the second class in May 1943.

Only one class of women flight cadets graduated from a field other than Avenger Field. This was the first class, which graduated in April 1943 and received its wings in a ceremony at the military base at Ellington Field, Houston, Texas.

The class designations 43-W-1, 43-W-2, etc., indicated the year of graduation as the first numbers, followed by the letter ''W'' for woman pilot and then by a number showing the order of the class graduation within the year. Thus, Class 43-W-1 was the first class of women pilots graduating in 1943. Class 44-W-2 was the second class of women pilots graduating in 1944.

The types of aircraft used for training changed considerably over the period of the WASP program. In the early phases of the program, military training aircraft were in short supply and the women pilots flew civilian-type aircraft. As training planes became available, and the curricula at Avenger Field changed, different training planes were required.

The first class started with a wide variety of light civilian aircraft similar to the military liaison (L) aircraft: L-3 Taylorcraft, L-4 Pipers, L-5 Stinsons, etc. Initially all training was to be given on these liaison planes, with transition to the military basic trainers, BT-13 Vultees, at the end of the course. While the curriculum called for instrument training in a Link Trainer, there was no Link Trainer available.[13]

As an example of this hodgepodge of light aircraft, twenty-six different types of aircraft were assigned to the 319th AAFFTD in Houston. With the move to Sweetwater, the liaison aircraft were eliminated and the types of aircraft more closely matched those of other military contract pilot training schools. Fairchild PT-19s were used for fifty-five hours of primary training, Vultee BT-13s or 15s were used for sixty-five hours of basic training, and North American AT-6s and the twin-engine Cessna AT-17s were used for sixty hours of advanced training.[14]

The length of the training program also changed. The program designed for class 43-W-1 called for completion within sixteen weeks. The trainees were to be given 115 hours of flight training, 20 hours of instrument training in a Link Trainer, 180 hours of academic instruction, and one hour per day of physical training. By January 1943, the program was extended to 22½ weeks, with 170 flight hours and 230 hours of ground school. In April 1943, starting with Class 43-W-6, the program went to twenty-four weeks, with 180 flight hours and 30 hours of Link instruction. In August 1943 the ground school program was increased to 406 hours.

This constant change in the training curriculum approached a leveling off in the middle of 1943. The start of this new training plan began with Class 44-W-1, which entered training in July 1943. The changes were made slowly and it was not until Class 44-W-5, entering training in November 1943, that they were complete.[15]

Class 44-W-2, the class highlighted in this book, was receiving training during this time of changes. Probably the most important of these changes were the following:

—Increase in training period to twenty-seven weeks
—Increase in flight program of instruction to 210 hours
—The Boeing Stearman PT-17 open biplane was phased into primary instruction after Class 44-W-2, which used the open low-wing PT-19 airplane
—Concentration of instrument flying into one phase
—Elimination of all twin-engine flight training
—Increase in navigation (cross-country) training
—Increase in ground instruction

Trainees were to move on to the advanced trainer, the North American AT-6, immediately upon completion of primary training.[16] The basic flight trainers, BT-13 or BT-15, were used for instrument flight instruction after training in the AT-6. Then the final phase called for a 2,000-mile cross-country flight made in the AT-6.

The number of cadets entering training varied from a low of twenty-eight to a high of 150 in any one class. The high point in terms of the number of cadets who were in training at any one time was reached at the graduation of Class 44-W-2, when 523 students called Avenger Field home.[17]

The recognition by the AAF of the piloting capabilities of its women pilots changed almost constantly. From the very beginning the WAFS were proving their ability to fly much more complex and faster aircraft than the liaison-type airplanes to which they had been initially assigned. As the graduates of the training school (WFTD) joined them, this trend continued. The first five graduating classes and part of the sixth (43-W-6) were assigned to the Ferry Command at one of four bases: Second Ferrying Group, New Castle Army Air Base, Wilmington, Delaware; Third Ferrying Group, Romulus, Michigan; Fifth Ferrying Group, Love Field, Dallas, Texas; Sixth Ferrying Group, Long Beach, California. After that, graduates went to various commands and Air Forces.[18] The high point of WASP utilization by the Air Transport Command was reached in April 1944, when 303 WASPs flew for the ATC.[19]

The AAF tested the abilities of WASPs to serve as pilots in jobs other than ferrying. To do this, an experimental program, initiated in the summer of 1943, was to determine if they could tow targets. During this program, fifty WASPs from classes 43-W-3 and 43-W-4 were sent to the Third Tow Target Squadron, Third Air Force, Camp Davis, North Carolina. Here they were trained to fly missions for anti-aircraft gunnery practice, flying primarily dive-bomber airplanes (Douglas A-24 Dauntless and Curtiss A-25 Helldiver). These missions required the gunners to track the aircraft, to fire at targets towed behind aircraft, and to use searchlights to search for, and track, aircraft flying at night.

The women proved so capable at the tow-target missions that it was decided to try WASPs on other, similar types of flight missions.[20] Thus, during the fall of 1943, WASPs were tested on other aircraft and on flying primarily tow-target missions for air-to-air and ground-to-air gunnery training.

They were sent to transition training in Boeing B-17 Flying Fortresses, Martin B-26 Marauders, and North American B-25 Mitchels; to B-26 copilot training; and to the highly classified program at Liberty Field, Camp Stewart,

Georgia, to fly drone aircraft by radio-control for live-fire practice by anti-air-craft gunners.[21]

The B-26 training at Dodge City, Kansas, involved three WASP classes. Starting in October 1943, a total of fifty-seven WASPs entered this special training. Of these, thirty-nine graduated. This included WASPs from Mrs. Cole's class, 44-W-2. Of the twenty who entered from 44-W-2, seven were reassigned to other duties at other bases, while thirteen graduated.

These WASPs at Dodge City proved themselves capable pilots in this fast and heavy bomber, as affirmed by their commanding officer, Col. Charles B. Root, when he was interviewed by the station historian:

We recently had at this station a group of Women's Army Service Pilots for training in the B-26, and we feel that it was a reasonably successful experiment. These women displayed a most cooperative attitude and were enthusiastic and tried harder than the normal student.[22]

Another comment came from Major John D. Todd, Commandant, Officer Student Detachment:

We have found them [WASPs] to be very anxious and willing to learn. I would say their eagerness exceeds that of the average officer student. From the standpoint of their ground school work, we have found them to be very conscientious with the result that the average grades of the WASPs in the ground school exceeds the ground school over-all average.[23]

The flying training program consisted of seventy-five hours of flying in the B-26, with forty-five of these as first-pilot training and twenty hours of Link Trainer instruction.[24]

B-26 copilot training was initiated early in August 1944 at three Army Air Fields: Kingman AAF, Arizona, Harlingen AAF, Texas, and Laredo AAF, Texas. All WASPs at these bases had to be at least five feet four inches tall, have experience on twin-engine aircraft, and hold an instrument card.

Another course of instruction in which WASP Class 44-W-2 participated was an advanced course in instrument training at Sweetwater. Graduate WASPs (242 of them) returned to Avenger Field to qualify ''for an instrument rating and receipt of Form 8 (White) as prescribed by AAF Regulation 50-3.'' The course included fifty-five hours ''under the hood'' or practice instrument flight time; fifty-four hours of ground school; and nineteen hours of instrument flying in a Link Trainer.[25]

The uniform worn by women pilots (WAFS, trainees, and WASPs) was another item that changed during the program. The WAFS wore a uniform of their own choosing. It was of gray-green material and included slacks, skirt, and a jacket with padded shoulders and patch pockets. These were worn with shirts and ties of tan broadcloth and an overseas cap. The arm patch of the Air Transport Command was on their left sleeve. Their wings were those of Air Transport Command Service Pilots.[26]

The women flight cadets of the first classes (WFTD) had no official uniform. They wore what civilian clothing they desired; there was, however, a restriction against wearing cowboy boots. When the first class graduated, some type of uniform was appropriate. It was decided that each girl would purchase, at her own cost, tan cotton gabardine slacks, a long-sleeved white shirt, and tan overseas cap. This became the "trainees' dress uniform" until February 1944. After graduation these early WASPs wore combinations of Army "greens" or "pinks" in slacks and shirts for a flying uniform. No insignia was worn except wings. Civilian clothing was worn for non-flying activities.[27]

There were no official wings for the graduates of the early classes. Unofficial wings, redesigned from Air Corps pilot wings, were provided as a personal gift from Miss Cochran to each graduate. These were unique to each class from 43-W-1 through 43-W-7. The shield in the center of the wings was polished flat and the class number was inscribed on it, i.e., W-1, W-2, etc. A scroll above the shield carried the detachment designation: 319th for the first two classes, and 318th for the remainder.[28]

With the graduation of Class 44-W-1 on February 11, 1944, graduates were provided with the new official WASP uniform of Santiago blue. The dress uniform (worn at graduation) was a straight skirt, white shirt with black tie, hip-length belted jacket, and beret-type hat. The insignia included the great seal of the United States worn centered on the beret, the new WASP wings, and on the lapels the crossed wings and propeller and the word WASP spelled out in gold. The winged arm patch of the Army Air Forces Headquarters and Commands was worn on the left shoulder.

The official wings designed for the WASP were slightly smaller than the pilot wings, and a diamond or lozenge replaced the shield in the center of the wings.[29]

Class 44-W-2 was the second class to receive the WASP wings at graduation.

The physiology of women in flight had concerned many officials. In the beginning, for example, WAFS had been forbidden to fly during menses and pregnancy.[30] By August 1943, while the pregnancy rule held, the other was subject to the decision of the individual WASP herself, who could refrain from flying only after consulting with her WASP squadron leader or the group flight surgeon.[31]

Attitudes toward mixing of the sexes went through some well-deserved changes. WAFS were first forbidden to fly copilot with male pilots (or pilot with male copilots). Likewise there were to be no mixed flight assignments or mixed crew assignments.[32] These rules were quickly rescinded and WASP pilots were given assignments like those of any other pilots.

The militarization of the WASPs, and their training to be officers, was a subject of continuous concern with the Army Air Forces Headquarters and with Congress. Anticipating that WASPs would be militarized, the ground school curriculum at Avenger Field, in the revision of May 1944, contained such new subjects as officer indoctrination training, plus duties and responsibilities of an officer.

Likewise, in April 1944 a special course was established at the Army Air Forces Tactical School in Orlando, Florida, to provide basic military instruction to WASPs who had already graduated from Sweetwater. Selected WASPs, including many from Class 44-W-2, were sent to this school for a three-week course in training to be an Army officer.[33]

The varied duty stations and flight missions assigned to WASPs would be impossible to recount here. Like all military personnel, the women of the WASP were not stationary. They were moved by the military as they were needed. This certainly included those of Class 44-W-2 as they spread throughout the country to duty in all stateside Air Forces and commands including the Air Transport Command.

Types of flying assigned to WASPs included ferrying of all types of airplanes from liaison through bombers; towing targets for anti-aircraft and air-to-air gunnery practice (both tracking and live fire); radio control; drone flying; smoke laying; simulated bombing attack flights; instrument instructor; instrument check pilot; instrument safety pilot; administrative flights; cargo flights; scheduled air-transport pilot; simulated strafing; and engineering flight testing.[34]

In the course of their duties thirty-eight WASPs lost their lives.

The WASP program terminated nine months before the end of World War II. In a press release issued by the War Department, Bureau of Public Relations, Press Branch, entitled "AAF to Inactivate WASP on December 20," the reasons were outlined.

Unless there are unexpected and much higher combat losses in the air war over Germany, the Army Air Forces will inactivate the Women Air Force Service Pilots (WASP) on December 20, 1944, General H. H. Arnold, Commanding General, announced today.

The decision to release volunteer women pilots from further service with the AAF was based on present indications that by mid-December there will be sufficient male pilots available to fill all flying assignments in the United States and overseas.

General Arnold said:

"I am proud of the WASPs and their record of skill, versatility and loyalty. They have done outstanding work for the AAF, even exceeding our expectations when the program was begun in 1942.

"The WASPs were accepted as volunteers at a time when the nation faced total mobilization and when a pilot shortage would have imperiled the mission of the AAF. They have been as much an integral part of the AAF as their civil service status would permit and have not only performed highly essential service but also have established previously unknown facts concerning the capabilities of women in highly specialized military flying jobs. This knowledge will be of inestimable value should another national emergency arise. Together with the women fliers of our Allies, the WASP have proved that women have the ability and the capacity to perform the most difficult jobs in flying."[35]

At the time of their deactivation, there were 916 WASPs on duty with the AAF at the following commands and headquarters:[36]

Hq. AAF. 1
Training Command 620
Air Transport Command 141
First Air Force 16
Second Air Force. 80
Fourth Air Force 37
Weather Wing. 11
Proving Ground Command 6
Air Technical Service Command 3
Troop Carrier Command. 1

When the WASP program was deactivated, the following conclusions were reached as a result of the AAF's experiment with women pilots:

1. Women can meet standard physical criteria for flying and can be trained as quickly and economically as men in the same age group to fly all types of planes safely, efficiently, and regularly.

2. The best women pilot material is in the lower age brackets, down to eighteen years.
3. Women pilots can release male pilots for other duties.
4. Physiology peculiar to women is not a handicap to flying or to dependable performance of duty.
5. The flying safety record of women pilots approximates that of male pilots in the same type of work.
6. Women pilots have as much stamina and endurance and are no more subject to operational or flying fatigue than male pilots doing similar work. Women pilots can safely fly as many hours per month as male pilots.
7. An effective women's air force could be built up in the case of need from the young women of our country.[37]

The WASPs were sent home, never again to fly for the country they had served so ably.

In 1949, WASPs were offered commissions in the newly formed United States Air Force. The rank each was offered was based on the time she had spent in the WASP.[38] Accepting these commissions, 121 ex-WASPs found their flying training led them to aviation support and administrative military occupational specialties—but not to flight assignments. Nine remained in the Air Force for twenty years to retirement. Thirteen ex-WASPs joined other services: U.S. Navy, five; U.S.A.A.F. Nurse Corps, four; Royal Air Force, one; U.S. Army, two; U.S. Marine Corps, one.[39]

In 1977 Congress finally acknowledged that WASPs had indeed been military personnel. They were issued honorary discharges and declared veterans.

When women were admitted again to flight training within the Air Force, thirty-two years after the WASP program had been disbanded, the Air Force was surely building on the success of the WASP program and the heritage the WASPs had established for all women in aviation and aerospace.

Notes

Most of the reference material listed below may be found either in the Air Force Museum, Research Department, Women Air Force Service Pilots Files L2, Wright-Patterson Air Force Base, Ohio, or in the WASP Collection, the Library Archives, Texas Woman's University, Denton, Texas.

1. "History of the Air Transport Command. Women Pilots in the Air Transport Command," 24. (No date, author or source indicated. Assumed author is Capt. Walter

J. Marx, Ferrying Division Historical Officer mentioned in introduction. Assumed date is 1945. Copy available in Air Force Museum Reference Dept. L2, Wright-Patterson AFB, Ohio.) Document is *unclassified*. Original classification was *classified*. Hereinafter cited as "ATC."

2. Ibid., 27.

3. Ibid., 13.

4. "History of the WASP Program, Army Air Forces, Central Flying Training Command," Historical Section, A-2, AAF Central Flying Training Command, Randolph Field, Texas, 20 January 1945, 8. Document is *unclassified*. Original classification was *secret*. Hereinafter cited as "CFTC."

5. "W.A.S.P. Women Air Force Service Pilots, WW II, 1990 Roster," published by Women Air Force Service Pilots, WW II, 95. Hereinafter cited as "Roster."

6. Cochran, Jacqueline, "Final Report on Women Pilot Program, (6–1262,AF)," Hq. AAF, Washington, D.C., 22. Hereinafter cited as "Cochran."

7. Roster, 116–17.

8. Cochran, 6.

9. ATC, 31, and Knight, Charlotte, "Our Women Pilots," *Air Force Magazine*, September 1943, 12.

10. Cochran, 10.

11. Ibid.

12. Deaton, Leoti, "The Gals of Fifinella, A Story of the WASPs," unpublished paper, 7. Hereinafter cited as "Deaton."

13. CFTC, 46, 63.

14. Ibid., 51.

15. Ibid., 53.

16. Ibid., 59.

17. Ibid., 16.

18. CFTC, 83.

19. ATC, 143.

20. Ibid., 92.

21. Cochran, 27.

22. CFTC, 96.

23. Ibid.

24. Ibid., 97.

25. Ibid., 102, and Ward, R. P. (Col.) and Doherty, Chs. (Lt.), "History of the 2563D Army Air Forces Base Unit. Avenger Field, Sweetwater, Texas, 1 Nov. 1944 to 20 Dec. 1944, Former Designation, 318th Army Air Forces Flying Training Detachment," 36–37. Document is *unclassified*. Original classification was *restricted*.

26. Scharr, Adela Rick, *Sisters in the Sky, Vol. 1 — The WAFS*, Patrice Press, Gerald, Mo., 1986, 85–87. Hereinafter cited as "Scharr."

27. Deaton, 6.

28. Ibid.

29. Ibid.

30. ATC, 83.

31. Ibid., 96, and Monserud, Nels, O. (Capt. M. C.), "Report of the Air Surgeon's Office on WASP Personnel," January 1945, 24–27.

32. ATC, 85, and Scharr, 368.

33. CFTC, 130.

34. Cochran, 28, and England, J. M. (CWO), "Women Pilots with the AAF, 1941–1944, Army Air Forces Historical Studies: No. 55," AAF Historical Office, Hq., AAF, March 1946, 73. Document is *unclassified*. Original classification *restricted*. Hereinafter cited as "No. 55."

35. Copy of this press release available in WASP Collection, Library Archives at Texas Woman's University, Denton, Texas.

36. No. 55, 76.

37. Cochran, 51–52.

38. Willenz, June A., "Women Veterans, America's Forgotten Heroines," Continuum Publishing Co., N.Y., 1983, 178.

39. Roster.

P-47

Acknowledgments

I wish to thank many people for their help in getting this book completed. First of all, Dr. Jessica Munns, whose idea it was, and who insisted that a true oral history "must be written." Author Carol Gelderman and editor Vicki Hay also gave me valuable criticism and suggestions. Members of my family were extremely supportive. My sister Edna drove me around New England and Florida to interview WASPs. Daughter Wendy flew me to interviews and WASP meetings in Texas in her Cessna 140, and daughter Sally made innumerable suggestions and corrections in the manuscript. Son Tom taught me to use the computer, and sons Stephen and Jeff helped with editing and encouragement. Stephen also supplied the fine pen-and-ink drawing of airplanes included in the book. My husband Jerry not only edited but was forced to put up with my long hours on the computer and absences from home on interviewing trips. Grandson Christopher also read the entire manuscript and made valuable corrections. Last but not least, my thanks to those thirty-four wonderful WASPs who gave me their time and their encouragement, but most especially, their memories:

Ruth Adams, Anne Berry, Ann Craft, Gini Dulaney, Margaret Ehlers, Doris Elkington, Marjorie Gilbert, Leona Golbinec, Millie Grossman, Kate Lee Harris, Sadie Hawkins, Minkie Heckman, Nellie Henderson, Kay Herman, Mary Ellen Keil, Fran Laraway, Verda-Mae Lowe, Kit MacKethan, Jean Moore, Marge Needham, Esther Noffke, Ruth Petry, Anna Mae Petteys, Lourette Puett, Clarice Siddall, Fran Smith, Mary Strok, Madeline Sullivan, Phyllis Tobias, Joanne Wallace, Ruth Weller, Joan Whelan, Ruth Woods, Lorraine Zillner.

Introduction

This is a book about women—women who flew military aircraft in the 1940s during World War II. They were called WASPs, Women Air Force Service Pilots, and, in this capacity, served the Air Force in a variety of jobs that required capable, well-trained pilots. These women established an enviable record of accomplishment in the field of aviation. They provided undeniable proof of women's abilities to handle aircraft—any and every aircraft flown at the time—from Piper Cubs to P-51 pursuits and B-29 bombers.

When the WASPs were disbanded in December 1944, they had flown roughly sixty million miles for the Army Air Force. The fatalities were thirty-eight, or one to about sixteen thousand hours of flying. These figures compare favorably with the rates for male pilots in similar work, but these women were not recognized at that time by the Army Air Force of the United States Government—not even the thirty-eight who gave their lives in service to their country.

These women, trained and used by the Army Air Force for the war effort, were ignored by the military at the time of their deaths. No military escort was provided for their remains to be returned home. No flags or military services were authorized for their funerals. No GI insurance benefits were available to them. No commendations were offered to grieving parents.

Many years later, on March 8, 1979, the U.S. Secretary of Defense announced that the service of the WASP had been determined "active military service" for the purposes of all laws administered by the Veterans Administration. The recognition came thirty-five years too late for those killed during service, including WASPs Betty Stine, Marie Michell (Robinson), and Susie Clarke. Betty was forced to jump from her disabled AT-6 in 1944 during a storm; she crashed into a rocky cliff in the southern California desert and died before she could reach a hospital. Marie Michell was killed later that year at Victoria Field, California, while serving as copilot on a B-25. The plane crashed in bad weather, and both pilots were killed. Susie Clarke was killed

1

flying a BT-13 in Fairfax, Kansas, according to Air Force records. These three women belonged to Class 44-W-2, one class out of eighteen, which provides the focus for this book.

The idea of women flying for the Army Air Force was the brainchild of Jacqueline Cochran. Already a noted aviatrix since 1938, when she captured first place in the Bendix Transcontinental Air Race, Cochran, who had already broached the idea to Eleanor Roosevelt, finally presented a proposal to General H. H. "Hap" Arnold, in 1941, with a plan to utilize women pilots. General Arnold did not think the time was ripe, however, and Cochran, at his suggestion, joined a group of English women pilots serving with the RAF Air Transport Auxiliary. Cochran brought with her twenty-four other American women pilots and was soon commissioned a flight captain with this group, in 1942.

By the time General Arnold called Cochran home to direct a program for women pilots, another flight group had already been formed by Colonel Robert Love, deputy chief of the Air Transport Command, with Nancy Harkness Love as director. Twenty-seven American women pilots, all with at least five hundred hours flying time, had been accepted into this program. Cochran, therefore, returned from England to find the Air Transport Command (ATC) program already under way. Based at New Castle Army Air Base in Delaware, Nancy Love's pilots, called WAFS (Women's Auxiliary Ferry Service), ferried planes for the military.

General Arnold then named Cochran director of the 319th AAFFTD (Army Air Forces Flying Training Detachment), based in Houston, Texas, with Leoti C. Deaton as chief administrative officer. These women were responsible for recruiting and training women pilots. The first class started training in November 1942, at Houston, Texas, and included twenty-eight accomplished pilots. At this point, the Air Transport Command and the AAFFTD operated independently.

In June 1943, General Arnold ordered consolidation of the AAFFTD (the Houston-based group under Cochran) and the Air Transport Command (Nancy Love's ferry pilots, the WAFS), into the Women Air Force Service Pilots, or WASPs. Cochran then became director of all WASP activities, and Nancy Love retained command of all original WAFS assigned to the Ferry Command. The training program for the WASPs, begun in Houston, Texas, was soon transferred to Avenger Field, Sweetwater, Texas.

Rigorous training was the order of the day at Avenger Field. WASPs lived in starkly furnished one-story barracks six to a "bay" (room), Army style. Two hundred and ten hours of flight training were crammed into the schedule along with four hundred hours of ground school. Some classes other than 44-W-2 were given different schedules of flight and academic hours. As an example,

Class 43-W-1 was given 115 hours of flight training and 180 academic hours. Classroom instruction included theory of flight, meteorology, navigation, math, physics, engines, aircraft design, Morse code, and instruments. Calisthenics and close-order drill on the outdoor training field exhausted every last minute of the trainees' time.

Flight training, the happiest part of a WASP's day, began with the primary trainer, the PT-19A. After completing seventy hours in this low-winged silver beauty, trainees advanced to the BT-13, a 450-horsepower basic trainer dubbed the "Vultee Vibrator" because of its penchant for shaking and shuddering. The next step forward brought the WASPs the AT-6 Texan, a powerful, smooth-flying plane that completed the trio of training planes. The AT-6 was a joy to fly and was everyone's favorite. Other classes, however, flew several different types of planes. Some flew the twin-engine AT-17s and UC-78s and some flew the bi-winged Stearmans, to mention only a few.

After graduation from training, WASPs were assigned a variety of jobs by the Air Force. Many went to the ferry command, but others transported military personnel, "slow-timed" engines, towed targets for gunnery practice, and served as flight instructors or as test pilots for planes that had been repaired or overhauled. In these capacities, the WASPs flew every type of aircraft from pursuits to bombers. Class 44-W-2 entered training in September 1943 and graduated in March 1944.

Sweetwater at that time resembled the standard movie depiction of a small Texas cowboy town. One hotel, the Blue Bonnet, graced its dusty streets, and a typical corner drugstore of that era occupied the lower floor of the hotel. Cowboys, complete with Texas hats, jeans, and boots with spurs, clanked along the streets adding to the Old West atmosphere; even a few guns were visible. Colorful and rough, these characters presented an impressive sight to incoming WASPs, many of whom arrived from eastern cities. Sweetwater soon became an influence in our lives; the people were invariably friendly and we grew to love this town and to appreciate its warm attitude toward us.

One hundred twelve women came to Sweetwater that first week in September to enter the 44-W-2 training program; one was killed in training, and forty-nine graduated. This class had the dubious distinction of having the highest washout rate in the program, but there seems to be no obvious reason why this was the case. It may have been that the war was already winding down, and fewer pilots were needed. Another possible reason was that twenty of the graduates from Class 44-W-2 were to be sent to B-26 school for advanced training and Cochran and Arnold wanted more rigorous training.

The class was fortunate in one way and that was the presence at the graduation ceremonies of many distinguished guests. General H. H. Arnold and six other general officers attended, as well as Jacqueline Cochran and Nancy Harkness Love. WASP Barbara Erickson was awarded the Air Medal at the ceremonies by General Arnold in recognition of outstanding service. It was a most impressive graduation ceremony.

Phyllis Tobias, graduating WASP, had this to say about the event. "My mother came for the graduation. She was able to sit in the audience and she enjoyed especially the part where General Arnold pinned on our wings. You may not remember, but he started pinning on everyone's wings. You know, reaching under your jacket. And Jackie [Cochran] said, after three or four of them, 'Never mind, General, you don't have to do that.' He said, 'Never mind, Jackie, I enjoy doing this.' And he pinned on every set of wings. Even down to Tobias.''

The last class of WASPs graduated on December 7, 1944. General Arnold was the keynote speaker and he said of the WASP program: "We will not again look upon a women's flying organization as experimental. We will know that they can handle our fastest fighters, our heaviest bombers; we will know that they are capable of ferrying, target towing, flying training, test flying, and the countless other activities which you have proved you can do. This is valuable knowledge for the air age into which we are now entering. We of the Army Air Force are proud of you; we will never forget our debt to you.'' WASPs know that General Arnold did all he could for us. After his death, his son Bruce carried on his tradition so that we finally became "veterans." The general didn't live to see this fulfillment of his goal, but Jacqueline Cochran and Nancy Love did.

Part of the pressure against militarizing the WASPs came from civilian male pilots who were dismissed when the Air Force cut back its training program. This action threatened the civilian pilots with induction into the infantry, the "walking Army." They formed a powerful lobby and the resulting pressures, both political and emotional, worked against the women. Although the Military Affairs Committee agreed with General Arnold, the Civil Service Committee reported that the authority of Congress had been bypassed and that the WASP program had never been authorized. The press then turned against the women pilots, and when the results of the voting came in on Bill 4219, militarization for the WASPs was defeated by nineteen votes.

Another low blow to strike the WASPs came from commercial airlines. When the war was over, the airline companies throughout the country scrambled to hire male pilots and denied female pilots entry into their training programs. Only men were allowed. Some of this prejudice, of course, could be attributed to societal attitudes prevailing at the time. (On commercial airlines, even now, female pilots keep a low profile.) Also, at the end of the war, probably enough male pilots were available to serve the airlines' needs. It was a bitter rejection, however, to the nine hundred women pilots who had served the Army Air Force so diligently.

In the following chapters, you will meet thirty-five members of Class 44-W-2 and read in their own words their adventures, their hardships, and their outlook on the WASP program. Unfortunately, in addition to the three WASPs who were killed in service, seven other classmates were deceased at the time of interviewing, two more died after the interviews, and five were unavailable for comment. Many of those not included, however, are brought into the story through the comments of their fellow pilots.

It must be remembered, however, that this one class of pilots represents only a small number of the total women pilots who served both England and the United States during World War II. In addition to those who served in England, and Nancy Love's WAFS, a total of eighteen classes finished the training program. Twenty-five thousand women had applied for flight training, 1,830 were accepted, and 1,074 received their wings. Graduates of Class 44-W-2, therefore, represent only forty-nine pilots out of those 1,074. In spite of this small sample, the following personal accounts of the training program and the service for the Air Force should, I believe, provide both a fair and an accurate portrayal of the life of women pilots as it was experienced during World War II.

"Grasshopper"

CHAPTER ONE

How It Began

"A dream to do something different." —Lourette Puett

Sweetwater, Texas, September 1943: One hundred and twelve women pilots arrived in this small, dusty Texas town, eager to start the Women Air Force Service Pilots training program. They were to enter Class 44-W-2, the second class of women scheduled to graduate in 1944. These women were a diverse lot. Some were entering the program with the minimum number of flying hours (thirty-five), while some held a commercial license or an instructor's rating, with several hundred hours of flying time. Some had started flying as early as 1936, and some had started only in 1943. Ages ranged from eighteen to twenty-eight. All, however, were pilots before they arrived. How could so many women have learned to fly on their own initiative (this was only one class out of eighteen), as early as 1943? Where did they come from, and how did they manage to become pilots?

I was one of them. As I was to learn, we came from all corners of America, from the small towns and the big cities, from the privileged classes and the not-so-privileged. For each of us, flying was a passion, and some combination of daring, rebellion, and determination took us into the air.

On July 3, 1942, I took my first flying lesson at Fair Haven, Vermont. The airport consisted of a grass runway just long enough to land a small plane, hangar space for two planes, and a one-room "lounge." When I arrived for my first lesson, I noticed the dusty parachutes stacked in a corner, the cluttered desk protruding from one wall, and the layer of pipe smoke hanging over the few old leather chairs strewn randomly around the room. Two elderly men (old World War I pilots, I discovered) sat smoking and boasting of their past exploits. The scene did not inspire much confidence. Nor did the old, red, oil-splattered Aeronca that soon wheeled into sight. Nonetheless, my instructor, Norm Grady, began explaining the airplane to me as though it were his prize possession, which perhaps it was. I can still remember, as if it were yesterday, the mixed odors of gas, oil, and fresh-mown grass as I climbed into the cockpit for our takeoff.

My first flight was a stunning introduction to a new world. Bounding along the grass runway, the Aeronca seemed ready to lift at a moment's notice. My feet were on the rudders, one hand on the throttle, one on the stick, carefully following the movements of the instructor who was flying the dual controls from the front cockpit. Suddenly the plane roared into the air, banked to the left, and swept, gloriously, into the deep blue of a clear June sky. The world opened up and I could see the green Vermont countryside spread below like a child's toy farm set. The first maneuvers—level flight, climbing turns, and gliding—seemed easy, but it was hard to keep my mind and eyes away from the magnificent world above the earth. This was now my world, this incredibly wide, amazingly beautiful new universe.

Those days, in the summer of 1942, were fraught with great upheaval. The war in Europe was in full swing. The battle of Midway had ended in June, and the methodical annihilation of all European Jews by Adolf Hitler and Heinrich Himmler was already under way. Fiorello LaGuardia was mayor of New York City, and photographer Margaret Bourke-White's book, *Shooting the Russian War*, went on sale at $2.75 a copy. U.S. airmen celebrated the Fourth of July by bombing Tokyo, and the U.S. Senate, on July 3, approved women for noncombatant duty in the United States Naval Reserve.

It was specified, however, that "women could not command men or go to sea." Eleanor Roosevelt, on this day, told a press conference that she saw no reason why women volunteers could not be used as price checkers for the Office of Price Administration. Also at this time, American women medical doctors were engaged in a campaign to be allowed to serve in the Medical Reserve Corps of the Army and Navy under equal rating with male physicians.

Perhaps inevitably during the wartime changes, many women began moving from their jobs and their domestic roles into fields that could benefit the war effort. The Women's Auxiliary Army Corps (WAAC) had been established on May 14, with Olveta Culp Hobby as director, and the first group was sworn in on July 10. Their pictures were shown in the *New York Times*, and they were an impressive group. All were career women, coming from jobs as varied as merchandise buyer, college teacher, agriculture agent, and dietitian. The youngest was twenty-two and the oldest, an executive secretary, was forty-five.

Back in Vermont, however, such events seemed remote. At nineteen, my attempts to return to college were thwarted by my parents—("girls" needed only one year of college, they believed), so I was confined to an eight-to-five job as a typist. Half my salary, nine of my eighteen dollars a week, went to my parents for room and board.

The rest was spent on flying. At eight dollars an hour, I could manage one hour's flight time a week, weather permitting—and the weather didn't always permit. Usually we flew only a half hour at a time, so my total often came to less than an hour a week. I spent every free minute at the Fair Haven Airport. The airplanes, the flying, even the weather fascinated me. My instructor could predict rain with uncanny accuracy, and I never tired of hearing about the flying mishaps and adventures that the pilots would brag about as we sat in the small lounge, rain pinging off the metal roof, waiting for the sky to clear so we could fly.

Finally, we were back in the air. I could delight in each new maneuver. Stalls—pulling the nose up until the plane would drop nose-first—left me breathless the first few times, but I soon learned to catch them before the plane fell off to one side or another. Keeping the nose falling straight was practice for landings, when the plane would stall out over the runway just as it set down. Spinning was the most fun. Stall the plane first, nose high; kick a rudder to force the plane to fall off to one side; hold the stick way back—and you brought on a full, nose-down spin. Around and around, with the landscape below rotating faster and faster the longer you held it, the spin wound ever tighter. With the ground moving up to meet you, you would finally ''pop'' the stick forward and the plane would recover into a dive, from which it was easy to level out. Spins were real exciting maneuvers.

Aside from the excitement, I'm not sure I can explain why flying held such a fascination. There is something about being on top of the world, looking down at everything and everybody below, that seems to put things into a proper perspective, one that makes sense. All those important places and people are relegated to the same flat earth, and a pilot looks down and sees it all as no more important than the sky and the clouds. The airplane itself, a wonderful machine that you can control and maneuver and cause to soar above the clouds, still excites me so much I can hardly wait to get in an airplane again, even now.

Besides, it is so beautiful up there, not like anything on earth, but like a whole different world, a world of glittering blues and whites, gold streaks of sun bouncing off the spinning propeller, everything in motion—a fluid world of color. Sally Van Wegenen Keil, author of *Those Wonderful Women and Their Flying Machines* (New York: Rawson Associates, 1979, p. 53), describes it as it seemed to her. ''To fly . . . permanently changed one's sense of space and one's concept of what the world looks like—not only an aesthetic experience, flight was an expression of independence and free will, a triumph over the eternal static hold of gravity.''

She was so right. Once you have flown an airplane yourself, your world is never the same again.

I would have done almost anything to get to fly, but, with no money and no car, it was not easy. The bus from Rutland (where I lived) to Fair Haven would drop me off about a mile from the airport. I walked that road many times that summer, in rain, dust, and heat, often arriving to find the ceiling too low or the gusts too strong to fly. I sat around the dingy old lounge, listening to flying tales and picking up bits of knowledge here and there. The men who flew there tolerated me as an oddity, but they were not unfriendly. Occasionally they would offer me a ride back to Rutland or to the bus station.

It was September before I could get enough hours to solo. Eight hours of flight time was average before a solo flight, and I was about average. Meanwhile, flying at Fair Haven had become a real joy. Much of our time was spent flying over the lush green countryside, where limestone quarries and streams dotted the landscape. With fall, the weather turned colder and we were wearing jackets in the plane. The first autumn frost painted only one side of the mountains. Flying to the west we watched the green of summer pass below us; but flying back, with the westerly winds at our back, the trees were miraculously displayed in their gaudy red and yellow tints. Flocks of birds were heading south. Occasionally deer wandered onto our runway, and we would dive down to chase them before landing. It was great fun; still, I yearned for the day I would be alone in the cockpit.

Finally, in late September, when I had completed eight hours of instruction, I was turned loose. It was almost dusk and the weather had turned very cold. I remember how light the plane felt without the bulk of another person in the front seat. It even bounced more buoyantly than normal around the sky, and for the first time I felt real freedom.

Someone said to me later that I must have felt some fear, but I don't believe I did. I was only twenty, and I loved flying that airplane. I never thought for a moment that I couldn't handle it. In fact, in all my flying career I never remember being afraid, except when flying at night. I'm afraid of a lot of other things—these days commercial flying frightens me a little, possibly because I have no control over the situation and no idea how qualified the pilot in the cockpit really is, especially on some third-world airlines. Flying by myself, however, never frightened me. Either I have a colossal ego, or I am just not afraid of the things I really love to do.

At any rate, my solo flight was successful but short, because it was getting too dark to fly. It was my last flight at Fair Haven Airport. My family was moving to Indiana and I had planned to accompany them. The future was uncertain. I knew only that I would continue flying.

I felt very much alone that day, the only woman I knew of who wanted to fly airplanes. My friends at work thought my flying was a bit strange, except for one girl. Thinking it might be fun, she came to Fair Haven with me one day. She went up on one flight, but I guess it didn't have the fascination for her that it had for me. She never came back. All over the country, however, there were many women like me. It just took me some time to find them.

In Minneapolis, for example, there was Joan Whelan. She had discovered flying at the age of seventeen. "I don't know what got me started," she says, "but I just wanted to fly." Fresh out of high school, she took a lesson the first time she went up, and that was supposed to be that, but she was hooked. "It took me a long time, because my dad didn't know I was flying. I had to take two buses and then walk a mile before I got to the field. It was bad in the winter and I didn't have much money, so it took a year—more than a year—before I soloed."

Joan's mother secretly conspired in the flying project. The two had to confess when Joan soloed, because her instructor brought her home—almost. "We landed in a grass field about a mile from where I lived, and my parents came and picked me up." At the University of Minnesota, she flew often and joined the Civilian Pilot Training Program (CPT). By 1942, she had earned a commercial license and an instructor's rating.

"I wanted to instruct, but I couldn't make much money at that time instructing," she recalls. She took an air traffic control job in Minneapolis, and afterward served in the control towers of airports in Chicago and Cincinnati. From Cincinnati she joined the WASP.

Joan was one of the few WASPs who entered the program with an instructor's rating and substantial flying time. Experience varied among the trainees, but most had fewer hours and some, including me, had not even a private license.

Many members of our class had been able to take advantage of the government-sponsored Civilian Pilot Training Program that was instituted at many universities. Although women were allowed to participate only on a one-to-ten ratio (one woman to every ten men—or, in some cases, to fifteen or more men), at least some managed to enter the program.

I wish I had known, at the time I was struggling to fly, that there were others like myself all over the country, some with more hurdles to overcome than I had. While I had to work and buy my own time, I at least had a supportive family. My mother was less than excited about the idea of flying, but my father thought it was the greatest thing outside of hunting and fishing that he could imagine. Indeed, it was my father who came racing into our house one day when I was six years old and my sister was eight.

"Come on, kids," he shouted, "there's an airplane out on Main Street in a big field, and the pilot's giving airplane rides." We piled into his old Chevy and drove out there, whereupon, instead of going up himself (which I thought he wanted to do), he dumped my sister and me into the back seat of that old plane. It took off with a roar, carrying just the two of us little children and the pilot. I guess my father thought it would be a great experience for us, and it certainly was for me. Perhaps that's when I caught the "bug," and maybe that's why I never thought of being afraid in an airplane. I leaned out of the window to look down, but the pilot made me sit down again. My sister was not afraid either, but she wasn't really impressed, as I recall.

Lourette Puett had no such help or encouragement when she started to fly. She was born in Fort Worth, Texas. "I started flying," she says, "when I was about sixteen. You know, it was a dream to do something different." Reared in an orphans' home after both her parents died, Lourette had a "tremendous ambition to do something." She started flying when she was in high school. She took a night job wrapping gifts and doing miscellaneous chores, and every penny went into flying. "I thought it was so exciting—how I loved it!"

Reflecting on the women's movement of the 1970s and 1980s, Lourette remarks that she has never worked in a position that wasn't a "man's job." Yet, she says, she has never encountered any prejudice. "I don't feel the same as some women, about being persecuted. In the WASP we were paid what the average government employee was paid; of course, we didn't have our commissions, but nevertheless it was a pretty good salary. In 1943, that $175 a month was marvelous.

"I joined the WASPs because that was the best place to get further flight training free. It wasn't very difficult to get in, because Jacqueline Cochran was in Fort Worth, in the headquarters of some command. [Cochran was the director of the WASP program and often interviewed the prospective trainees herself.] I was eighteen at the time and I wasn't very mature, but I didn't have many problems in training. I loved flying."

Madeline Sullivan came from an entirely different background. "I had one year of college," she says, "and at the end of that year, my father took a look at my marks and said, 'Madeline, that's the most expensive fun you've had. Now get out and get a job.' So I did." Her family was in merchandising, so she got a job at Best's Department Store on Fifth Avenue. "I was going to be the hottest fire to hit New York since my aunts had been there, but it didn't take me long to look around and see the gal who had been head of stock for the past fifteen years and to figure, 'This is not for me.'" Nevertheless, Madeline was earning a good salary and living at home, so her only expenses were transportation and lunch. "I had to do something with all this leftover money," she says. "I started going out to Roosevelt Field to take flying lessons. It just sounded like fun."

About the time America entered the war, Madeline realized she hated Best's. She got a job at United Airlines, joining the second or third group of women who were taken on as passenger agents. She loved working there, but she soon started seeing notices about the WASP program. In its early months, the program required five hundred hours of flying time for eligibility. The figure later dropped to three hundred, then to one hundred, then to thirty-five. "By this time," she recalls, "I have maybe eighteen hours. One day I see in the paper that Maxine Howard is going to be at the Hotel Lexington interviewing, so I get Monday and Tuesday off and race in. First crack off the box, she says to me, 'Now, before we start, I have to tell you, unless you have thirty-five hours of signed, logged time I can't sign you to a class. How many do you have?'

" 'I have about thirty-one,' I lied. 'But if you're here until Friday, I'm sure I can get the rest.' "

Howard promised to put Madeline into the first opening as soon as she had thirty-five hours, and that opening would come up in September. On Thursday, Madeline went to her instructor and said, "You've got to sign my log book. I have from May to September, and I'll certainly be able to make up the time." He was reluctant at first, but, after much pleading and promising, he gave in. Then he remarked that he had another student who wanted to enter the WASP and asked if Madeline would drive her to New York City to meet Howard. She agreed, but only if the girl could be ready to go in fifteen minutes, for she could not take off any more time from work.

"Twelve minutes later, who shows up in my car but Jo Wallace [another 44-W-2 WASP]. That's how Jo and I met.

"Well, I listened to Jo on the way down—oh, she was so good-looking and very impressive—and I was sitting there thinking, 'I don't seem to have any of the right answers.' The last twenty minutes of the drive, she was saying what she thought of people who pad their log books, and let me tell you, it wasn't much. I was thinking, 'How am I going to lose this babe so I can finish the last few things I have to fill in?' My instructor had just signed his name. As I was parking in front of the Hotel Lexington, I finally said to her, 'How many hours of signed time do you have?' She said, 'I have about thirty or thirty-one.'

"I said, 'I have news for you. Unless you have thirty-five hours of signed time, she's not going to put you into the next class in September.'

" 'Oh, my God,' she said, 'have you got a pen?'

"The two of us went into the ladies' room and finished padding our log books. Then we went upstairs, met Maxine Howard, the WASP interviewer, and were both assigned to the September class."

Madeline was by no means different from many of the girls who entered our class that September. Many of us took the attitude that we would do "whatever it takes to get in." In my case, although I had more than thirty-five hours of flying time, I was a little bit short of the required height demanded of women pilots. This was my biggest worry when I went to Dayton to take my physical exam. Fortunately, however, the Army lieutenant who tested me was a friendly, jolly young man. He noticed that I was stretching up on my toes when he measured me, so he asked, "What's the matter? Not tall enough? How tall do you want to be?" I told him that the minimum height requirement was five feet two and a half inches, and he said, "Well, honey, that's just what we'll make you," so I was saved.

Many of the thirty-four WASPs who spoke with me for this account squeezed in by various methods, not all of which were aboveboard. World War II was a very popular war. The country was totally involved and everyone wanted to be "in it" or helping in one way or another. No holds were barred when it came to "getting in." Besides, most women pilots had an additional ambition: to fly—any way possible.

Nellie Henderson was one WASP determined to get in by any method. Her problem was poor vision. As an advertising manager for Muller's Department Store in Lake Charles, Louisiana, she earned forty dollars a week—a fortune in those days, for a woman. She took flying lessons at a nearby field and loved it. Shortly after she obtained her pilot's license, she learned that the government was interviewing for WASPs in Shreveport. "I drove all the way to Shreveport, brought my little log book and got my interview, and cheated on the eye exam. Couldn't see bats for beans. Everybody who checked me all the way through said, 'You really don't see, do you?' I said, 'No, but don't tell anybody.' I had good medical officers who never reported the fact. All my flying glasses had correction in them. You know, being nearsighted, you can squint momentarily and make out what it is. I cheated like crazy to get in—but I got in."

Like Joan, Doris Elkington got her start through the Civilian Pilot Training program, which had been started by President Franklin D. Roosevelt shortly before the United States entered the war. Doris began flying with the CPT program at a junior college in Highland Park, Michigan. She was about eighteen years old. "They had classes of ten where they allowed one woman for every nine fellows," she recalls. "I was the one gal in a class of ten, and there were two classes, so there were two gals and eighteen fellows. I think every one of the fellows went into the Air Force at the start of the war. We received our private license and we had approximately fifty hours of flying time." The cost, she says, was twenty-five dollars. "Ten dollars was for insurance, ten dollars for ground school, and I don't know what the other five dollars was for. We had to provide our own transportation, and that was difficult for me because I didn't have a car and my dad wasn't about to let me use his. I could fly an airplane but not drive his car." Doris usually got a ride with one of the male students and then waited her turn to get flying time.

After finishing junior college and completing the CPT program, she went to work. A year later, the WASP was formed. "As soon as I heard about them, I wanted to get in, and I met Velma Baumann—we were both part of the Civil Air Patrol. She and I took our physicals together and went into the WASP together. This was from Detroit.

"We had an interview in Chicago with Nancy Love, and then we took the train together, to go into the WASP. I can remember going across Texas with the train's windows wide open. We stopped at every little crossing, and it seemed to take forever to get there."

Leona Golbinec began flying very young. "I started flying because my brother flew. He flew way back in 1928. He had gone into the Air Force back in 1929, but he was washed out in 1930 because of his eyes—after he had started his training. I was only seven years old then. He'd tie a handkerchief over my head because my head was too small for a helmet, and he'd take me up. I always said, 'When I grow up, I'm going to fly.' "

At Bowling Green University, Leona discovered the Civilian Pilot Training Program. Here, too, they took one woman for every ten men. "I had an instructor named Mike Murphy. He took us up one night in a Ford Trimotor—all his students, when he was advertising Marathon gasoline. We flew all over. We flew clear to Cincinnati one night. We had to stay over the night and here I was, the only girl with all these boys. Oh, it was great. This Trimotor—you couldn't hear a thing in it, but still it was marvelous." She obtained her pilot's license in her junior year, and, like other CPT graduates, taught ground school to get more flying time.

"I went for an interview when Jackie Cochran came to Cleveland," she recalls. "At that time, she was looking for pilots to go to Canada, and boy, that was for me, but she wouldn't take me because I was in college, and she wanted me to get my degree first. She was strong on education. She didn't have a degree, but she really thought that education was very important. That's when Jackie told us that she was going to try to get a group of women started in the United States. She said, 'When I do, I'll let you know, and I'd like you to join us,' but I was disappointed not to be able to go to Canada and fly with them right away.

"Later I got my telegram from Jackie. It was a notice that I was to come in September in the 44-W-2 class. I met Doris Elkington on the train—she was coming down, too."

The Civilian Pilot Training Program also was a start for Ruth Adams. She was a Wellesley graduate living in Boston and working as a research assistant for a company in Wellesley. She got into flying almost by chance.

"I had a friend doing graduate work at Smith," she said, "so I would drive over to see her and spend the night. Once, when I was coming back, I passed a little roadside school where they were offering flying lessons for under five dollars. I was saying disparaging things to myself about it and then about five miles beyond it I said, 'Are you afraid to go up?' I turned around and I went up in this little airplane—it was an open cockpit biplane—and I saw that the fields were very different from up there. I didn't feel at all afraid. It was simply an interesting sensation and also, intellectually, it appealed to me. I liked it so much. I kept going back there, not building up time particularly, but to explore the experience.

"Then I heard about this flying school, I don't know how, and I saw this pretty little lady, Nancy Love, who had gone to Vassar. She was the wife of the owner. I found out it would cost two thousand dollars. I thought that would be nice but didn't know where it would lead, so I got another job as a research assistant at Wellesley. As the war began to heat up in Europe, the Civilian Pilot Training Program came on line. I thought, 'That's something I can do, and it's free.' " As a college graduate, Ruth had only to pay a registration fee at Northeastern University. "I got into their CPT program and got my private pilot's license—free."

Later, she joined a flying club, accruing flight time at about three dollars an hour. "Of course, I didn't think I would ever get five hundred hours, but then I got word that the WASP were getting organized and that the requirements were much lower. I somehow managed to get an interview for WASP candidates with a lady in a hotel, and I survived the interview."

Mary Strok also got her training through the CPT program. "I started flying when I was sixteen years old, and I was deeply influenced by my brother Michael. Mike was always interested in flying. I think I was a sophomore at Cornell when they started CPT. Mike suggested that I try for it, so I did. I barely passed the physical, because they told me I had to be five feet two inches, and I was only five feet one and three quarters. But the doctor was very kind and said, 'I can see that you really want to get in this program. I suggest that you stretch yourself for several days, then come in early in the morning before you do anything. I'll measure and I'm sure you'll make it.' "

She passed the physical, went through the program, and emerged with a private pilot's license. Then she began flying Piper Cubs in Ithaca, New York.

"Shortly afterward, I read that famous article in the July 19, 1943, issue of *Life* magazine about the WASP program. I just couldn't believe I might be eligible, but I applied. Ruth Petry, who applied at the same time, went down to New York with me by overnight train. It was an adventure for me, a little hometown girl who never left Ithaca, never went anywhere. We were interviewed by

Jackie Cochran. I haven't the slightest idea what I said. I'm sure I babbled, and I went home crestfallen. Of course, she would never take me—why would she? Then I got a letter saying I was accepted, starting in September 1943.

"I still couldn't believe it. I thought they'd made a mistake, but I didn't want to call because I was afraid they would check the records and find I really hadn't done it."

Other women got into flying in less formal ways, or, without the help of CPT, by more expensive or circuitous routes. Really, the members of Class 44-W-2 had only one strong similarity: they wanted to fly. Some came from flying families; both Ruth Woods and Frances Smith had fathers who were pilots. Fran's father was an early airmail pilot and an instructor during World War I; that was one reason, she told me, that she took up flying.

"After the war," she says, "my father became a commercial pilot flying the airmail in the old Jennys. Then, in 1929, the government asked him if he would go to China to start an airmail service there—which he did, with the help of other people. After three years or so, one of the companies (I think it was Trimotor Ford) asked my father if he would demonstrate a plane to General Chiang Kai-shek. If the general would buy it, my father would get a commission.

"Dad said, 'Sure.' He took the general and his wife up, flew them all over Shanghai and around the country, and told them what an advantage it would be to have an airplane in China. When he brought it in, the general said, 'I'll tell you what, Mr. Smith. I'll buy the plane if you'll fly it.'

"That's how my father became personal pilot for General Chiang Kai-shek, and he continued that for three years. After six years in China, my father decided that my two brothers and I should learn something about the United States, so we came back." Fran and her family stayed in California, but her father kept up his connections in China. During one trip, he contracted typhus; he died in China in 1938. Although his love of flying was one reason Fran took it up, she says, "He never knew I went into flying."

Fran started flying before the war, in Monrovia, California, just after her high-school graduation. When World War II began, she had only had about ten hours. "I had soloed, and my brother had joined the Air Force. I thought to myself, 'He's not going to learn to fly before I do.' At the same time, I saw the article in the *Los Angeles Times* about the WASP, so I went out to Blythe, California, and got my fifty hours (in a flight school) and then applied to the WASP. I was supposed to start in the August class, but they had overbooked that, so they sent me a wire saying to hold off until September.

"I remember going down to Los Angeles to get the train to Sweetwater. They wouldn't let me on, because all the military personnel were waiting to get on. I said, 'But I've got my orders.'

" 'We've got too many other people,' they said.

"Another fellow who was standing there heard all this, and he said, 'Come here a minute.'

"He took me aside and said, 'I'm supposed to take my wife with me, and she's not coming. Come on.'

"Well, we got on the train together as husband and wife." She laughed when I asked where his wife was.

"I don't know. I lost him right after we got on the train. He was just nice to help me get on. Then of course I went on to Sweetwater and joined the ranks. Now that I know all the girls in our class, I'm glad I didn't get in the August class."

Ruth Woods's flying father became a pilot as a hobby. "I came by this naturally," she claimed. "I started flying legally at about age sixteen, but I had flown before that in Dallas, Texas.

"I was born in Dallas and raised there, and when I was in college I had a good friend whose father had flown with Eddie Rickenbacker. He and I flew a little forty-horsepower Cub all the time and we went everywhere. When we ran out of gas, we landed in the nearest pasture, and, while Clyde hitchhiked into town to get some more good old East Texas gasoline, I kept the cows off the airplane.

"I have actually run in front of the airplane to keep the cows out of the way so he could get enough speed to take off—and I'd jump into the airplane as he went by. He did the same for me. This was back before the Civil Aeronautics Administration cracked down. They wouldn't let you do those things."

Speaking of the difficulties women had in learning to fly, Ruth observes that she felt exempt because the men at the airport, who ordinarily might have treated a woman who hung around airplanes as "a floozy or something," knew her father. "They also knew the guy who became my instructor, so I didn't have the prejudice problem that others experienced back then.

"I joined the WASP, but—it seems terrible for me to say this—it wasn't particularly out of patriotism, although that had something to do with it, at the time. Primarily it was because I could get to fly aircraft that I couldn't get my hands on any other way. No matter how much money I had, I wouldn't have been able to buy time on them, because they were military planes. I had no trouble at all getting in. I had a commercial license and I was twenty-two when I went in."

Fellow Texan Sadie Hawkins says she can hardly remember when she didn't want to fly. "I had my first flight when I was about five years old, in an old Ford Trimotor with one of those old barnstormers who came around," she recalls. "My father liked it, but my sister and my mother were terrified. I thought it was great, and from that moment I wanted to fly."

18

Sadie grew up in Quanah, Texas, where her father was a sheriff. "I remember being so excited once because there had been a bank robbery. Dad went out and rented the only local aircraft to fly up and look for this guy. I can still remember that thing—I'm sure it was put together with chewing gum and baling wire—but they found the guy. They spotted him in a field and caught him. I was envious that I didn't get to go with them."

After graduating from Amarillo High School, she spent two years at Texas Technological College (Lubbock), where she was a journalism major with a photography minor. "I went right from there to flying school in Blythe, California. I lived there in Blythe and roomed with Lorraine Fiedler, who was in Class 44-1. When I graduated from that flying school, I put in my request to join the WASP and was accepted. All the girls there were trying for the WASP, and I think all of them became WASPs."

Gini Dulaney started flying very young—at about fifteen, she stated. "I had this old pilot who taught me to fly in an old World War I Waco. This was in Atwater, Ohio. This airplane was put together with hairpins, I swear! He used normal gas out of the gas pump and he used spark plugs out of his car to put in the plane. This old guy didn't have a license, the airplane didn't have a license, and he used three farmers' fields as landing places. I was good at gliders later because I didn't know anything but a dead stick landing. As soon as the plane quit, we had to land in the nearest farmer's field, so we stayed within the area of these three farmers' fields. That's how we did our flying!"

Jean Moore, in Kirklin, Indiana, tried out for CPT. At Hanover College she asked to be the one girl per nine boys allowed in the program, but her request was denied because she did not have a B grade average. The following year she dropped out of school and went to work for her father. Unable to get the government-sponsored training, she spent twelve dollars of her fifteen-dollars-a-week salary on flying. "It was six dollars an hour, whether you had an instructor or not," she says. She flew at Frankfort, Indiana, ten miles from Kirklin. "I was twenty-one when I soloed; my mother came and sat in the car making her afghan and watched. My family didn't object. My father just thought I was a little strange.

"On my solo flight I had carburetor ice on the next-to-last landing and the engine died on the base leg. I landed it anyhow, and they came out and propped it. I went around and shot another landing. Yes, I only had six hours before soloing. They lied and said I had eight [required]. They had an instructor only part-time, and he wanted to turn me loose so they could make more money for their airplanes."

In January 1942, Jean went to Indianapolis to join the WAVEs. "I had heard about the WASP, but you needed two hundred hours at that time, and I knew it would take me years to get two hundred hours. I walked in and said, 'I'm learning to fly and I would like to have something to do with airplanes.' The lady said, 'Did you know that they have just lowered the hours for the WASP to thirty-five?' I said, 'No.' She gave me the address in Washington to write to, and I said, 'You just lost a recruit.' ''

I wish I had known about Jean at the time, because when we moved to Indiana that September after my first solo flight, I had to start all over again. She was in Kirklin and I was in Richmond, only about seventy miles away, but we didn't meet until a year later, at Sweetwater.

By this time, the war had escalated on many fronts. The Russians were advancing through the ruins of Stalingrad. Back in America, we did not know at the time (and many still do not know) that Russian women pilots were playing an important role in the Battle of Stalingrad. Women were flying combat planes, some even without the benefit of parachutes, and many were shot down.

Back in the United States, rationing of fuel oil, coffee, sugar, meat, gasoline, and tires was a reality to every family. Our planes had pounded Tunisia and Guadalcanal, and the American-made P-47 had set a record for planes in a power dive: 725 miles per hour. Benefits were being held for the war effort by various celebrities, including sports figures and film stars. Even the New York Philharmonic Orchestra, with Arturo Toscanini conducting, attracted an immense audience to benefit the Red Cross. Child-care centers were urged for New York City to benefit mothers engaged in war work.

Meanwhile, I got a job at a war plant, the National Automatic Tool Company in Richmond, Indiana, to earn enough money to fly. I could see that it was going to take a long time to get the hours I wanted just by renting planes at the airport. I had heard of ''flying clubs,'' so I thought if I bought an airplane with other people we could all fly at less expense and get in a lot more time. I knew of an inexpensive Piper Cub for sale, but I didn't have any money (this old plane cost about a thousand dollars). My father suggested that, since I had a good job, I go to the bank and ask to borrow the money.

The next day I did exactly that. I was turned over to an elderly gentleman who asked why I wanted a thousand dollars.

''To buy an airplane,'' I answered. I outlined my plan to get some other fliers and form a club to pay for it.

There was a long pause—a very long pause. Then after a few minutes, he looked at me carefully and said, ''I just bet you can do it,'' and he loaned me the thousand dollars.

The club—five men and I—bought the airplane. Only two of the men ever flew much, so I had a plane practically to myself, although it was a poor excuse for an airplane. The tires were always flat, so we had to keep putting patches on them, and the engine often spit drops of oil onto the pilot in the cockpit. One day when I was flying, the fabric tore loose from the windshield and ripped off a strip about a foot and a half wide all the way to the tail. I was looking at the sky overhead, but it landed okay, and I did get in thirty-five hours of flying time. Before I left for Sweetwater, we fixed it up and sold it for only a little less than we had paid for it.

About that time, I was fortunate to meet Marge Gilbert. She was also flying at Richmond, but I don't think I knew that until she came and told me about the WASP program. We were in the Civil Air Patrol together. We both went to Wright-Patterson Field in Dayton for our physicals and interviews. Then we went on down to Sweetwater on the train together. Also with us was a girl named Carol White. Carol was excited about the WASPs and flying, but she was an early washout. Marge and I didn't fly with her because she was in Flight Two and we were in Flight One, but I know she was heartbroken to have to go home again.

How very unlike these women were, in personality, in education, and in flying time! When I think of them heading for Sweetwater in September 1943, I can hardly imagine myself as one of those fortunate individuals. I never dreamed that more than half the class would wash out, or that I would be one of the lucky ones to graduate. I was among the youngest, and I had confidence oozing out of my ears, so I'm certainly glad I didn't know that many of my classmates had several hundred hours of flying time, not to mention college degrees. I had only forty hours, one year of college, a very provincial background, and a greatly overinflated ego. We were all optimistic in those days, however, and all we wanted was to fly.

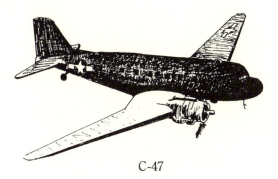

C-47

CHAPTER TWO

Avenger Field
and Primary Training

"The engine was in the front seat. Both wings were torn off. There was one thing left and that was the little rear cockpit!" —Nellie Henderson

WASP Class 44-W-2 was to report to Sweetwater the first week in September 1943. During that week much was happening on the war front. On September 3, 1943, the Allies landed in Italy, and by the ninth, Italy had surrendered. Many Germans remained entrenched in Italy, however, and the fighting continued on many fronts. At that time, MacArthur was in New Guinea, and the RAF was bombing Berlin with thirty tons of bombs a minute. Women's War Services made the news with a full-page spread in the *New York Times* about a variety of their activities. Nothing, however, was mentioned about the WASP. One woman writer, Elinore Herrick, wrote an item about "Women After the War." Her premise stated that women should be free to choose home, children, or career—or all three. A pretty advanced idea for 1943. Betty Smith's best-seller, *A Tree Grows in Brooklyn*, made its debut, and on September 7 a full-page ad in the *New York Times* entitled "An Open Letter to President Roosevelt and Prime Minister Churchill," begged for help to aid the Jews in the Warsaw ghetto. No response was forthcoming, at least as far as could be learned from news articles, to that poignant plea.

Meanwhile, WASPs from all over the country were heading for Sweetwater, Texas. Marge Gilbert, Carol White, and I arrived in Sweetwater tired and dirty. The ride across Texas had jostled us unmercifully, and the open windows had assailed us with wind, dust, and the odors of Texas sage, gas and oil. Having lived in the East and the Midwest, I had never before seen anything like this wide, empty landscape, these miles and miles of open range. Surprised and fascinated, I could not keep my eyes away from this unusual and captivating scene.

At the station, "cattle wagons" from Avenger Field greeted us. The "cattle wagon" was a large, primitive sort of bus. All windows and hard seats, this "people-mover" transported WASPs to auxiliary fields or to any other place they needed to go. We loaded our belongings into its spacious interior and hung on as the monster lurched into gear and rattled its way along the highway to our base, Avenger Field.

"Avenger Field," a magic name for all of us hopefuls, certainly lived up to our expectations. The roar of the planes, the low, wooden barracks so close to the flight line, the mess hall, the huge marching field—and the sand—everywhere, the sand. As Lorraine Zillner says, "It was so wonderful. We all were bright-eyed, excited; it was all so new to us. The routine, the militarization, the way we had to march to classes, and the hours we had to keep—most of us weren't used to that."

One of the first things the officers did (which will be familiar to anyone who was ever in the Air Force) was to line us up and tell us to look at the person on either side of us. We were then told that both of those people would wash out. Of course, someone would be looking at you from each side. We were supposed to be impressed that this was a very difficult program. More than half did wash out, but Sadie Hawkins was not at all impressed. "Remember," she says, "when they told us to look on either side of you, because probably both of them would wash out? I just thought 'Poor things.' It never occurred to me that I would wash out."

After an orientation, we were assigned to our barracks, called "bays." The bays were a series of one-story rooms, two rooms connected by a smaller room with showers and toilets. Six girls were bunked in each room, so twelve of us shared the two showers and two toilets. In our bay were housed Handerson, Harris, Hascall, Hawkins, Heckman, and Henderson. Only one washed out, "Hank" Handerson. None of us ever heard from "Hank" again, to my knowledge. The five who remained became great friends and remain so today. Kate Lee Harris and I, Jean Hascall, always had a difference of opinion about the windows. Kate Lee was from North Carolina and always wanted them shut. I was from Vermont and always wanted them open, especially at night. We would both try to be considerate, but I remember many nights when I would wait to hear her breathing deeply in sleep before I would surreptitiously open a window. We still share a room together at reunions, and somehow the problem has disappeared.

Anne Berry remembers the Saturday morning inspections. "What eager beavers we were when we first got there," she relates. "All these regulations—you were supposed to have your sheet turned down two hands' width over the blanket and you were supposed to have your blankets so tight that they could bounce a quarter on them. I remember the first week we were under our beds, tightening the sheets—and then, in three weeks' time, we were trying to see how much we could get away with.

"I can remember, though I didn't drink at the time, that on Saturday morning the girls would be out in those little alleyways between the two rows of barracks, burying all their liquor. They had learned they couldn't hide the bottles inside the barracks. Then, they'd put little sticks in the ground to mark where they had buried them, so they could dig them up again. We had these little cemeteries and tombstones, showing where people's liquor was buried.

"I also remember Ruth Adams—this tickles me to this day—Ruth Adams, who in her later years became a psychiatrist. Our shoes all had to be placed under our bed with the toes facing out toward the center of the room. For some reason, Ruth never could get this—she was absolutely brilliant, but she couldn't get this through her head, so it was somebody's duty, always, to check Ruth's shoes. She invariably put them with the heels pointing out, which meant we might get a demerit and not get off the post that weekend. Somebody always had to check Ruth's shoes!"

Anne recalls the strenuous physical training we received. "I can remember, with fondness, the PT instructor," she laughed, "Lt. William LaRue. He was a nice guy and he put a little fun into what we were doing. We went through our routine and our drill was what it should be; he didn't let us get away with anything, but he would inject a little humor into it. I remember that we had to do something called side-straddle hops and these would go on for a few minutes, and then he would stop and say, 'Okay, pull 'em up,' and everybody would. [In those days we still wore brassieres.] Everybody would reach in and haul up their bra straps and then we would go on."

The story about Ruth Adams and her shoes reminds me of Ruth's attitude toward primary training. Ruth was indeed very bright, with an analytical mind. Petite and very attractive, she was smart enough to realize, right from the start, that there would be a lot of washouts. She was going to figure out a way not to be one of them. "I sensed very quickly," she told me, "that it was going to be a highly competitive situation. I remember thinking, if they're going to wash a bunch of us out, they can't tell who is really good or bad. They might be able to recognize the very outstanding upper 10 percent, and they could probably pick out the really bad fliers—uncoordinated, bad judgment, et cetera— but the whole middle mess of us, they would not be able to discriminate among at all. They were going to do it on personal prejudice. I have my own prejudice, about not really liking men. I really had a thing about men. I didn't like being around them. They spoiled my day, so, in primary training, I knew I'd have to watch myself. I set out to comb my hair right. You know: I must not in any way offend anybody, any of the men who had the responsibility for failing or passing me, but I had a very nice instructor, Ray Booth. A lovely man. Really nice."

Kate Lee Harris, Marge Johnson, and I also had Ray Booth as an instructor. A tall, heavyset Texas rancher, Ray wore cowboy boots, spoke in a Texas drawl, and went "all out" for his students. An excellent pilot, he was a joy to fly with. He and his wife were kind enough to invite all four of his students to Christmas dinner at their home. It was such a treat for us that we still talk about it.

Ray Booth really saved me when I went up for my first check ride. I was unlucky enough to get an Army Lieutenant named Pinkston (not to be confused with Flight Commander Harl Pinkard, a delightful man). Somehow, I thought I could pass the test best by being real tough. I started manhandling the plane around and he failed me. Ray Booth went back and talked to him and found out that Pinkston thought I wasn't a very "smooth" flier. Ray took me up and spent over an hour with me showing me just how to fly for Pinkston. The next time I passed. If it hadn't been for Ray Booth, I never would have graduated. Pinkston had a reputation for being a tough check pilot. I think he washed out a lot of students; many of us remember him with something less than affection.

Ruth also had a bad ride. "At one point," she says, "I had heard this examiner saying how you had to keep turning your head to left and right—keep your head on a swivel at all times. I went up on a check ride with him and I took him too literally and I was turning this way and that and, by God, he failed me. Just because of that. Then I realized I had made a mistake, and I should have used my judgment. You know, if you fail your check ride, the second ride is just routine, then they kick you out—but Ray Booth stood up for me and said, 'No, she's really a good flier.' This very same man had to take me up again. This time, I was very calm, and very smooth, and it was a calm day. I still remember he had me doing figure eights and it was all as smooth as silk. When we finished our check ride he commented, to somebody, 'She's a honey,' so, I felt, that was it. I passed. But that was the closest I came to not making it."

Ray Booth contrasted sharply to an instructor shared by Nellie Henderson, Anne Berry, and Ann Craft. Nellie describes her instructor as a "mean, mean blond. He was tall, thin, and thought he was God's gift to women. He was the one who beat your knees."

In dual-controlled aircraft, when the instuctor shoved the control stick back and forth rapidly, the control stick in the student's cockpit would hit her knees. "Yes, I got the stick beatings. He drove me crazy. He was determined that we would be shatterproof when he got through. Well, here we were going on like this, and he was fussing at me and he said, 'Take your feet off the Goddamn rudders.' I thought, 'My feet are on the floor.' He said it again: 'I said, take your Goddamn feet off the Goddamn rudders.' Well, I just took both hands and pulled back the throttle so it was dead calm, and put one foot up, and the other foot up, and yelled, 'I haven't got my feet on the Goddamn rudders.'

"I thought, 'Well, this is it, I'm washed out,' but he didn't say a word. We just flew back. He was great to me from then on. He was marvelous. He was one of my best instructors, finally. Loved me. I loved him."

I'm not sure I would have been as forgiving as Nellie. I saw the inside of her knees and they were both black-and-blue. Anne Berry remembers him as "tall; he really looked like a cowboy. This guy could have fit into a Clint Eastwood movie—no trouble at all. What his philosophy was in instructing I don't know, but he could be pretty mean. I can remember he would take the stick and whip your knees with it. Then sometimes, if you weren't doing something he wanted you to do, he would take the earphones and hold them over the side of the open cockpit. The wind would come whipping through these earphones and right into your ears, which could be pretty unpleasant. Happily, I have forgotten his name."

Ann Craft was his other primary student. Ann was a beautiful girl, and for some reason or other we all thought she had been a beauty queen at Ohio State University. It was just common knowledge. When I interviewed Ann, I asked about that and she said, "No, no." I said, "You mean it wasn't true? That's what we all thought. Where do we get these ideas?" She answered, "I guess because I was so beautiful?" and she laughed uproariously. She actually graduated from the University of Nebraska in education. Because she also had the "mean" instructor, I asked if she also got the "stick beatings."

"I don't think he did that to me," she answered. "I was awfully sweet and I don't think anyone would have done that to me. He used profane language, screamed and yelled—there was nothing you could do about that; and he was very strict, but did you know that all of his students graduated? He couldn't believe that I would graduate. He made me think that I was his worst student. I thought I was pretty bad, and how I stayed in just amazed me all the time, until I flew with some of the other girls. Then I realized I was better than some of them."

Jean Moore switched instructors three times in primary training. "My first instructor," she told me, "drank too much and sometimes he'd show up for work and sometimes he wouldn't. They finally got rid of him and gave me to the mad Russian, Emilie Cernich. He was very verbal and he thought I was so great that he sent me up too early for my Army check ride, which I busted. Then he was really verbal. He nearly had a fit about it, and he gave it to me in the ready room. Mr. J. Pollard heard him and came over afterward and said he would give me Mr. J. R. Smith, who was an instructor to instructors. Smith was great. He taught me aerobatics and all kinds of stuff. I never had any problems with check rides after that."

Most of the people I talked with were enthusiastic about their instructors.

Some of them, like myself, felt we owed our success to good instructors, but there were a few men who either did not like instructing women or were just "mean and ornery," and who probably should not have been instructing. Some women instructors also taught 44-W-2 pilots. As far as I know, they were assigned exclusively to Flight Two. I am not sure why. Women pilots were enough of a rarity in those days, to say nothing of women instructors. Clarice (Sid) Siddall had a woman instructor whose name was Jennie. "It really surprised me," she says, "that they were able to instruct at Avenger Field. Jennie, I think, later became a WASP herself. The other woman instructor was Lewis."

Several women pilots became WASP instructors. Jennie, I believe, was Jennie Gower, later a WASP graduate in 44-W-5. Lewis was Dottie Swain Lewis. Ruth Woods, who was in Clarice's flight, told me she had yet another woman instructor, Helen Montgomery Hine. Ruth thought Helen was the only woman instructor at that time. "She was good, you bet," Ruth tells me. "She was the world champion glider pilot at that time, and so was her husband. He was the male champion. Man, she could fly." I have heard of two other woman instructors, at other times during the training period, Helen Duffy and Ziggie Hunter, but there may have been more.

We all loved our primary plane, the low-winged, 175-horsepower Fairchild PT-19A. For many of us the PT was the largest plane we had ever flown, and we enjoyed the open cockpit, the extra power, and the maneuverability. It was a plane that was fun to fly—so much fun that we often got into trouble with it. When Clarice Siddall (Sid to us) was on her cross-country flight, she felt as though she had been set free with the airplane. "Maybe you did the same thing," she says, "and I'll bet Mary Ellen [Keil] did too. That was fence-hopping."

Fence-hopping consisted of flying your airplane so close to the ground that when you came to a fence, you had to hop over it. It could get dangerous, of course, because large bushes would sometimes appear suddenly as well as fences. You had to watch closely. There was another hazard as well—as Sid discovered—getting lost. "I got so caught up with this fence-hopping," she tells me, "that I really wasn't watching what I was doing and where I was going. We were flying almost in formation—and all of a sudden I was there all by myself. I didn't know what else to do, so I landed at some Army base. I can't remember where it was, someplace in Texas, and I had to call and let them know that I was there. I got called in when I got back. I was ashamed, and I had to tell them the truth; I had to tell them what I was doing. They probably laughed, but I got a lecture and was told to behave myself."

Asked about the reaction of the people at the Army base, she says: "Oh, that was really funny. When a woman got out of that Fairchild they were just agog. Then they thought it was pretty funny, too, that I got lost, that I didn't know where I was. But, you know, you get that feeling and you kind of panic, and you'd better get yourself down and out of it.''

Nellie Henderson had an even more exciting experience in the PT-19. ''I smashed up one of their little airplanes, and that was funny,'' she laughs. ''It was our first cross-country that we had in the open-cockpit PT-19, and I was in the first shift to leave for someplace in Oklahoma. I went to the flight line and the guys who check you in and out weren't open yet. But an officer was standing there, and he said, 'Yes, I know you're supposed to be going. Go on and get an airplane and take off.'

''Well, I got my little PT-19 and I looked in the front seat and the compass wasn't working. It was all screwed up, so I just said, 'Well, I'll just fly from the back seat.' At the time, the place was under construction, if you remember. I had to take off directly toward the construction. I got everything warmed up, and checked everything. I had a compass in the back seat and I was in great shape. 'Here we go,' I thought, with all of my five cushions that it took to see out of anything, and my little parachute and all my junk. Well, it took off fine, and then it went 'eh heh, eh heh' and died. I remembered that you're supposed to shut off the gas and turn off the switch and go straight ahead.

''Straight ahead was where all the construction was, but I had to go there. I sure as hell couldn't turn. I remember taking my glasses off—I was so proud of that—to protect my precious little nearsighted eyes. Then we went 'hoop de hoop' and *wham!* I just sat there and then got out of the airplane. I thought, 'Gee, it's going to be marvelous.' I'd always wondered what it would be like to have all the staff cars coming with their flags, all the ambulances and everybody coming.

''Well, nobody even knew I was down there. I was down right off the end of the runway. I didn't even get more than eighteen feet off the ground, maybe twenty feet, and there I was down in a ditch. I mean all the digging part. Then I looked at the airplane. It was a good thing I was flying in the back, because the front—well, the engine was up in the front cockpit. Both wings were torn off. The tail assembly got ripped off. There was one thing left, and that was the little rear cockpit. I'd hit my head up there and it made a little dent in the instrument panel.

''I thought, 'My God, I'm going to have to walk back to the flight line and report that they've got an accident.' No little red flags waving, nobody saw me. I'm just down there. I got my parachute—I leave my cushions, there're too many of those to take back—but I do take my parachute.

''Then I walked back, and they were open, but you couldn't see back there, where I crashed. A couple of people were in there and they said, 'What happened?' I answered, 'I just tore up one of your little airplanes down there.' They replied, 'Oh? How are you?' I said, 'I'm just fine.' Then they said, 'Well, the best thing for you to do is to take that plane out there and shoot a few landings.' I said, 'Fine,' and I went out and was merrily going around having great fun when they came on the radio and they said, 'RV 222, please land and report to the hospital.'

"They'd seen the plane by then, and they told me, 'You could not be able to fly again.' I answered, 'But I feel fine. I've got a little tiny bump on my head.' They sent me over to the hospital and kept me over there even though I insisted there was nothing wrong with me.

"Well, the sweet old gal who ran the cafeteria knew I liked avocados, and she went through the salad for the day and picked out all the avocados and brought them over for me to eat. I finally got out by that night.

"Later, when I told them I didn't know what was wrong with the plane, they told me that it was maintenance. Of course they wouldn't now, but they admitted it then. A mechanic had left an oily rag in the engine. That was the story, and that was my only problem."

Nellie was fortunate to have survived that accident. All of her baymates went over to the "cemetery" where they dumped the crashed airplanes, and when we saw what was left of that poor PT-19, it was hard to believe that she had walked away from it. Her story was true—nothing was left except that rear cockpit. Looking at that smashed airplane sobered us a bit, but if I remember correctly, we sang a chorus of "Blood on the Cockpit" to regain our usual jubilant spirits. "Blood on the Cockpit" was sung to the tune of "Blood on the Saddle," a Western ditty popular at the time. The song ended up, "Pity the pilot, all bloody and gore, for she won't be flying the pattern no more." It was, of course, all bravado, but such a song was okay to sing as long as Nellie was unhurt. I really think we were more careful after seeing that airplane.

Lourette Puett, whose primary instructor was Dotty Swain, had a rather close call in the PT. "I went up once on a solo flight and forgot to put my seat belt on. I was practicing spins. As I pushed the stick forward and came out of the spin, I rose up out of my seat and went over the canopy, but just then the plane straightened out and the wind blew me back in my seat. I was so scared, I don't think I ever told anyone. I probably wouldn't have graduated had anyone known. I'll tell you, even on airlines, I don't undo my seat belt now. I think it was a very good lesson."

Phyllis Tobias's instructor in primary training was named Jenny (Jenny Gower, 44-W-5). "I don't remember her last name but she was a friend of Margaret Wakefield [one of Phyllis's friends]. I'm sure if it hadn't been for that she would have washed me out in the first week, because I was just terrible, flopping all over the sky. Oh, she was wonderful to me. Finally, I did solo.

"I'll never forget when I passed my test to go from primary to basic. The military pilot I had, and I can't remember his name, flew us upside down and he said, 'You can pass. But if you don't let go of that seat belt, I'll never pass you.' I threw up my arms, and I didn't fall out, of course, so all went well. But what a graphic way to learn."

Ruth Woods also had a woman instructor, Helen Montgomery Hine. But Ruth had a lot more experience than Toby had. "I got through everything in primary ahead of time," she said, "and I still had a lot of hours to fly. I used to go over and fly the PT inverted on rectangular courses. Helen knew I was doing it. She told me, 'Just know what you're doing.' I'd get up there and have no problem. I'd come in and land and lie down on the ground under the airplane and think about it. Then I'd go back and do it again. When the gas would start fading, I'd roll her back over 'til the gas started feeding again. Then you could roll over again. I had a lot of fun with that one. That was a challenge—and someone in my class challenged me to do it, and that's why I did it."

Once, a professional photographer came to Sweetwater and took a picture of some of us throwing Kate Lee Harris into the Wishing Well as the first to solo the PT. I always thought Kate Lee had soloed first because of this photograph, but apparently the picture was taken after an AT-6 solo, when Kate Lee ended up as the only student of her instructor. "So, consequently," she said, "I got my time in faster, and I was the first to solo the AT-6, only because I was his private student." As for the Wishing Well photograph, Kate Lee says, "We 'posed' that—it was in the wintertime, so you didn't actually splash me in. We have a good picture, anyway."

After talking with Kate Lee, I finally understood why Sadie Hawkins had told me that she was the first to solo the PT-19 in Flight One. She was indeed— I had thought it was Kate Lee only because of the picture. "We were flying out of that little auxiliary field where we used to shoot landings," Sadie said, "and no one had soloed yet. The chief pilot, who was head of instruction, said, 'Can I ride over to Avenger with you?' Naturally, I said yes, and I remember a few things he did on the way back, such as shutting off the fuel, and when we got back and landed he said, 'Take it up, you've just passed your test.' " In Flight Two, Lorraine Zillner was the first to solo the PT-19. "Yes," she said, "I was thrown into the Wishing Well."

That photograph of Kate Lee, posed as it may have been, shows a group of Flight One pilots dressed mostly in "zoot suits." Mary "Minkie" Heckman remembers our first encounter with these famous costumes. "When we first went into Sweetwater, we were assigned these old Army fatigues—a heavy

31

twill. We tried them on and I don't care how big the girls were, the suits were all too big. I don't know anyone who had one that fit. We just rolled up the sleeves and the pant legs and tied them up. The seats just swished along as we walked, but we hitched them up the best we could. We used to send them to the laundry and never got them back in time. Finally, we learned what we could do. The air was so dry there in Sweetwater, we'd just get into the shower and scrub ourselves with the zoot suit on, and have somebody scrub our back. Then we'd just rinse them out and hang them outside. They'd be dry in about two or three hours."

Let us not forget the turbans, either. How we hated them. Whoever was in administration simply could not handle the fact that we had, most of us, long hair. It became almost as much an issue as it did for young men much later, in the sixties. I don't see why there should have been any real concern about long hair; the chances of its getting tangled anywhere were minuscule. But ''they'' (we never knew who) were determined to ''do something'' about it. At first our hair was confined in hairnets, but that just wasn't good enough. Next, we were required to wear ridiculous-looking turbans. We were all so eager to fly we would have dyed our hair green, if it had been required. Many of us, however, wished we could have found out the name of the person who thought up that particular bit of insanity.

Another time, someone decided we needed some publicity. Newsreel camera crews came down to Sweetwater. First they showed us at Physical Education, then they showed us sunbathing. Then they piled us into the cattle cars and took us out to some lake about fifty miles out of town. ''I remember them telling us, 'Run to the water, run to the water,' '' Fran Smith says. ''Remember, at that time, you'd go to the movies and you'd see fifteen minutes of newsreels? It was shown in the theaters, and I used to get calls from people saying they saw me in the movies.''

It was already early November before Class 44-W-2 completed PT-19 training. In less than two months' time we had racked up roughly sixty hours of flying time in the PT-19. During those two months, the Germans were driven from Naples and the city celebrated the Allies' arrival. British and American bombers were blasting the Ruhr Valley, and U.S. bombers were attacking Germany from Africa. Meanwhile, the Germans were sacking Rome as the Allies advanced across Italy. In the Pacific, U.S. Navy planes pounded Wake Island, and U.S. ships sank a Japanese cruiser and two destroyers off the Solomon Islands.

Women doctors had finally won their fight for equality in the U.S. Army Medical Corps, as Capt. Marion C. Loizeau became the first woman M.D. to receive a commission. Lt. Mary Ann Sullivan, an Army nurse, won the Legion of Merit for her devotion to duty in the Tunisian campaign. Eleanor Roosevelt gave a talk to the Congress of Industrial Organizations Auxiliary where she stated that the American woman's greatest opportunity was "to count as a citizen and be reckoned with as a political entity." Out in Portland, Oregon, the Kaiser Shipyard was the first to pioneer child care at the shipyard where mothers were employed.

Rationing continued to be a serious issue in the United States. At one point, when shoe rationing was considered, Americans were told to "use it up, wear it out, make it do, or do without." Bill Mauldin had come on the scene with sardonic cartoons that deglamorized war and poked fun at the Army brass. The four leading powers of the United Nations, the United States, Great Britain, Russia and China, agreed at Moscow to fight their common enemies to submission on terms of unconditional surrender. The new airplanes of the day—the P-51, the P-47, the Corsair, and the Sikorsky helicopter—were displayed in the *New York Times* in a full-page ad by the manufacturers, and the huge B-29 bomber was nearing its final test for the Army.

Meanwhile, the WASPs of 44-W-2 were engaged in their own struggles. Most of the heartbreaking washouts took place during those first two months of training. Of the three who started out from Indiana in September, two of us still remained. Marge Gilbert was next door to me, but Carol White had washed out early in training. She was in tears, as I remember, and we felt sorry for her, but we felt lucky, at the same time, that we were still there. There seemed to be so much "luck" involved in the washouts. We later found out that many good pilots didn't make it. Frances Laraway said, "I was amazed at the numbers as they shrank—when different people washed out and they impressed us into smaller and smaller space. I don't think that you ended up in my bay, Jean, but you must have been next door, because we really did get smaller in number."

We were settling down to a solid group, about twenty-five in each flight. We knew all the girls in our own flight well, because we flew together, went to ground school together, ate together—and we played together, too. Did we ever! The WASPS had a club in town where we could gather. The music was just recordings, but we could dance. Officers from Camp Barkely in Abilene used to come over on weekends and a lot of partying went on. One person in each flight owned a car, fortunately, so we were able to get to town on weekends. Nellie Henderson, in our flight, was our "driver."

Her car was a convertible with a rumble seat. We would put about six people in front and six in the rumble seat, and off we'd go into Sweetwater. "I had the only car in Flight One," she says. "I was very popular."

In Flight Two, Clarice Siddall had the car. Her mother, whom she

33

described as "something of an adventuress," liked to travel, and they drove out to Sweetwater together in Clarice's car. "I was very popular with that car," Clarice recalls, "because it was a good way to get to the Army bases where the guys were. We also filled the car up one weekend to go down to San Antonio where there was a base. I knew this guy from Cleveland; I had gone with him before, and when he found out that I had access to all these girls, he asked me to get four or five girls together and come on down, because they had dances every Saturday night, so I did. But you know what those guys did? They didn't know what to expect, in women fliers—what we would look like and what we would be like—so they told us where to meet them. Then they drove by and looked us over before they came to meet us. I think they even kind of picked whom they wanted. That was one of the things that happened that was fun."

It was more than fun, though. It was a special time in our lives, and we were a special sort of group, luckier than most. Mary Strok sums it up: "It was just the height of anything I had ever done in my life, and even since. It was a marvelous experience. Everything about it appealed to me immensely. I loved the comradeship of the girls, the trainers, the people who taught us. There was not a single one of them that I didn't care for, or thought wasn't doing his job. Every day was a new adventure. I can remember getting up at the crack of dawn in those cold rooms, because we got there in September and the nights were very chilly. We had snow in November or December. It was mighty cold and one of us would have to get up and turn those heaters on—those noisy heaters—and check our shoes to be sure no animals had gotten in during the night to keep warm. I couldn't wait to get on the flight line to get into the airplanes. It was such a wonderful, wonderful feeling. Every morning I'd say, 'I can't believe I'm doing this.' "

Mary speaks for all of us. It was a wonderful time in our lives. All of us worked together toward a common goal, and primary training was where we first "got it all together." Here we first met our lifelong comrades, flew our first "big" 175-horsepower planes, struggled to master the intricacies of flying, sweated over ground-school problems, labored with our instructors, and finally won out—staying the course to advance into basic training. Tough, fun, exciting, exhilarating, we loved it all—Avenger Field in its entirety, and our beautiful, open-cockpit, primary trainer, the PT-19. We were ready, now, to tackle the formidable BT-13s. We knew their reputation, but we would master the monsters!

CHAPTER THREE

Ground School and Basic Training

"The rudder cables had been cut." —Lorraine Zillner

Primary training and the delightful PT-19 airplane had occupied most of our thoughts and efforts during those first two months at Avenger Field. It would be a mistake to think, however, that our training was all flying, all excitement. Many hours were spent in the classroom, on the marching field, in daily calisthenics, and in mundane chores such as cleaning our barracks, washing clothes, or writing letters home. Ground school was tough for some of the younger girls who had not had the advantage of a college education. The courses, which included a lot of math, physics, navigation, and aircraft engines, seemed formidable to women who had received little education along such lines.

Madeline Sullivan found it difficult. "I was just as happy as my father when he said he wasn't going to pay for another year of fooling around. I wanted no part of school, that's for sure, but I had always been arrogant enough to think I could do it. He used to call up the school all the time and they'd say, 'She could do it, if she wanted to.'

"I can remember saying to myself from grammar school on, 'They're right, but I don't want to.' When we got out to Sweetwater, I thought we were just going to fly. I didn't realize they were going to send me to ground school. I really struggled, because I had no good study habits. Joan Whelan worked with me like crazy in navigation and some other courses. I really got scared. I thought to myself, 'I was stupid enough all my life to think I could really do it, if I wanted to. If I don't do it this time, it really shoots a hole in my big theory.' I was afraid I was going to wash out, but I just squeaked through."

Minkie Heckman had few difficulties, but even for her it was not easy. "Mathematics and I are not the very best of friends, but I managed to get through it. Morse Code was another tough one. It was hard getting it into my head, but I did finally get through that."

Women like Joan Whelan and Anna Mae Petteys, who had graduated from college, spent a lot of time coaching some of the other girls so they could get through the ground school. "I'd already had a lot of education," Anna Mae said, "so I thought it was pretty simple. I had a master's degree at the time, but some younger people that I was helping didn't seem to have enough education to deal with ground school. The high-school background didn't equip them well for that."

Marjorie Gilbert had learned a lot before she got to Sweetwater, although she did not attend college. She was very bright, however, and that made a difference. "They had these Civilian Pilot Training courses for people going to college," she explained. "I didn't get to go to college, but CPT also had a non-college class in ground school. You had to pass all your ground work before you got to take a flight—to take any flying lessons at all. Those who got the best scores were the ones who got to fly. We had more than fifty in our class and the top five got to take flight training. I was one of the top five—four men and I. I didn't have a car at that time because my father had died, and I had to hitch a ride with one of the other four. We went up to Muncie [Indiana] to fly at Ball State University. After I finished the training I got my private license, with the government paying for it."

Ground school certainly was difficult for most of us, but we all seemed to help each other. Morse Code came easily to me because I had already memorized it back in Girl Scout days. Engines, another tough one, took a lot of effort, and math was a bugaboo for many, although I enjoyed the math instruction, and especially the meteorology.

Mr. Christopher, who taught us meteorology, was a fascinating character. He walked with a mincing gait, wore his dark, curly hair combed back neatly, and always smiled, no matter what was said to him. Nellie Henderson remembers him. "Mr. Christopher was so prissy and so serious about the thing, because the airplane would not kill us, but the weather would! Oh, my God, he was a devoted weather man. He just had to see that we understood weather. He was good. We used to wear dark glasses all the time. Then one of us would cross her legs. That was the signal for us to reach up and put our dark glasses just off-center on one side, so that the glasses were all going off to the right side. He would lean over to that side and start talking to us. Then somebody else would cross another leg, and then we'd all reach up and move our glasses over to the other side of our noses, and he'd lean over to the other side. He never caught on that we were driving him crazy. Whenever I get together with Minkie, we get our glasses off-center and start giggling, because they do look funny. They're not really wrong, but they're not right, so you sort of lean over that way to talk to somebody."

"Nellie made up this little poem for him," said Anne Berry. "He must have been one of the ones that we liked. The poem went, 'Drink, Mr. Christopher, drink, be gay, we can afford this on our fabulous pay.' Which was, of course, practically 'zip' in those days. We must have given him a bottle of wine when we completed the course. We would not have given it to him while we were taking the course."

Another instructor, Mr. Ted Merchant, was supposed to be an "instructor for instructors." I always thought him a fascinating man. Short, tough-looking, and harsh, he seemed incapable of speaking without using triple negatives, poor grammar, and pronunciation that would curl your hair. He taught us instruments (ground school) and he kept emphasizing, with pictures on the blackboard, that we should just "step on that little ol' ball. That's how you keep that plane level. Just step on that little ol' ball [meaning the needle/ball device on our instrument panel]."

We were a bit intimidated by him because he was so certain of everything. Minkie Heckman recalls, "That awful man, the one who said, 'It don't make no difference nohow, it ain't writ in no book'? Ted Merchant. He was such a fusspot about these things. We were kind of a little afraid of him."

Finally, because he was so grim and stern and never cracked a smile, we decided we would straighten him out. I was flight leader at that particular time, and we made plans. When he came in to class the next day I said, "Exercise position, take"—and we all went down on our knees and said, "Allah, Allah." As Minkie recalls, "It really cracked him up and he was human after that. He was okay. He was a good instructor, too."

Other strange stories popped up from time to time. This one concerned Ruth Adams, but she never mentioned it when she was talking to me. Instead, Anne Berry, who has a marvelous memory about what happened that far back, tells the story. "I really think it should be recorded—for the annals of military history," she insisted. "We were doing a cross-country in the PT-19, and of course we wore parachutes. Ruth told me this after it happened. She's on her cross-country and she has to urinate. What is she going to do? You remember, if we landed—if we made a forced landing—then we weren't supposed to take off again. We were supposed to call the Army and an Army pilot had to come in and fly the plane off. We would have to go through all of this interrogation as to what happened and why we were doing it, so she didn't want to land the plane.

"She said to herself, 'If I urinate in my uniform and onto this parachute, I may ruin a two-hundred-dollar parachute. I don't want to do that.' She figured her only alternative was this: she unzipped this great big fleece-lined leather jacket. Then, we wore a sort of bib overall thing—a big fleece-lined leather overall. She had to get rid of that. She had a flight suit under it and we wore these zoot suits that were left over from the men. They didn't have any drop seats in them. Whenever we had to urinate, we had to take the whole uniform off, and drop it down around our ankles. Then she had on some kind of winter underwear. She managed to get all that off, scoot over to the edge of her seat to where she could pee without getting it onto anything. Then she got all this paraphernalia back onto herself and never got off course. She kept her direction, and ended up where she was supposed to go. Anyone who ever wore those outfits can realize what she had to go through.'' Not to mention how cold she must have been in that open cockpit in winter with no clothes on!

Anne also remembers our flight lieutenants' problems in getting us up in the morning. She recalls Muriel Lindstrom, who would get up early and try to get the flight moving. ''She'd start out in this brisk voice shouting, 'All right, everybody, on the double.' There'd be absolutely no response from any of the barracks and Mimi would come out five minutes later and in this authoritative voice shout, 'On the double.' Nothing would happen again. Finally, about five minutes later, she would come out and, in this pleading tone, say, 'Oh come on, you guys, on the double.' At that time, we would probably come out. I remember, there were some trainees who were many classes ahead of us. They were down at the end of another row of barracks, and they had the same time to get up for breakfast that we did. The cafeteria was sort of equidistant between the last barracks and the first barracks. We would march toward the cafeteria and we could see this other flight marching toward the cafeteria, so Mimi would up the cadence a bit and we would march a little faster, because we wanted to get to the breakfast line first. Then their section marcher would jazz them up, and at the end we would both practically be running (but not quite, because we weren't supposed to run) to see who would get to this single walkway that would lead us to the breakfast line first.''

Lorraine Zillner, flight lieutenant for Flight Two, remembers William LaRue, our physical education instructor. ''I had to give all the orders like 'Hup, two, three, four,' and all that, and march everybody over to the Armory. I'd get everybody marched in and then I'd go off to the side. I'm not the athletic type. One day, Mr. LaRue, our PE instructor, said, 'Lorraine Zillner, I've been watching you for days. You get in here with the rest of your class, and quit sitting in the shade out here.' After that I went in with the rest of the group.''

Much of our flying in primary training took place at the auxiliary fields. With so many flying, it would have been impractical to have everyone practicing out of Avenger Field. During night flying (which could be done only at the main field), we had to fly in specified quadrants and at specified altitudes so we wouldn't collide with one another. Several auxiliary fields dotted the dry Texas landscape that surrounded Avenger Field, however. These were used for daily practice flying. Early morning often found us piled up inside a "cattle car," bouncing over the rough roads leading to these auxiliary fields. A few lucky ones got to fly the airplanes over. More pilots than airplanes were needed, because we took turns flying. Nellie Henderson remembers one incident that took place at one of the auxiliary fields.

"We'd gone over there and were fooling around, and this Navy plane came in. It was gorgeous—just beautiful—and out came the pilot. We all came out saying, 'Look at the pretty airplane, look at the pretty man.' He was going to really show us, so he got in his airplane, he taxied down to the end of the runway, and opened the throttle. I knew what he was going to do—he was going to fold his wheels up and clap the hydraulic button. But instead of that, his little wings went 'chung, chung' and came up over his head. He'd forgotten to set them in lock position. Instead of flying off with his wheels up under him, he was flying off with his little wings coming up over his head. He stopped at the end of the runway, and when he came back we were waving, 'Good show. Good show.' He didn't look at us. He just went straight by us and down to the end of the runway. He checked everything and took off, and he didn't even pull his wheels up. How humiliating!"

In early November (the third, if my log book is correct), Class 44-W-2 moved on to the infamous BT-13. This airplane had a 440-horsepower Wright engine, a sleek appearance, and a bad reputation. Many names were applied to this aircraft, one being the "Vultee Vibrator," or, more often, "that bucket of bolts." I don't know if new BT-13s were any better, but ours were all old ones. Many of us thought they were Army rejects, but, in any case, they certainly were far from new. They rattled, they shook, they were unreliable in spins, the cowling always seemed about to come loose, and, for some reason, the radio reception was often poor. Most of us, however, were happy to be moving into something more powerful, whatever its condition.

Again I was fortunate to draw a delightful flight instructor. John Hosier loved to fly, was a good teacher, and was always ready to hop a fence, zoom through a cloud, or try an exciting maneuver. Flying with him was always fun, and I never recall a cross word from him.

We all soloed the BT within a week, but we had flown it for only two weeks altogether when it was decided, for some reason, that we should move on to the AT-6 and learn to handle that too. Then, while we were still flying the AT-6, we were sent to Link training.

The Link looked like a miniature airplane, but it was just a box full of instruments that simulated instrument flying. You really felt as though you were flying an airplane, however. The training itself was like ground school in that we took the training in conjunction with our real flying.

After completing three weeks in the AT-6, simultaneously with Link, we again switched back to the BTs for instrument training. We never knew the reason for switching back and forth. Confusion reigned for a while, but we soon learned to cope. The reason for switching from AT-6s to Link to BT-13s, I learned later from Dora Dougherty Strother, Class 43-3, was due to a new curriculum, which had been started with the previous class and which was gradually put into effect until it was fully implemented with Class 44-W-5. This curriculum concentrated instrument flying in one phase, eliminated twin-engine training, increased navigation training, lengthened the training period, and provided increased ground and flight training.

The BT gave many of us some anxious moments. Every spin was a surprise; something or other invariably went wrong. Sometimes the plane simply wouldn't spin right; other times, it would wind up so tightly, you were uncertain whether or not it would recover. Every plane seemed different. Lorraine Zillner had a frightening experience in a BT. "I went up and was trying aerobatics—I thought all by myself, but Kit MacKethan saw what happened and she later called in to the field to tell what she saw.

"I was up there doing maneuvers and all of a sudden the plane just went completely out of control and flipped into an inverted spin. I stayed with it, I worked with it, I did everything possible. I stayed with it as long as I could, and then I tried to get out. That was a big surprise. It was difficult to get out of the plane because, in this case, I was underneath, being in an inverted spin, and in getting out one of my legs was hit by the rudder. I have a picture of my leg, bandaged, and that was the result of being hit. Then I counted 'one-ten' and pulled the ripcord. No counting to ten. It was just one and ten. I was so close to the ground. Later they told me I had stayed with it too long. Kit saw the plane going down and she saw it crash, but she never saw my chute open. That's how close I was. My chute had just barely opened when I hit the ground.

"I lay there for I don't know how long. Then, all of a sudden, two cowboys came galloping up. One of them said, 'Oh, there's the pilot.' He came over and pulled my helmet off and my long hair fell down, and he said, 'My gosh, it's a little girl.' When he said that, I don't know if I was in shock or what, but I started to cry, and he said, 'Don't cry, don't cry.' The other cowboy went galloping off and came back with a branch of cotton to dry my eyes. It was a cotton field that I had landed in, and he said, 'Here, don't cry, don't cry. We'll get help.'

"In the meantime, Kit MacKethan had called the field and I don't know how long it took or just where I was, but the ambulance came and took me back, so I spent that night in the hospital.

"Later, there was a board meeting and I had to get all dressed up in uniform and they questioned me and asked why I left the airplane. I said I stayed until the last minute, and then one of the officers said, 'Well, how did you manage to get out of a plane that was in an inverted spin?' I didn't know how I got out. I just looked at him and said, 'Have you ever prayed?' He didn't say a word to that and they excused me at that point.

"Still later, I found out that the rudder cables had been cut. They grounded all the BTs at Avenger Field and also at Randolph Field.

"Yes, the rudder cables had been cut. That's what they told me, so there was no problem about my doing right or wrong. You know, they were cut through just part way, so I took off and went up and then, just when I was doing some maneuver, they snapped, and that was it. No rudders.

"That was the end of that airplane, but I still have my ripcord. I never let go of it all the way to the hospital. To this day I have it. My leg was just bruised. I wore the bandage on it for quite a while, but two days later I went right back to flying."

Zillner still beamed confidence, even after her accident. We all admired such hardiness and wondered if we would have been able to continue as non-chalantly as she did, so soon after that harrowing experience.

By the time we suffered through BT training, most of the washouts had taken place. But there were one or two girls who did wash out in basic training. One was Fran Hollander. She was a good friend of Kay Herman, and Kay had tried to help her before her last washout flight. Kay said, "Fran had been criticized quite a bit for coming into the pattern wrong."

We always flew a rectangular pattern, a standard method of entering airport space and landing. We would enter the "downwind" leg of the rectangle at a forty-five-degree angle, flying downwind and parallel to the landing strip. Then we would continue along that leg until it was judged time to turn onto a "base" leg. From the "base" leg we would turn onto our "final" approach to the landing strip. Apparently, Fran had experienced trouble in the way she entered the "downwind" leg. Some people do have difficulty in visualizing this pattern and the approach to it. Kay was trying to make her "see" this pattern.

"I remember," Kay continued, "the night before, we had a flashlight, and we were hand-flying in the bay, trying to get her into the pattern—stuff like that. I was up for my first check ride in the BT the next day, and I remember the field was being repaired (again), and I was very upset because I knew Fran had been called and she was going up for this last ride.

"Then my name was called for my check ride, and I was so angry, you know, thinking that she was probably going to get washed out, which she did. When you got in the plane, prior to takeoff they would give you all these instructions—and then hope to heck that you wouldn't remember them. I

41

wrote them all down really quickly on my knee pad, and I went through the thing and hit everything off as I had never done before—I was so angry. Because I thought this was one of the check pilots who had given Fran a 'down.' I remember coming in on this short field, when all of a sudden I realized I was too high. I started putting the flaps all the way down, and I felt his hand on the stick. I got on the intercom and said, 'Get your hands off my controls. This is my airplane.' Then, after I said it, I took it down, and made the best landing I've ever made. When I was securing the airplane, I looked back and I thought, 'He's going to get me—for insubordination, or something' and then I decided, 'The hell with it, I don't care.' He came out and I said, 'Well?' He said, 'That's the best ride I've had,' turned around, and walked away. That was the end of it."

Ruth Woods had a terrifying ride in the BT-13. "I was on my check ride in the BT," she explains, "the old Vultee Vibrator, and I was planning to go home for the weekend, and this was on a Friday, and I was riding with Pinkston. Man, he was tough. Well, we took off and he told me to climb to some altitude. He wanted me to do a left, climbing stall. I started in this left turn, climbing to stall it out, and the damned airplane caught on fire.

"Now, if there's anything I've had a fear of, it's fire. Anywhere—not just in an airplane. He said to me, 'Take it in.' I said, 'All right.' I called the tower and told them my problem, and they brought me in and we landed. I never made as good a landing in my life. That thing was so greased in we didn't know for sure we were on the ground—and I was out of it almost as soon as it hit the ground. My only concern, then, was whether or not I was going to get to go home. I went up to the day room and waited and waited, and he finally came in. When I asked him whether I could reschedule my check ride for that afternoon, he said, 'No, you can't reschedule it—there's no need to. You passed it. You remained really calm and cool and you did a good job and you brought the airplane in. You never panicked.' He didn't know what was happening to me inside."

Most of us had very little good to say about the BT-13. "I have heard that some people thought the BTs were quite a dangerous airplane," added Ruth Petry. "Mary Strok's young husband was killed in an accident in a BT, not too long after they were married. The cowling came loose, and pieces of it were chopped off by the prop. I've heard since that one of the WASPs had that happen, but she didn't know anything was wrong until she landed and they saw the cowling was chopped up. Mary's husband stuck his head out to see what was going on, and was hit by a piece of the cowling, they think. The plane crashed and killed him and a cadet. That was the only fatal accident I knew of with a BT."

Madeline Sullivan remembers her BT instructor, William Tischler. "We were flying out in the back of Texas someplace, following the little dirt roads that seemed to go noplace. Suddenly this little pickup was coming at us with two cowboys in it. We could see them coming, so we went down until we weren't very far aloft, and we just kept going at them. They started making S-turns, and the first thing you know, they went right off the road!

"But that B-13—that bucket of bolts. That really put the fear of God into me. After Zillner had trouble and jumped—I mean, from that time on, when they sent you out to fly in one of those quadrants, I stayed in the corner closest to the field. They weren't going to lose me that easily."

Ruth Petry tried an unusual maneuver in a BT once, although it was after her basic training at Sweetwater. "Mary Strok and I were taking off from an auxiliary field in what seemed like a pretty good wind. The wind shifted or died away, and when I got the plane off the ground it began to turn and was on the verge of a stall. I couldn't hold it. I was trying to hold it but it was coming dangerously close to the fence. I had heard of this trick that you use in a Piper Cub, bouncing it over a fence. I cut the throttle back and put it on the ground and bounced it—and as soon as I throttled back it was all right. It was the torque that was turning it, so when I cut back the throttle it went very nicely. Some of the people who were there at the field came running over when I came back and asked about it, and I said, 'Well, I thought I'd better not hit the fence and I thought I'd bounce it over instead, the way you do in a light plane.'

"They'd never heard of that. It's a trick they teach in the Grasshopper squadrons for getting into a field. When you have two fields and neither one is long enough to land, you come in on the first, and put the plane in a big bounce and land it in the second field. Mary's brother was a big shot in one of those squadrons so we'd heard a lot about it."

"How many people have bounced a BT?" I asked her.

"Oh, they bounce nicely," she laughed.

During basic training, Leona Golbinec had a bad reaction to a typhoid shot and ended up in the infirmary while the rest of us went to Dallas for a fun weekend. She broke out in fever blisters all over her face. They brought in a plastic surgeon from Dallas, but fortunately surgery was not required. To make up for her lost time, an Army officer flew with her, putting in three to four hours a day in BTs and ATs so she could catch up.

"Our original instructor in BTs was let go," she explained, "and they washed out the other four students in our group. They kept me because they didn't want the group to be a complete failure. It wasn't fair because one of those girls could fly circles around me. She was a wonderful pilot. I'm beginning to see that maybe a lot of those that were washed out really weren't bad pilots."

Sometime in November 1943, new uniforms were chosen for the WASPs by General Hap Arnold. The *New York Times* showed Jacqueline Cochran modeling one of the lovely Santiago blue outfits, and the article stated that "WASPs averaged four inches narrower in the hips than other selected women's groups because of the exercise and training they get." I could well believe it. It seemed we never had enough time to get everything done that needed doing, and there was plenty of exercise. The other women's service groups were in the news a lot—more than the WASP!

One *New York Times* photograph showed an enlisted WAVE who had qualified as an air gunnery instructor at Pensacola. WACs (by now they had dropped the auxiliary designation) were turning out "peppy, photogenic, popular" military police. Recruiting for the WAC, however, failed to fill the need for their services, and compulsory service was being discussed as the only way to raise the corps to the desired size.

In other news items was a plea to ease the "Jim Crow" laws, which segregated the races on streetcars and buses. Even white Virginians were voting three to one in favor of scrapping such laws. Plans for the postwar world began to crop up, especially regarding veterans, housing, and inflation.

War news continued to dominate the headlines, and much was made of the parley at Cairo between Chiang Kai-Shek, Roosevelt, and Churchill. Then the "Big Three" conference at Teheran, with Stalin, Roosevelt, and Churchill, followed shortly and held the spotlight. Meanwhile, bombing was stepped up. Tons more bombs were dropped on Berlin, and the Eighth Air Force bombed Bremen. In the Pacific, U.S. carriers sank two cruisers and downed seventy-two Japanese planes in the Marshall Islands.

The draft was upped with plans to take two million, including one million fathers, but shortly after, President Roosevelt signed a bill to postpone the drafting of fathers. The *New York Times* posted daily lists of U.S. casualties as well as men imprisoned by the Germans. During the month of November, 1,000 four-engine bombers and 7,789 other airplanes rolled off U.S. production lines.

We often wished we would see a few of those new airplanes, but we always got the leftovers. The BTs especially were thought to be in pretty bad shape. "I don't think they were kept up as they should have been," said Fran Smith. "All of the good mechanics and people in the know were on the front lines. My instructor said he had lost his license and was helping out. He was probably 4-F or deferred for some reason, like most of our instructors, or they would have been in the service. I think that's why we had the Army check pilots—to make sure they were teaching us Army flying. I feel the same way about our mechanics, but, again, how many of us really thought it was dangerous? To me, it was like driving a car. It was fun."

Most of us would agree with Fran. I didn't take it too seriously at the time, but the girls who experienced the bad maintenance, like rags in the engines or exhausts and severed rudder cables, were really concerned. The talk of sabotage seemed unlikely to me, but after Zillner was told that her rudder cable had been "cut," we didn't know what to think. Mary Ellen Keil had two bad experiences with maintenance at Avenger Field.

"I needed to fly at night in AT-6s to pick up some extra time," she said, "because we'd been delayed by weather. On one flight the engine caught fire and they found out that a mechanic had left an oil rag on top of the engine. We never knew whether it was sabotage or carelessness. I had just taken off and got up into the air, just turning on my forty-five-degree angle out of the field, so all I had to do was to come on in and land. I know I was scared pea green. It was hard to know whether to jump, to land straight ahead, or to come on in, when you had a fire.

"Then, another time, when I took off, all the flight controls came loose from the side of the airplane and I was left holding them in my hand—the prop, mixture, and throttle controls. In the AT-6, the controls were all secured on a metal plate which was itself screwed on the metal wall on the left side of the plane and operated by the pilot's left hand. I had no engine control because the right hand was on the stick controlling the plane's attitude and direction. All three controls are on that set of wires. I just had full flaps on for takeoff (later we didn't use flaps for takeoff), and I just got everything shaped up and got nicely in the air and went to pull back on the mixture and prop, and the whole thing came off in my hand. I had no controls because I didn't dare touch them—I didn't know what might happen next. That plane just staggered, with full flaps, but I couldn't raise the flaps and I couldn't use the radio because I didn't have any hands left to use. I was holding onto this group of controls with one hand and I didn't dare to let go of it. I finally climbed up and leveled off with the whole plane shuddering. Then I stuck the control stick between my knees, where I could hold it in level flight, and managed to reach the radio and tell them I had an emergency.

"I came in, got around the field somehow, and landed. I still couldn't change the mixture, prop, or throttle settings. I came in full blast. I can't remember how I did it, with the mixture full rich and the prop full pitch and the throttle full forward.

"I don't think that could have been anything but sabotage. Nobody could be so careless as to leave the whole throttle quadrant unscrewed from the airplane, and it could not have been unscrewed all the way when I took off, because I checked the plane. Several others had bad experiences, too."

I am glad that I was so unaware of much that was going on. My own experience with the BT-13 was a good one. Even though it rattled and shook and was a bit scary during a spin, I enjoyed some wonderful flights with John Hosier in the old Vultee Vibrator. One day when we went up, the clouds were the kind of beautiful "fair-weather" clouds that roll into huge, billowy masses; some of them reached tremendous heights, forming passageways between one another. They looked like mountains made of snow. John said, "Let me have it."

Then he wove that old airplane in and out between the clouds, up and down, flipping it over and rolling us along the sides of those "mountains." I have never seen a more beautiful sight, flying close up to those clouds with the clear, blue sky in the background. I remember that day when I hear stories from other pilots about some particularly beautiful flight they experienced. Sometimes I think that pilots fly more for those glorious moments than for any thrill they get from speed, acceleration, or aerobatics.

By now, we were well settled in at Avenger Field. We really did not expect any more washouts after surviving ground school, solo flights in the BTs, and the ATs. Our rapport with our baymates grew closer; we exchanged funny anecdotes and tales of close calls on our flights. We had accepted (or conquered) our many flight instructors and ground teachers; we could even tolerate PE and marching. Our next challenge would be shutting ourselves into that little box of a Link, and flying blind under the hood in that BT Vibrator. We were ready and eager, and our confidence was still riding high.

BT-13

CHAPTER FOUR

Instrument Training and Link

"They had all those wreaths up there for the people who had 'died' on Link flights." —Millie Grossman

It was already mid-December and growing cold by the time we started our Link training and "under-the-hood" flying in the BT-13. We were now one of the upper classes, although we still had a few months to go before graduation. Surprisingly, most of us enjoyed instrument flying. Link we could do without, but flying under the hood had many attractions. Aside from hearing the "A" and "N" sounds in our sleep (dot-dash and dash-dot, over and over), we liked the challenge of "riding the beam" and hunting the "cone of silence." This old system of flying "beams" on instruments has long since been scrapped. Newer and safer methods are now used, and it is hard to believe that all of that training is now obsolete. Nevertheless, it was all we had at the time, and we tackled it with enthusiasm.

Part of instrument training—a necessary prerequisite to flying the beam—involved flying a complicated course while under the hood. "Under the hood" meant exactly what it sounded like. A black hood was pulled up over the pilot's section of the cockpit. She could see only her instruments—nothing else. In the rear cockpit of the airplane, an instructor (or later in training, another WASP) could see out and prevent any collisions or any tendency on the part of the "blind" pilot to slip into a dangerous maneuver or to fly too far afield.

It involved climbing five hundred feet on the first leg, flying level on the second leg, descending five hundred feet again on the third leg, and flying level on the last leg. Each leg had to be the same length. Then, each corner had to be maneuvered accurately, by degree of bank and number of degrees of turn (270 degrees on two corners and 450 degrees on the other two), in order to come out onto the square at the proper place. Timing was also important so that the distances for each leg stayed the same. We flew by the clock, the airspeed indicator, the altimeter and the gyroscope (compass). By the time the procedure was finished, the pilot was supposed to end up exactly where she had started, barring the wind factor.

The square course looked like this:

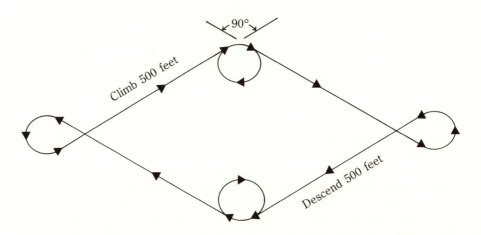

It was challenging, but we loved it, and somehow, in the final analysis, most female pilots were much better at this intricate flying than male pilots. Perhaps it had to do with women's early training—more concentration on small hand-eye coordination feats than on the gross-motor activities in which men were more frequently involved. At any rate, women consistently rated higher on instrument flying than men.

Following "pattern" flying, we started flying the "beam." In those days, the entire United States was interlaced by "beams," which radiated out from individual radio stations, centered at airports located near cities. These beams sent out a solid "hum" on the beam. To the right of the beam, one would hear an "A" (dot-dash) sound. To the left of the beam, one would hear an "N" (dash-dot) sound. Thus, when a dot-dash and a dash-dot signal meshed together, there would be a solid sound, or the hum of the beam.

A pilot could tell from the radio signal which beam she was trying to bracket (which city or airport). We were provided with maps showing all the beams and radio signals. When trying to zero in on a beam, and hence on an airport at a particular city, a pilot would fly back and forth from an "A" signal to an "N" signal gradually cutting down the distance between the two until the steady hum was heard to signal that one was flying "on the beam." That course would lead one to the "cone of silence," the exact location of the airport, where all sound would cease. It was tricky, because the wind played an important role in figuring out the exact direction one must fly to stay on the beam, but it was fun, like a puzzle, and very rewarding to hit the ''cone of silence.''

The Link Trainer was another story. Link was a miniature airplane with an enclosed cockpit; it simulated flying while remaining on the ground. Most of us disliked it. Being shut into a small box for an hour, or even half an hour, was not exactly pleasant, but we did learn from it. We all spent at least thirty hours in the Link Trainer. A few WASPs had had previous Link training and they breezed through it while the rest of us struggled. Ruth Petry was one. She had worked in Link before she became a WASP.

She told me she had been working in New York City first, but then got a job as a Link operator for Pan American. The WASP was in existence then, but she didn't have enough flying time to qualify. When the WASP program ran out of candidates and lowered the requirements, she applied. ''I don't think I was in Pan Am even a year,'' she told me, ''before I got assigned to a class—44-W-2. When I got there and got into instrument flying, the very first question the instructor asked was, 'Were you ever a Link operator?' They could tell a Link operator immediately. We were sort of 'by the number, one, two, three.' We got so used to it, needle, ball, airspeed, needle, ball, airspeed. Twitch, twitch, twitch, all the time.

''Kit MacKethan was a Link operator too, I think for American Airlines. They asked her the same thing. We can fly instruments quite well, but we don't do it the same way a person does who has never flown a Link. In Link they don't emphasize coordination, they just say to keep all those needles where they belong, but I had the same training as anyone else. Of course, you tell people now that you did all these things with only a needle, ball, and airspeed and they say, 'Oh, boy'—have you noticed this?''

Ruth Petry also had some conversations later, with male pilots at the base where she was sent, concerning instrument training. ''They asked about our instrument training,'' she said, ''and we explained that two girls flew together. We would take off the first period and fly to Abilene. There would be two girls together in one plane and the instructor with one girl in another plane. Then he'd fly with the other girl while the other two would fly together and practice. Then they'd come back. We described this to them, and they asked, 'You mean they let two students fly together?' We answered, 'Why, yes.' They said that in their training two students were never allowed to fly together. Apparently they thought with two students, they'd go off and show each other how good they were in aerobatics, so the men were just amazed. They asked, 'Didn't you have a lot of accidents?' When I said, 'No,' that just floored them.''

Verda-Mae Lowe was one of the few who really didn't like instrument flying or Link and had a bit of trouble with both. "I hated Link, just hated it," she told me. "When the Army checked they found I was weak on finding the 'cone of silence.' I would always miss it."

The check pilot told her he would check her again on Monday. Her instructor then kept her in all weekend flying Link and under the hood so she could pass.

"That was hard," she acknowledged, "because everyone was out partying. There wasn't a soul around. He had me in with the Link Trainer with the hood off so I could see what I was doing and he kept me in there until I could bracket the beam. Then he was satisfied, and he said, 'When you get in with that check pilot just remember how to do that, and you'll be all right.'

"On the second check ride, I discovered about an inch gap under the hood. 'Old Shorty' Lowe could look right out and see where she was. I flew the beam and I hit the cone of silence—which was the first time I had hit it. Then I flew partly back and the fellow wanted to know if I could tell where Avenger Field was. I just looked out and saw where the field was and shook the stick. 'Good,' he said, 'You've got the feel.' That was passing by the skin of my teeth."

Madeline Sullivan was happy to move into instrument flying because she was having trouble soloing the AT-6. The unexpected switch came just in time, she told me, to save her from washing out in ATs. "When we got to advanced, on the AT-6, everyone else was soloing in four to six hours. I was up to eleven hours, and my instructor was a Texan, and he sang that Texas song all the time—'Pistol Packin' Mama.' Finally he said, 'Sully' (he was the only one who called me Sully and I couldn't stand it), 'I think I'll have to send you over to the flight surgeon and have your eyes checked.' I was at least nine or ten hours then, and he hadn't let me solo. At that point I figure, oh cripes, I'm not going to make it. I'm going to be sent home. The very next morning we got out to the flight line and they changed us from AT-6s to instruments."

Madeline, in the meantime, had been spending extra time over on the Link Trainer, because she was so worried about not soloing. She thought she would try to get in all the training she could in case she washed out. When we were switched to instruments she was delighted.

"I was golden," she told me. "I was so far ahead of everyone else that for the one time in my life the kids were coming to the bay to check with me, because I must have had six or eight hours at least on Link, ahead of anybody else. I breezed through the instruments and then, when I went back to the AT-6, I made it."

Madeline told me about another strange event. In spite of being one of the best students in instruments, she became mixed up on one of her Army check rides. When she came out from under the hood there wasn't even any field in sight and she failed.

"I remember going back to the ready room in a state of shock," she said. "When I told Bill Tischler, my instrument instructor, I flunked, he replied, 'Knock it off, I haven't time to fool around. I've got other students I'm worried about.' It took me fifteen minutes to convince him that I had flunked. Then he went to bat for me and talked to the check pilot. He was able to get me another check ride, which I passed."

Kate Lee Harris and Anne Berry were flying an instrument practice flight one day when they had a rather funny experience. They were flying instruments, around Abilene, working the beam, and when Kate Lee finished her time she raised the hood and turned the controls over to Anne.

"Anne started circling around," Kate Lee says, "flying lower and lower, making tighter and tighter turns, and I looked around and we were near the Abilene air base. I asked her, 'What are you doing, buzzing the air base?' She looked at me in shock and said, 'Don't you have the controls?' We both laughed at that, but it could have been serious; we were getting pretty wound up."

Ruth Woods came into the WASPs with a commercial license and was quite a bit ahead of the rest of us because of all her flying time. But she also credited her success to the kind of instruction she had received before she got to Sweetwater. "When my Dad said I could fly," she explained, "there was a stipulation—that this guy we knew, Les Simpson, would be my instructor. Les was an old Army instructor—*old* Army instructor. If he told you to turn ninety degrees, you'd better turn ninety degrees. You wouldn't turn eighty-nine and a half, or you'd be afraid he'd knock your brains out. I mean, he was precision—absolute and total precision. That's why I didn't have any problems when I got out to Avenger. I was good at instruments. I had been taught precision to the point that there was never a moment when I didn't trust the instruments implicitly. I didn't have any problem with Link, either. I didn't like it very much. It was boring, but you had to do it if you were going to fly instruments."

We all had check rides during our instrument training, but Doris Elkington got an extra one. "Saunders was my instrument instructor," she told me. "He was kind of slow-going and easy, and nice to have as an instructor. When we were all through instruments, they came around and said the Army was going to give us a spot check, and they would pick one from each flight. Unfortunately, I was the one picked from our flight. I had just come in from flying when they told me I was going to be the one for the spot check. It just scared me to death, and they said, 'Don't even put down your parachute. Go right out. He's waiting for you.'"

51

This was to be an Army ride. Before that, all of us had been given only civilian check rides on instruments. Doris and the Army pilot flew over to Big Spring, Texas, where he handed the plane over to her, under the hood. She had to fly the beam into Big Spring.

"I guess I did all right because he flew it back, but he didn't say a word until we landed. Then he said, 'Why did you wait so long before you started your turn here?' (pointing to it on the map). I answered, 'Okay, this is where I thought I was,' and I showed him on the map. He said, 'Okay, *up*,' and he left.

"I was shaking like a leaf, but I remember Gini Dulaney said they'd carry me over to the mess hall on their shoulders if I passed, so I did, and they did. They carried me. There were a lot of good times."

We were all very happy that Doris had to take the Army check ride instead of any of the rest of us. We really appreciated her efforts. As much as we enjoyed instrument flying, we certainly didn't enjoy check rides with Army pilots. In fact, Lorraine Zillner said, "They were very unhappy being associated with a women's field. They wanted to be out there being gung-ho. I really think they were embarrassed about it." Most of us felt the same way about those Army check pilots. I'm sure they were essential and kept us up to the qualifications for the military, but most of them were pretty tough on us. The only military check ride I remember, however, is the one that I failed and had to repeat. I must have passed several others, but I can't remember them. I'm sure I've forgotten many other incidents. One I had forgotten concerned Link training, and Millie Grossman reminded me of it.

Millie remembered the "wreaths" they had hanging up in the Link-trainer room. "In Link flying," she recalled, "they get you up there under the hood and they give you this thing and that thing to do, and you forget you're flying, and you fly right down into the ground. I think I did that once, or came awfully close to it. I remember when I got into the Link room, they had all those wreaths up there for the people who had 'died' on Link flights—or who would have died if it had been an actual flight. Usually, though, they would bring you out from under the hood before you 'hit the ground.'

Millie told me of one incident in instruments that she has never forgotten. It concerned Sadie Hawkins who was in Flight One with us. "Sadie was quite a pilot," Millie recalled. "She was really good. I remember the day that she learned her boyfriend had been killed in action. It was the day that she was supposed to take her instrument flying test, and her instructor said, 'You don't have to do it today,' and she answered, 'No, let's do it.' When they came down he said to me that that was one of the best flights he had ever experienced, bar none—from man or woman. She really could produce a skillful job of flying. It made a great impression on me."

For Mary Strok, however, instruments were just the greatest part of flying. "I loved it," she said, "it was one of my favorites. I enjoyed it tremendously. As a matter of fact, after I graduated, that's one of the things I did— check out pilots in instruments. It was exciting because it was a new and different challenge. It was a little more exciting than just plain flying."

Clarice Siddall was another WASP who thought instruments were great. "I really loved instruments," she told me. "Some of them hated it, but I just thought that was the most exciting thing. The biggest thrill to me was to come in over the runway, and we could do that from a pattern and flip over and there you would be."

Lourette Puett liked instruments too, but she was amazed at how different things are now. "They certainly have changed," she commented. "Heavens, I couldn't begin to fly instruments today. All we had was needle, ball, and airspeed. Now they have all the instruments that tell you where you are. It looks to me as though the pilots now sit so far in front of the plane that they're on instruments all the time. They have no visual reference to their wings. How would they know if they were level or not? They need the instruments to tell them so. I imagine they fly instruments most of the time."

Instrument training, according to Ann Craft, could sometimes be a bit dangerous. "When we took instrument training in the BTs," she related, "it seems we just had narrow escapes all the time. I think it was dangerous the way we were landing—we were heading toward each other on the base leg."

She was right on that! We had two traffic patterns set up to land on two parallel runways. Both downwind legs headed in the same direction, heading south, for instance. Then each would turn, one to the east, one to the west, and head toward each other. Then, each would turn north to land. On the base leg before the last turn to land, the planes would be heading toward each other. You would often see another plane heading straight toward you just before you turned (and the other pilot turned) to land on parallel runways. It was pretty safe providing everyone knew what she was doing, and for which runway she was heading. During our time at Avenger Field, no one crashed because of this particular approach to landing. I cannot speak for the other classes, but Ann and several other of our classmates worried about the situation. Perhaps that made them more careful on their base legs and final approaches.

Ann mentioned another funny thing that happened. "I used to write all the love letters for the girls," she laughed, "and sometimes I would just get carried away, but there was this guy that I had gone out with who was a general's pilot. He called me and I told him, 'You can't land here. They won't let men land on our airport,' and he just said, 'Don't you worry about that.' He came in and landed, and they were just furious until they found out that he was the general's

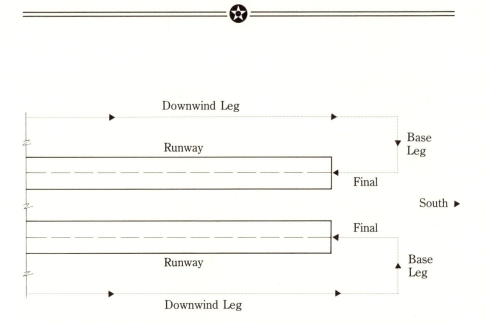

pilot. That was a kind of funny thing. Then I went in to dinner to see him and I looked so terrible with my hair in pigtails and that horrible zoot suit. He was just shocked when he saw me. Remember how ugly we looked?''

Well, I can't imagine Ann looking ugly under any circumstances, but by now it was getting close to Christmastime. In fact, I note that I finished my Link Trainer time on December 27, and did not finish instrument flying in the BT until mid-January. Madeline Sullivan had a Christmas story to tell that I had never heard before. The story is entitled ''Beatrice.''

''I'll tell you a story that most of the class never knew about,'' she laughed. ''At Christmastime—first time away from home for a lot of us—all of a sudden who arrived on the scene about three or four days before Christmas but Zillner's younger brother. He was about seventeen, and so she's ecstatic. Her family felt that she shouldn't be alone during the holidays and that he should come out and have Christmas Day with her. He was staying at the Blue Bonnet Hotel.

''We decided that he didn't have enough money to stay at the Blue Bonnet. We somehow got another zoot suit and a turban, dubbed him ''Beatrice,'' and put him in the bay with us. Of course, he loved it! When our night checker came around—you know how the two bays were connected by the john?—well, we'd run him into the other side, and then she'd go out the door, and we'd run him back into our side. I've got pictures of him somewhere in my book. In fact, in our yearbook, the one with a sort of collage—he's in it. Most of the kids don't know who it is, but it's Beatrice.

"We really kept it between the two bays, because we were afraid if it got beyond, you know, that it would somehow leak out and we'd get into big trouble. He stayed for at least five or six days, and it was absolutely a riot. I remember Mary Strok going out a couple of days before Christmas, and, thinking it was a bit depressing being away from home, she bought herself a black slip, which we thought was very exciting. Then, all of a sudden she walked in and said, 'Wait 'til you see this.' We yelled, 'Get out of here. Beatrice is in here.' That's the way it went. It was great fun."

Christmas was not really depressing at all. In the first place, we were busy flying—which we loved. Then, Sweetwater families hosted many of the WASPs on Christmas Day. My primary instructor, Ray Booth, as I mentioned before, invited four of us for Christmas dinner. It was a beautiful family dinner in a lovely home, so we felt a part of the holiday celebration. During that time, my husband-to-be spent a lot of time with me in Sweetwater (he was stationed at Abilene) so I didn't feel at all lonesome. In addition, WASPs had a Christmas party of their own, held in the new gym. Officers and cadets from nearby fields were invited, and a twelve-foot Christmas tree was decorated. Madeline Sullivan was head of the Christmas decorations and Mimi Lindstrom was in charge of refreshments.

We all felt very fortunate, especially as we kept hearing about the many soldiers overseas who had no opportunity at all to be with their families or to celebrate Christmas. Many were fighting even on Christmas Day. The *New York Times* reported that three thousand planes smashed the French coast on that day, but the article also added that all craft returned. Also at Christmastime, it was announced that General Eisenhower had been named commander for the invasion of Europe, and General Sir Bernard L. Montgomery was named commander-in-chief of the British armies serving under Eisenhower. Just before Christmas, however, the United States lost sixty Flying Fortresses with a total of 581 men missing. Later, 346 of the fliers were reported alive, but prisoners within Germany.

It was hard to imagine how extended this "world war" really was. Fighting was spread over many countries. Besides the tremendous amount of fighting going on in Europe, Americans downed thirty Japanese planes at Rabaul, and Japanese shipping was attacked frequently by American bombers. In the North, Red Army troops were fighting even above the Arctic Circle, using reindeer to draw their sleds through deep snow. In New Zealand, a report came from Wellington that Allied Warhawks had downed five Japanese Zeroes over Bougainville.

The most noted "pin-up" girl, Betty Grable, was playing in a war film, *Victory Through Air Power*. Hundreds of GIs had hung posters of the curvaceous Grable above their bunks, and certainly "victory through air power" was no myth. General H. H. Arnold stated that a major turning point in the war was the struggle for air supremacy and that the survival or ruin of the Nazis hung on the balance of air power.

Meanwhile, back at home, President Roosevelt was forced to take over the railroads as three union brotherhoods rejected mediation. On December 28, the Army seized the railroads on the president's order. Roosevelt said that the war must come first; he must make sure that troops got goods without halt. The railroads functioned smoothly, it was reported, with officials wearing Army uniforms taking over the operations.

Women were not overlooked. King George of Britain, in his New Year's honors list, mentioned not only political leaders and soldiers, but several women in the armed services, as well as "the gallantry of housewives and factory workers." President Roosevelt was pictured at his home in Hyde Park at Christmastime with his grandchildren. Shortly afterward, the Roosevelts deeded the homestead with its more than thirty-three acres to the federal government as a national historic site.

Finally, we finished both our Link time and our BT instrument time, bringing us into January. At that time my log book shows two instructors who had signed for my time, instructors I cannot remember. This came as a blow to my ego, because I have such clear recollections of most of the instructors I flew with. I could not believe I had forgotten some of them. Most of us, however, have forgotten several of our instructors, or at least a few, and I must admit I am no exception. George Hight signed for my AT-6 solo, and O. A. Martin signed for my BT-13 instrument instruction. Unfortunately, I can remember neither, but I do know that we continued to fly the BT for another week or so before moving back into the AT-6 near the end of January.

I specifically remember having two instructors during this AT-6 training. One was Kenneth Willingham, who was young, good-looking, and very warm and friendly. He was a fun person who loved to fly and could slow-roll the AT-6 with the greatest of ease. Unlike most of the instructors, he usually wore a white silk scarf, like aviators we would see in old movies, and he was always dressed meticulously. He seemed very young, but he certainly could fly!

The other was a man who seemed not to like women very much. He was reserved and taciturn, and really unpredictable. I had him during night flying, and I remember we were all so tired during those night flights that we would often fall asleep on the low wooden benches while waiting for our turn to fly. I also remember one night being sound asleep and being rudely awakened by this instructor who shoved me to the cement floor with the comment, "Get up, it's time to fly."

Perhaps I should have been forewarned by this type of behavior. I still wonder why I did not ask for another instructor. Somehow it never occurred to me that I could do such a thing without some sort of reprisal. At any rate, I had one extremely unpleasant flight with this man. We were up in the AT-6 and suddenly, without any warning at all, he flipped the plane into a maneuver that was so violent that I was knocked unconscious almost instantly. In that brief moment before unconsciousness, I realized that I was not ''blacking out,'' but experiencing a ''red out.'' I saw red just as I went unconscious. That meant, I later figured, that we had been thrown into either an outside loop or an inverted spin. Such maneuvers force blood *to* the head, rather than *from* the head. Knowing ahead that such a maneuver is planned, a pilot can tuck her chin down, or otherwise prepare herself to prevent the blood from rushing either from her head, or to her head. Also, most such maneuvers are not as violent as this one must have been.

The next thing I remember was that my hands were flopping around loosely inside the cockpit (we must have then been upside down), and I was hearing a voice in my earphones saying, ''Are you all right? Are you all right?'' When I finally regained complete consciousness, I answered in the affirmative, but my nose was bleeding and there seemed to be blood oozing from my eyes. I was nauseated as well. This instructor said nothing else, but flew us back to the airport. He pulled the plane into its parking space, climbed out, and with no other explanation whatever said, ''You write it up,'' meaning that I could make whatever comment I wished on Form One, which had to be filled out after each flight.

I did not know what to say. I had no idea of what had really occurred. I felt sick and I was angry. I thought, of course, that it was deliberate. On the other hand, I was not about to risk being washed out at this date. I simply wrote on the form, ''All Okay.'' I went back to the bay and went to bed. I don't think I even mentioned the incident to anyone. Somehow, when one is mistreated (as I believed I had been), there is always the question of ''why?'' and ''what did I do to deserve this?''—some sense of ''I must have done something wrong''— so I said nothing to anyone.

It did not occur to me at the time, though it certainly has since, that this man may have simply flipped us into some maneuver that was dangerous or so violent that he had trouble handling the airplane himself. I thought, at the time, that an instructor would know enough about the airplane to make such a mistake impossible, but after talking to many pilots, I know now that our instructors were not infallible, and some were not as well trained as they should have been.

I don't recall ever flying with that instructor again. To the best of my recollection, he left Avenger Field shortly afterward. Perhaps he had frightened himself more than he had me, but, as an interesting footnote to this affair, I remember receiving a congratulatory card when I graduated, signed by this man who was no longer instructing at Avenger Field. He is not listed, even now, as a former instructor of WASPs. I still don't know what to think about the incident, so I reserve judgment.

Night flying in the AT-6, also called the "Sweet Six" or, more often, just the "Six," frightened some of us, including me. I remember the first time I went up at night I flew in the back seat of the Six, with the instructor in the front. I don't know why that happened; usually the student was in the front, especially when learning a new procedure. At that time, our runways were lighted by flares, so as we took off all I could see from the back cockpit was a row of flames racing past the plane before we took off. I remember tears of pure fright rolling down my cheeks, or maybe I was just overtired. I was glad it was too dark for the instructor to see me. Once aloft, however, the moon streaked across the silver wings of the Six, glistening and shining, turning the whole black night into nothing more than a background for this brilliantly illuminated powerhouse, roaring across the Texas desert. What a thrill! Thereafter, night flying fascinated me; its beauty was captivating. Nothing could really touch night flying for sheer beauty.

Jean Moore, however, really did not enjoy night flying. "I cheated a lot on night flying," she confided. "When we were supposed to take our cross-country flight—from Lubbock to Odessa—there weren't any lights showing for Lubbock, so I just turned around and flew between Odessa and Midland until my time was up, and then I flew back to Sweetwater. I didn't like it out there, all dark, so I didn't bother to get to Lubbock. I never told anybody I didn't. I didn't have to check in so it didn't matter. I didn't much care for night flying."

Night cross-country flying offered new adventures. Fran Laraway was flying one night, she told me, when "I had all my electrical systems go out and I had to fly contact all the way back on my last leg." She never did tell me how she landed without radio contact.

I had a similar thing happen to me one night. My radio contact went dead. Everything else worked, but the radio produced nothing except Mexican music. I thought to myself, "What a great excuse to buzz the tower." It was really necessary, after all. I came zooming in low, buzzed the tower with a roar, and came around to make a landing. As I headed in on my final approach, a flashing red light greeted me. Well, I couldn't see anything wrong, but I dutifully went around the pattern again and came back in another time. Again a flashing red light. Well, I was in no mood to stay up there forever and I certainly could not contact the tower to see what was wrong, so I decided to land anyway.

58

The runway was clear, but I kept getting red lights all the way down to the runway. As I neared the ground, I noticed I was going pretty fast. I put down more flaps, but I was still speeding along. Finally, with full flaps, and nearing the end of the runway, I managed to get it on the ground. Using all my strength, I shoved on the toe brakes, noticing at the same time, that the fire engine and ambulance were speeding down the runway beside me. I swerved to miss the flares at the end of the runway, and luckily was able to avoid a ground loop as I swung around and brought the plane to a stop.

As soon as my wheels hit the ground, the radio came back on to its proper channel and I could hear the tower saying, "Make your approach to land 180 degrees to the south," and I immediately realized that the wind had shifted 180 degrees from my time of takeoff and that was why the tower had been giving me a red light. I was landing downwind with a pretty strong wind at my tail. Well, I decided there wasn't much else to do except to try to bluff my way out of this one. Fortunately, Hal Pinkard, civilian flight commander of the base, was on duty. He came out and jumped up on my wing and asked, "Didn't you see the red light?"

I answered, "Yes, but it's late and I was tired and I wanted to go to bed." (It was about 2:30 A.M.)

He gave me a sort of "knowing" grin and said, "Well, I guess they hadn't got the Tee turned around to the south yet." The wind Tee was a large, lighted, miniature airplane pointed in the direction a pilot should land.

With that remark, I realized I had an "out." I'd been too dumb to look at the lighted Tee, but it was still pointing north, the way I had landed, so I was more or less in the clear even though I had come in against a red light. In reality, I had landed north only because I had taken off north and I assumed the wind was still out of the north. At that point, after noting Pinkard's grin, I remembered that I had always bragged to my baymates that someday I would land the AT-6 downwind at night. I realized that he probably thought I had done it on purpose—and such an act was much more acceptable than to have done such a thing out of stupidity. What a piece of luck! All I had to do was say nothing.

Luck was with me, also, because I could have run into some other person, or the Army officer in charge that night. Hal Pinkard was an easygoing, competent commander and he kept his ear to the ground. He always knew what was going on and he seemed to really enjoy his female charges. He was unfailingly kind to us. I was not even seriously reprimanded for that downwind landing, as I recall.

Most of our instructors, both air and ground, as well as the other personnel at Avenger Field, did their best, I believe, to help us. There were very few "bad apples." The flight instructors, in particular, must have found it difficult at times to instruct, rather than to fly, especially in the AT-6. Often they did not resist and took over the plane for the pure joy of it. Minkie Heckman told me, "In advanced training I had that wonderful instructor, Mr. Ingram. For some reason or other, he was never called by his first name. He was a little, short fellow and he had two thick cushions that he put under his parachute so he could see out of the back seat of the AT-6.

"One time we were out flying and he said, 'Just let me have this thing for a minute,' and he took it and he went down, and if we'd had the wheels down I think we'd have been taxiing. We went up and over the fences and around the trees and it was a fantastic thing. Then we went by a railroad station and zipped right past it. I called him up and laughed, 'Mr. Ingram, you know we're not supposed to be doing this—I'm objecting.' Just at that time a voice said, 'Oh, I can't help it if we're lost, can I? I have to see where we are. That's why I went by that railroad station.' Of course we weren't supposed to be doing anything like that—and no aerobatic training—but I'm sure everybody tried some. They didn't train us in aerobatics; we got the cross-country flying instead. I never got to do a slow roll. I rode through them but I never did one myself."

Nellie Henderson remembered Kenneth Willingham taking over the controls of the AT-6. "He was so sweet," she told me, "a really sweet guy. You know the dry riverbeds that were there? The farmers farming on each side? We used to like to fly down those, and then just come out of the ground when we were right next to the farms so they'd say, 'Where did that come from?' Oh, we were mean."

That kind of flying was such fun that many of us tried it ourselves. Millie Grossman was up flying with Ruth Woods one day and Millie said, "Ruth was a very capable gal and was usually talking bravely about this, that, and the other thing. I guess I'm a kind of feminine person, so they didn't expect too much of me. We were flying along and she said, 'Come on, let's buzz!' I said, 'Okay, you go ahead.' Ruth buzzed, and then she said, 'Okay, you do it now,' and she was very impressed, I guess, because when we came back to the field she told people, 'You know what that Millie Grossman does? She wets the belly of the plane in one field, and she dries it off in the next!' I'll never forget that. She couldn't get over that buzz. Here I am this feminine person and I was doing these things. Ruth was an excellent pilot, but I didn't feel I was that good."

We didn't know whether we were good pilots or not. We had little chance to fly with one another, but we usually were impressed with our classmates' flying abilities—the ones we did get to fly with. I always thought everyone could do aerobatics and I knew I couldn't.

Of course, we never got any instruction in aerobatics. This was frustrating so one day, flying solo, I took the Six up to ten thousand feet and tried a slow roll. Well, I couldn't manage to keep the nose from dropping and the plane fell into a "split S," which means that it simply dropped nose first straight down out of the sky. I was sure glad I had gone up to ten thousand feet because I was below five thousand feet before I was able to pull it out. I never tried that again, but I always wanted some instruction in how to do it. I know others tried aerobatics and I certainly hope they had better luck than I did.

The rationale behind not teaching us aerobatics, I believe, was that we would not be flying combat and we needed cross-country training much more than we needed aerobatics. Cross-country flying would be a big part of our work after we graduated. Anyhow, it was always fun to be going someplace, seeing new country, new places. We made cross-country flights in all three of our training planes, but the longest would be the flight to Blythe, California, in the AT-6, just before graduation. We all looked forward eagerly to that trip.

AT-6

CHAPTER FIVE

Cross-country and Advanced Training

"Here came a Navy torpedo plane with the prop not spinning. This thing was dropping like a rock." —Kay Herman

Nothing else in flying can really match the excitement and anticipation of a cross-country trip. Waking up in the morning, knowing you are to take off alone for some new place, plotting your course, then climbing into that beautiful machine for a roaring takeoff into the morning sun—nothing else can compare to it for pure enjoyment. Every trip opened up new possibilities, a new adventure to be relished, a different countryside to be explored, an unknown place to discover. Often, of course, pilots became lost. Getting lost was not really a big worry in itself. It was part of the adventure, and we felt pretty sure we could find a reasonably safe place to set the plane down. The big worry was being reprimanded or even washed out.

Anna Mae Petteys said she had one "embarrassing experience." She became lost on a navigational flight to Tyler, Texas. It was getting dark. She was almost out of gas and couldn't get a response on the radio. The only choice was to land in a farmer's field.

"I went in and called the air base from the farmer's house," she said. "They sent out several personnel from the air base where I was supposed to have landed, and they set up this little camp to guard the plane. Then the area was weathered in. That same night a group of grasshopper pilots in Cubs flew in to the air base and were also weathered in. [Grasshopper pilots were so named because they resembled grasshoppers the way they hopped in and out of grass fields in small planes.] We were posted to the one hotel in Tyler and these young pilots started going out, having fun, and they dragged me along with them. I was happy to be dragged!"

The weather didn't clear up for days, she told me, and the pilots found girls to play with. Anna Mae would trundle along with them in her zoot suit until they suggested that she borrow some clothes, which she did. Regulations required that an Air Force officer fly the plane out of a forced landing, but the weather was so bad no one could fly in to the base to do so. Finally, an officer risked the weather and landed at Tyler, but he couldn't fly the plane out because by then the field was too muddy to lift off.

"Every day the officer would want to get out of there and get home," Anna Mae explained, "but every day he couldn't do it. He was getting so unhappy and so cross that finally he just decided to fly it out. He got in and gunned the engine. The plane nosed up and burned. He got out of the plane with only burned trousers. The plane was a loss. I had to fly back with this cross man, in his plane. I believe that I could have been washed out for that episode, but happily they didn't do that, maybe because it was very near to graduation from training."

Several other classmates had strange adventures. Verda-Mae Lowe got lost on the California trip and Nellie Henderson thought it was one of the funniest stories she had ever heard. Nellie said, "Verda-Mae was just flying around lost, and it was mucky and she couldn't see through the clouds and so she said, 'Dear God, just give me a break in the clouds so I can see a place to land and I'll be a good little girl all the rest of my life.' About that time, the clouds parted just as if God's magic had worked, and she saw the longest green field you've ever seen in your life. She put that little AT-6 right down on that little green field, saying, 'Dear God, thank you, thank you.' Then all of a sudden she was surrounded by these little people with slanty eyes, and she thought, 'My God, I've overshot the Pacific. I'm a one-woman invasion of Tokyo.' She'd landed on the parade grounds in a Japanese internment camp—perfect place to land. So funny."

Verda-Mae went on with the story. "Yes, I landed in the Japanese camp. It was Camp Two, one of a series of Japanese relocation centers. The Commander of the base came out and I was in a 'zoot suit,' and I had a turban on my head and the canopy open, so I must have looked strange. They put guards on the airplane and they phoned back to the base where everyone else had landed [in Blythe] and told them that I wouldn't be coming in. I ate at the table with the officers, and they took me to the men's barracks and had everyone get out so I could wash up before I came to eat.

"I stayed there until after the lunch meal. I was a curiosity for them. Lieutenant colonels, majors, and other officers asked about what we were doing. Then they got an Air Force pilot to take the airplane out and I got in the back seat. He flew it out but he had a devil of a time and took a lot of shrubbery with him, because there were two of us in there so the plane weighed more."

Verda-Mae later explained another reason that she got off course. She had been told that if you cross a river you're in Mexico, and if you cross the mountain range you're too far north. She was in desert country and saw a big irrigation ditch. "It seemed like a river," she explained. "I didn't know about irrigation ditches then, so I thought, 'I'm in Mexico. What am I going to do?' I turned around—and I think if I'd been higher I'd have seen where we were supposed to land, in California. It was that close."

Ruth Adams tells about a cross-country experience and the instructor she had who really taught her a lot. "He was a perfectionist," she explained, "and he demanded a really good performance. We'd be doing chandelles and he'd say, 'What do you think you're doing?' He'd yell at me and the tears would be streaming down my face and, by God, I did what I had to do to make that ball stay in the middle. Helen Ritchie, another WASP, once said, 'You do whatever you have to do to make the plane do what you want it to do.' People talk about 'don't cross your controls' and all these damn rules, but you just do what you have to do!

"On our cross-country flight, that instructor wanted me to identify everything along the way. He'd say, 'What's that town over there?' I'd say, 'Well, I think it must be——,' naming a small town, although I could hardly see it. He said, 'What the hell else could it be?' I learned a lesson from that, too. You don't have to go down and read the water tower to be absolutely sure. You have to draw certain conclusions on the basis of what you know—it has to be that. You have to trust in your own judgment. I learned a lot of things from him. He was very good, so I was grateful to him. I don't know why I can't remember his name, the little toad, but he was a good instructor."

Pilots also got lost during night cross-country flights and they ran into other problem situations peculiar to night flying. Kit MacKethan told me, "I had an electrical failure and the procedure was to buzz the tower. They would give you a green light for landing. Well, according to them, someone else had exactly the same problem at exactly the same minute, and we crisscrossed around each other and we each got a green light and came in. I landed somehow and I know I walked back. I was glad to be down. Neither of us was hurt, but I don't remember who the other pilot was."

Perhaps it was Fran Laraway. She told me, "I was flying the night line and had all my power go out and had to fly contact all the way back on my night leg. Another time, a mechanic left a rag in the exhaust so I had a fire in the plane when I landed. You always hated it when you had to draw attention to yourself on the flight line, but I did that time. There was smoke pouring out."

Two unusual accidents plagued Anne Berry. "I sometimes think I was successful by the grace of God, or dumb luck," she complained. "On our long cross-country trip we landed at Tucson. I don't know what happened, but the plane veered off to the left for no apparent reason. It went shooting across this apron for a few seconds (which seemed like twenty minutes) before I was able to bring it under control. Fortunately, it was a great, big, empty apron, but I thought afterwards that it could have been full of airplanes. Now that was luck!''

Another time she told me she had forgotten to ''ess.'' When you taxi small airplanes, it is necessary to move back and forth in an ''S'' in order to see ahead. You can't see straight ahead because the engine and spinning prop are directly in front of you.

''All of a sudden the tower became very quiet,'' she said, ''and when the tower became quiet it was usually an indication that something was amiss. I thought, 'What's going on with those guys?' I looked out over to the right and there had been a lot of thin sticks with flags on top of them, and my right wing had just mowed a whole line of those things down. Nobody said anything, so I guess it wasn't too bad.''

Marge Needham told me about forced landings on cross-country trips. ''One of the instructors at Avenger told me, 'You've got to visualize the flying that you're doing in that particular airplane. It's only you and the individual airplane. You've got to know just what that plane can do for you.' I haven't had a scratch yet on an airplane. I've always landed in a place where they could get the airplane right out.''

One funny incident was told me by Kay Herman. This was on her long cross-country flight to California. She had stopped at El Paso to gas up and heard sirens screaming.

''Here came a navy torpedo plane,'' she informed me, ''heading in with the prop not spinning. It had run out of gas, I guess. This thing was dropping like a rock, and he came in and hit—bang, bang—and just made the runway. All the hatches opened up and everybody was getting the heck out. Coming out of the bottom of this thing was a WAVE. She had bummed a ride, and she was white as a sheet. She was so scared.

''We ran out to see what the deal was and she was saying, 'You'll never catch me in another airplane. I bummed a ride and I almost didn't make it.' At the moment it was quite funny, but of course it would have been terrible if it had turned out otherwise.''

The cross-country trip to Blythe, California, was not only our longest flight, but our first over the Rockies. It was also the first mountain flying for many of us. Each pilot plotted her course carefully because, although we would take off with a large group, we were on our own immediately after takeoff. Sometimes we would plan to fly along with one friend or another, but usually that didn't work out because it was hard to keep another plane in sight. We seldom saw one another from takeoff to the next landing. We all thought we were trained and ready for this long trip, but many strange events occurred and not all of them happy ones. On this trip, we lost one of our classmates, Betty Stine. It was our first and only fatality during training. Fran Smith was a close friend of Betty's.

"We don't know really what happened to her plane," she told me. "There was a malfunction of some kind, or she would not have jumped out. On that cross-country, she and I were going to fly back together. I took off ahead of her and I was circling the field waiting for her and you could tell by the voices who was flying, taking off and all, when you called the tower. I kept waiting and waiting for her and finally I had to go because of fuel and so forth. None of us knew what happened to her until we got to the next base and she didn't show up.

"We had gone to Mexico the day before, because we were at El Paso, and Betty had bought a bottle of wine and a big straw hat. She couldn't get them in her plane so she put them in mine. When we found out what had happened, we had a hard time deciding, as a group, what to do with that bottle of wine. I think it was just about at graduation time that we all got together and drank it, you know, kind of in her memory. I think we gave the hat to her parents. They came to the base. I'm afraid I was chicken. I couldn't talk to her parents, but I think they did talk to some of the girls. I don't think I could have handled talking to them—Betty was an only child."

Another close friend of Betty's was Mary Strok. "Betty Stine was my baymate," she said. "She was my best friend. I heard, I suppose, what everyone else did. We took our final cross-country just before graduation, which was our trip to eastern Texas and then to Blythe, California, and then back again. Each group took off, roughly, at the same time. Much to my astonishment, when we were getting ready to take off from Blythe, the Stines appeared. I had met them before, her parents, and they came over to say something to me, and they started to weep. Her father took me in his arms and wept, and I said, 'What's the trouble?' He said, 'Betty's gone.' I said, 'What do you mean?' Then he told me what had happened.

"She had flown out of Blythe, as I understand it, in her AT-6, and experienced flames coming out of her engine, so she went out over the side. Of course, this was in a heavily mountainous area and she landed very hard, apparently injuring herself seriously—as it turned out critically. They took her to a hospital in Blythe and she died shortly afterward. I guess her parents had gotten the word. They were on their way to the site of the accident. They had not told me because I was a very close friend of Betty's. That was a shock—and to fly back all the way. But what can you do? It happens. There were some miners working there who saw her. They went to the site and she was very seriously injured, a head injury. She died later at the hospital."

Many of us did not learn of Betty's death until after our return. She was in Flight Two. Some of the girls in Flight One, which was my flight, did not know anything was wrong while we were on our trip, and learned of the tragedy only after we returned to Avenger Field. Others in Flight One told me later that they were told of Betty's death in Tucson where some of us had been weathered in. Betty had been in the very first group to fly the cross-country trip, and those of us who followed, later, had different experiences. The group that I was with landed in Tucson because of bad weather and we were put up in the Santa Rita hotel for two nights. I was talking to Marge Gilbert about that and she asked, "Isn't that where they put us all up in the ballroom because the hotel was full and 'Mother' Gilbert had to go around and check to be sure everyone was in at night?"

That was correct, as I remember. Most of us were wandering around Tucson, looking for fun, and Marge was the one who always kept an eye on us and checked to be sure we made it back at night. She was just enough older than most of us so that she worried about us. We all thought she was great—like a big sister.

Ann Craft remembered being with us in Tucson. "I can remember that mountain coming closer and closer, but I just stayed on the same level and I think finally I had only about two hundred feet of altitude over the mountain and all of a sudden here we were at the Tucson airport. Then those navy pilots came zooming down and kept landing right in front of us so that we'd have to go around again. We'd get ready to land—and here they'd come again. I thought that was a fun thing. We got weathered in, and we had such a good time. We all slept in one room."

Ann remembers being told about Betty Stine's death in Tucson, but I know I was not told until after my return to Avenger Field. They must have told some, but not all, of the girls. Ann said, "They told us that someone had been killed and we had to have a buddy to fly with. I think Anne Berry was mine. We took off and I saw Anne flying in the completely opposite direction from where I was going and I thought, 'I can't follow her—what if I lose her? I'll never know where I am.' I did my own navigation and I never did see anyone. We got to Blythe and had lunch and they wanted us to rendezvous over the lake. It was the funniest thing because here we were going around and around the lake. Then the leader took off and we all took off afterward. I think they were afraid of the weather and of having one person killed, but then they put us in a more dangerous spot by trying to have us fly close together. We really hadn't been trained to do that. It seems to me we just had narrow escapes all the time."

Mary Ellen Keil was on one of the later flights to California and she was another who became lost on her return. She knew of Betty Stine's death before she left Sweetwater. "We took the very same route," she told me, "only it was later. I was curious to see where she had gone down and how it happened that she got lost. Everyone had told me about where it had happened, so when I got out in that area, I made a fifteen- or twenty-degree turn off course to fly over and see the spot where she had been killed. I flew around and saw the area where it had happened and then I turned around to get back on course. We had had plenty of instruction on how to do that, but instead of doubling my correction, I misfigured my course to get back on track. The result was that before I could decide where I was, I got myself lost. By the time I found out my location and got into Phoenix, I think I had fifteen or twenty minutes of gas left. Those AT-6s—when I think they sent us out on those long flights, over mountains with no mountain experience, and very little AT-6 cross-country time, it makes me mad. Also, we didn't have what the FAA requires now—a forty-five-minute gas reserve. I misfigured my course correction and almost ran out of gas, so there was only a short time of extra flying. There was very little room for error."

On her return from the California cross-country, Gini Dulaney told me she had trouble getting over one of the passes. "Being a practicing coward," she said, "I got as high as I could to get over the pass." When she gained enough altitude to clear the pass, however, her engine quit. Then, as soon as she descended to a lower altitude, it caught again. "I went so far as to undo the safety belt, and I rolled back the canopy and was just about ready to jump." After her engine caught, she went back up to higher altitude again and it quit again. "By then I was a cot case," she announced, "and I still hadn't cleared the pass!" Her engine failed her three times, she told me, before she figured out that it must have been carburetor ice. She thought maybe that could have happened to Betty Stine's airplane. "Our carburetor heaters didn't work in those old planes. That's why those engines would quit." Gini finally did make it over the mountains, but then she had a dust storm blocking her vision near Sweetwater. It was already dark and the flares were lit before she arrived at Avenger Field.

Millie Grossman remembered that she had been told about Betty's accident when she landed on her first leg of the cross-country flight. "At that time," she said, "they thought she didn't know how to get out of the plane properly. They told us what we should do was to unstrap ourselves from the plane, turn the plane upside down, and fall out. Well, I remember that scared me so much! I thought, how in the world am I going to do that? I thought you should just slide off the back of the wing; that's what they had told us before. I suppose they didn't realize that what happened to her was that she had jumped properly, but it was close to a cliff and her parachute just smacked her against the cliff.

"On the next leg of the flight I think we landed in Phoenix. It took me about three tries to get down. The first time I bounced so high I had to go around, and the second time there were big planes that had to come in. I think I went around about three times. I was scared. It shocked me to realize all of a sudden that someone could be killed doing this. You don't think about it usually when you're young."

Phyllis Tobias remembered different stories about the pilots we'd met on our cross-country trip. "I had a lot of fun with that cross-country, because we kept meeting all those pursuit pilots everywhere we stopped. When we landed at Tucson we had all those fancy guys in the bar, and Betty Stine, I know, had one that followed her all the way from Tucson to Blythe. They were playing tag all the way going west to Blythe. He was in a P-38 and was flying circles around her, but he was really leading the way, so coming back she could have had trouble finding her way. That was pretty rugged country, too."

Phyllis also became lost on her way back between Midland, Texas, and Sweetwater. She told me she had been flying over "those nice round circles they use for bombardier practice" when she realized she was lost. She tuned her radio in and landed at San Angelo. "I didn't get washed out," she said, "because I brought my plane and myself back safely." She added, "They didn't make me pay for the extra gas."

Everyone felt upset and sad about Betty's death, but I think it would be a mistake to say there was any blame attached to anyone. Betty was a good flier, but a combination of bad weather and bad luck put her into a dangerous situation. First, her plane had a serious enough problem to force her to jump. Then, the terrain and the weather combined to place her in jeopardy. She did everything she could, but circumstances beyond her control brought about her death. It could have happened to any of us and that thought remained in our minds from that day on. None of us will ever forget her.

During those last few weeks at Avenger Field, we were too occupied with finishing up our flying to pay much attention to what was happening in the rest of the world. A lot was going on, however. Early in March, U.S. troops took over Admiralty Isle, north of New Guinea, where three thousand enemy soldiers were reported killed, and for the first time in the war an American flag flew over Japanese territory at Kwajalein Atoll. Allied planes were pounding islands in the Pacific; near the island of Truk, U.S. battleships were destroying fleeing vessels. Many Japanese cruisers were sunk off Truk Island—a place now frequented by scuba divers.

In the European theater, fighting was raging at Anzio, bombs were still falling on London, and American bombers were trying to clear a path to Berlin. Long-range P-38s made their first reconnaissance flight to Berlin and returned safely. The following day the U.S. bombed Berlin for the first time and a few days later eight hundred bombers smashed the city. On the fourth Berlin raid, which took place on March 9, two thousand B-17 Flying Fortresses and B-24 Liberators bombarded the city, but thirty-eight planes were lost in the attack.

At Anzio, five American Army nurses were reported killed during a bombing raid on the hospital where they served, and many American wounded were moved to hospital ships in the Anzio harbor. Nazi casualties were reported to be nine thousand since January 31 in the area of Cassino—the equivalent of four German divisions eliminated.

Meanwhile, back home, General Hershey stated that the Selective Service was "scraping the bottom of the manpower barrel" in its search for more than a million people needed for nonfighting jobs. Results of a survey showed that voters backed, by over 75 percent, the drafting of single women rather than taking fathers for such service. Returning veterans were already finding that "wives" with more seniority than the veterans were holding jobs that the veterans wanted. "Is this the kind of thanks to be given boys coming back from the war?" one veteran asked. Women were already striving for equal pay, and it was becoming obvious that the changing role of women, triggered by the war, could become a serious problem for the postwar world. Women were also struggling in Congress to remove the limitation of funds for care of children under the Lanham Act for child-care projects. This project had aided women working for the war effort in the care of their children.

Reading through old *New York Times* newspapers I was impressed, as well as depressed, at how many Americans died daily in this all-out war effort. While we in the WASP were often upset by the fact that we were not militarized, and thus not able to be part of a military group, such as the WAC and the WAVE groups, we felt great sorrow for the many fighting men who were killed daily so far from home. The WACs, as of March 11, the day of our graduation, were to be stationed at airfields in Hawaii. These women were to release men for service in the field, according to Major Geraldine May, WAC staff director for the Air Transport Command of the Army Air Force. Too bad that our Air Transport Command ferry pilots could not have joined in this endeavor.

When we finished our California cross-country trip, we had only to complete the total flying time required and we would be ready to graduate. In the meantime, our new Santiago-blue uniforms had arrived and we all gathered around, trying on and fitting ourselves into the beautiful new outfits. Those last few days before graduation remain just a blur in my mind. I was thinking not only of graduation but of my own upcoming marriage. Jerry and I had planned on marrying right after the graduation ceremonies, and my parents were coming down for the event.

In addition, the big question of where each of us would be sent after graduation invoked a lot of speculation. One person who was "in the know" about it all was Madeline Sullivan. She was group commander when the assignments came in and she was friendly with Mrs. Ethel Sheehy, who worked in administration. She told me, "You know, they hadn't had any requests for more pilots in the Ferry Command for three or four months—and Jo Wallace and I had always dreamed of being assigned to Wilmington and flying around and 'saving' the country, and then zapping up to New York and dazzling our friends, and all that. Then it came out, for the first time, that they had three or four openings in Wilmington. They were also assigning 20 WASPs to B-26 school in Dodge City, Kansas. I decided, if I was going to do anything with this training later, I wanted the horsepower rating, so I decided to go to B-26 school. Jo was a little upset with me, but she went to Wilmington and that's how we separated."

I was surprised when I talked to Madeline because none of us, that I knew of, had any choice; we did put in a request, but we didn't know what we would get. "I really did have a choice," she told me, "I really did. I saw the list before it was posted."

As it turned out, twenty members of Class 44-W-2 were sent to B-26 school at Dodge City, Kansas. The story, as we all heard it, was that the men were complaining about flying B-26s. Many of them were afraid to fly it. The B-26 was a hot plane, difficult to fly, and the landing gear was narrow, contributing to danger in landing. The answer to the problem was to send a group of women up to fly them, and it certainly worked. One other class of WASPs had already completed B-26 school successfully. The men could hardly refuse to fly an airplane that women could handle, and time proved that the women could handle it very nicely. Out of the twenty members of our class who entered B-26 training, thirteen graduated and flew B-26s for most of their active service. The other seven were sent to other bases.

Besides the B-26 assignment, five were sent to the Fifth Ferry Group at Love Field, Dallas, five to the Sixth Ferry Group, Long Beach, and five to the Second Ferry Group at New Castle Air Force Base in Wilmington, Delaware. Two each were sent to Courtland AAF, Courtland, Alabama; Jackson AAF, Jackson, Mississippi; Napier AAF, Dothan, Alabama; and Aloe AAF, Victoria, Texas. Three California bases, Merced AAF, Mintor AAF, and Stockton Field, received one WASP each. Two Arizona bases, Williams Field and Douglas AAF, also received one WASP, as did one Texas base, Randolph Field.

Later on, a short time before the WASPs were to be disbanded, some were transferred to different bases, including Dyersburg, Tennessee; Victorville, California; and others.

On March 10, the night before graduation, Class 44-W-3 entertained W-2 with a traditional graduation party. Our group commander, Madeline Sullivan, insisted on a St. Patrick's Day decor, as any good Irish lass would do, so a large four-leaf clover decorated the walls along with various clouds and "Fifi" figures, to represent the theme of the party, "Off We Go Into the Wild Blue Yonder." Music and tasty food added to the general gaiety. The Fifi (or Fifinella), by the way, was a cartoon female with wings, designed by Walt Disney especially for the WASPs.

The introduction to this book has already described our graduation ceremonies, but Anne Berry had another statement to add—another reason, she tells, why General Arnold decided to pin wings on all of us when he had originally planned to hand them to us. "I think we were probably one of two classes, out of the whole lot, who had General Arnold pin our wings on. That was because of Kate Lee Harris. If you remember, Kate Lee was always 'bringin' up the reah' because they put the tall girls in front whenever we marched. When we got ready to graduate, they reversed it and put the short girls in front. I don't remember who the first one was, but General Arnold was only going to do a symbolic thing—just pin the wings on the first one. Then he was just going to hand out the wings to the rest of us. Kate Lee was the second girl, and when he got to her she said, in that lovely North Carolinian accent, 'Well, don't stop naow.' General Arnold, bless his heart, didn't, and he pinned the wings on all the rest of us, and it took him some time. He was delightful."

It has always annoyed me somewhat that our class had the highest rate of washouts—more than 50 percent. During these interviews, I asked many of my classmates why they thought they succeeded when more than 50 percent of the trainees failed. Surprisingly, many of them thought that luck played a big part in their success, but others attributed it to good instructors, and others to pure determination.

Kate Lee Harris said, "It seemed that every time you turned around someone was gone, and you kept thinking, 'Am I next?' I think I was lucky—if half the class washed out and you didn't, you think it was probably luck. What was so bad was that both my brothers were in flight training. We were all three in at the same time, and both of them washed out. That was a big disappointment for them. But, they went on; one was a navigator and the other a top turret gunner on a B-24 that was shot down over Austria. He was lost. But you know, it sort of put the burden on me when I learned that they had washed out."

"I'll never know why I made it," Doris Elkington told me. "I think we were praying every night that we'd stay in, that we'd make it. A roll of the dice, perhaps. I think Dulaney was the only one left in her group, and I think her instructor was very tough on them. I think some of the gals couldn't take that. I didn't find any of my instructors tough on me. I felt like they were all there to help me and they did. They really did.''

Lorraine Zillner said she really didn't know why she didn't wash out, but she added, ''I think some of the girls had personality clashes with their instructors, and then some of the instructors were good friends with the check pilots. I really don't know. They were very rough on us, but I was thankful for it. I always thought they were getting us ready for being out alone in airplanes. I never held any of that against them.''

One reason for so many washouts in 44-W-2, according to Fran Smith, was because the armed forces were beginning to need fewer women pilots. ''I think it started with our class. They began washing out more because we were getting to the point where they didn't need us. At that time, I think it was getting to be a wind-down. The fellows were coming back and they needed the jobs that we had.''

Fran Laraway had another point of view. ''It was kind of interesting,'' she stated. ''They had people who were very good who washed out because they couldn't tell their right from their left. Also, there was a kind of 'factory' going on, if you want to get into that, producing pilots in the private sector. I know that after I left home and came down to Texas, I kept meeting people who had been relieved of their money and given thirty hours of casual instruction, which profited the private airports very beautifully, but didn't necessarily turn out a good product. I think that probably happened all over the country.''

There was, also, a wide discrepancy in flying hours. Some trainees in 44-W-2 came in with five hundred hours flying time and others with a bare thirty-five, quite a difference in experience. Still, many with only thirty-five hours flying time successfully completed the course. Nellie Henderson said she thought many of the girls who passed the course ''were pretty gutsy in taking it! We just fought back and kept fighting. Really. Just guts and stubbornness. Mainly stubbornness and the love for flying, but I didn't think it was easy.''

When asked why she didn't wash out, Mary Ellen Keil said, ''I'm sure there are some natural-born hot pilots, and some who learned. I think I was one who learned. I don't think I was a natural hot pilot. I think I used my brain to get through more than my natural ability.''

Sid Siddall had a different thought. ''I know there were other women who were better fliers than I, but I'm a good 'read,' and quick on picking up. I'm kind of cool in times of stress. I can handle that. I don't know, maybe they pick that up. As for directions, I've always had that—knowing where I am.''

Leona Golbinec's experience was somewhat different. ''They washed out all of the girls in my group,'' she told me, ''but then they let that instructor go and they kept me because they didn't want that group to be a complete failure.

It wasn't fair because one of the girls was a wonderful pilot. She flew circles around me. I'm beginning, now, to see that maybe a lot of them got washed out that weren't bad pilots.''

Millie Grossman said, ''I guess I didn't *want* to wash out. It was like the end of the world to wash out. Everyone who did felt awful; but I always felt that if I wanted something, I could do it, and I did.''

Joanne Wallace wanted to stress that we had double check rides. ''We had both the civilian and the Army. None of the men had double check rides. We had two men—both of whom had one idea and that was to wash you out—giving you those check rides. One man, coming in to just do check rides, said to me, 'I'm going to pass you, but my only idea when I came here was to see how many of you women I could wash out.' He said that! He was an Army check pilot. I said, 'Well, then, how come you passed me?' He said, 'Because I had to.' Don't you love it?''

Ruth Woods came into the WASPs with a lot of flying time, and she said, ''Well, I had a head start. Let's be honest. I had a lot of good experience and had been well trained. Helen Montgomery Hine, my instructor, was a 'precision' pilot and when I started flying with her she asked me who had taught me to fly, and I told her, 'an old Army instructor.' She said, 'I thought so.' It's too bad they don't still teach that way. We probably wouldn't have so many near misses and hits as we have, even though the skies are more loaded.''

At the time of graduation, however, we certainly weren't worrying about the washout rate. Our main concern was where we would spend our leave and what it would be like in our new base. Packing and getting rid of the many superfluous items we had amassed during our six-month stay occupied a lot of our time, and saying good-bye to all our baymates became a hurried and flustered event. Everyone was rushing off to someplace, usually home for the short leave before our assignments. Jerry and I were married in Sweetwater, the evening of March 11 following graduation ceremonies. It was not a large wedding because most of the WASPs had already left. It would be a very long time before many of us would meet again.

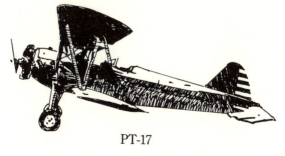

PT-17

75

Doris Elkington, Gini Dulaney, Ann Craft, and Twila Edwards in pregraduation dress uniforms.

Flight I of Class 44-W-2. Top Row: Gini Dulaney, Minkie Heckman, Marjorie Gilbert, Twila Edwards, Muriel Lindstrom. Third Row: Margaret Ehlers, Ann Craft, Betty Le Fevre, Millie Grossman, Kay Herman, Leona Golbinec, Anne Berry. Second Row: Jean Hascall, Kate Lee Harris, Ruth Adams, Nellie Henderson. Bottom Row: Susie Clarke, unidentified, Mary Ellen Keil, Kay Cleverly, Fran Laraway, Marjorie Johnson, Sadie Hawkins.

Calisthenics at Avenger Field, Sweetwater, Texas.

Top: Ann Craft. Middle: Doris Elkington, Twila Edwards, Susie Clarke. Bottom: Gini Dulaney.

Kate Lee Harris and Jean Hascall in winterwear.

Yvonne Stafford models "zoot suit."

Overlarge features of the "zoot suit."

Left to right: Kay Herman, Minkie Heckman, Millie Grossman, Jean Hascall, Leona Golbinec, Sadie Hawkins, and Margaret Ehlers.

Virginia Flugel and Gini Dulaney model their red winter underwear.

Sadie Hawkins, Lyle Rose Handerson, and Minkie Heckman.

"Beatrice" (Lorraine's brother) and Lorraine Zillner.

Lyle Rose Handerson, Jean Hascall, Marjorie Gilbert, and Leona Golbinec in their fleece-lined flightwear.

Mary Saunders studying.

Kate Lee Harris, Jean Hascall, Ann Craft, Nellie Henderson, and Sadie Hawkins with a "cattle car" at the auxiliary field.

Millie Grossman, Marjorie Gilbert, Anne Berry, Ann Craft, Jean Hascall, and Barbara Drew (reclining).

Eleanor Patterson, with instructor, aboard an AT-6.

Marion Lambert, Eleanor Coonley, Millie Grossman, and Frances Fisher, at the Auxiliary Field with a PT-19A.

Jean Hascall, Kate Lee Harris, Ray Booth, Marjorie Johnson, Ruth Adams.

Top: Doris Elkington. Middle: Marion Lambert, instructor, Virginia Flugel. Bottom: Margaret Ehlers.

Anne Berry, Nellie Henderson, Instructor Moore, Lois Cutler, and Ann Craft.

Instructor J. Hosier and Jean Hascall.

Nellie Henderson climbing aboard a PT-19 at Avenger Field.

Jean Hascall just previous to her first solo flight aboard a PT-19A.

Kate Lee Harris receives congratulations from Jean Hascall after first solo flight, at Avenger Field.

Kate Lee Harris getting tossed into the wishing well after her first solo flight.

Ruth Woods going over a preflight checklist on an AT-6.

Lorraine Zillner filling out a Form I after flying an AT-6.

Mary Strok aboard an AT-6.

Mary Strok and Ruth Petry on the wing of an AT-6.

Minkie Heckman in a PT-19A.

Joan Whelan standing on an AT-6.

Mary Ellen Keil in an AT-6 at Avenger Field.

Twila Edwards poses with a Stearman.

Ruth Woods.

Kit MacKethan.

Verda-Mae Lowe with plane named for her after she landed it on fire at Williams Air Force Base.

Susie Clarke (in front), with Ruth Adams, Jean Moore, and others.

Squadron returning from drill in pre-uniform dress clothes.

Clarice Siddall upon graduation.   Verda-Mae Lowe upon graduation.

J. Cochran, Gen. Henry H. Arnold and Lorraine Zillner at graduation ceremonies.

Madeline Sullivan, Gen. H. H. Arnold, Jacqueline Cochran, Gen. Barton K. Yount, and Susie Clarke (right) at dinner, graduation day, 11 March 1944.

Tow pilots, Aloe Field, Victoria Texas, 1944. Front: Rita Darcy, Hank Henry, Jean McFarland, Bert Paskvan, Carol Webb. Back Row: Liz Watson, Dottie Allen, Minkie Heckman (44-W-2), Ruth Weller (44-W-2), and B. J. Overman.

Minkie Heckman and Nellie Henderson at Aloe Field, Victoria, Texas.

Marjorie Gilbert and Millie Grossman.

Mary Ellen Keil, pilot aboard a B-26.

Mary Ellen Keil, Ruth Woods, Mary Saunders, and Millie Grossman at B-26 school, Dodge City, Kansas.

Ruth Adams after delivering a P-51.

Front row left: Clarice Siddall and Lorraine Zillner on assignment.

Gini Dulaney with a UC-78 ''Bamboo Bomber.''

44-W-2 Class Reunion, Leland Hotel, Richmond Indiana, March 1946. Left to right: Jean Hascall, Eleanor Patterson, Jean Moore, Marjorie Johnson, Millie Grossman, Kate Lee Harris, Mary Ellen Keil, Anne Berry, Minkie Heckman and Marjorie Gilbert.

Reunion, Sweetwater, Texas, 1986. Top: Jean Moore, Madeline Sullivan, Marjorie Gilbert. Middle: Anne Berry, Millie Grossman, Kay Herman, Jean Hascall, Elizabeth Price, Minkie Heckman. Front: Nellie Henderson, Lorraine Zillner, Kate Lee Harris, Mary Ellen Keil, Leona Golbinec, Fran Smith.

Minkie Heckman, Jean Hascall, Sadie Hawkins, Nellie Henderson, and Kate Lee Harris in "zoot suits" and at reunion September 1978 at Colorado Springs.

CHAPTER SIX

B-26 School

"She was trying to wave to the jeep to stop for her and her arm went into the spinning prop." —Fran Smith

Imagine a sleek, shiny, streamlined twin-engine bomber, so beautifully designed that it earned the name "The Flying Torpedo." The B-26 Martin Marauder was all of that and more. Described as a "hot" airplane, it landed at 130 to 135 miles per hour, and it took a very good crew to fly it, by all accounts. Powered by two 2,200-horsepower Pratt and Whitney engines, it zipped along at 320 to over 400 miles per hour, and carried a bomb load of 5,800 pounds. Restricted from such maneuvers as loops and rolls, it still demanded constant attention in flying. This B-26 served as a medium bomber, dropping its heavy load from medium to low altitudes. A nose enclosure for the bombardier, made of a one-piece clear plastic molding, afforded a spectacular view. During combat a turret gunner sat in the tail. When the war was over, the B-26 was found to have been one of the safest planes in combat, but it was still tough to fly, and not popular with some pilots. "At Boise," Marge Gilbert told me, "the squadron commander told the men, 'It takes a man to fly this B-26. Boys can fly the B-24, but it takes a man to fly this plane.' Then we came in!"

"The first time I went up in the B-26," Madeline Sullivan said, "I remember thinking to myself, when we were making our first landing, 'Oh, this son of a gun! He's trying to scare me witless, and he's pretty well achieving it. Is he going to land this thing? The runway is almost behind us.' Then he dives at the runway and flattens out and I thought, 'Hotshot, he's trying to scare me to death,' but it turns out that's the way you land the thing. It didn't float at all. I mean you really did come down with almost no approach, and then it dropped like a brick."

She went on to describe her first introduction to B-26 school at Dodge City, Kansas. "When we first arrived, potbelly stoves were used in the barracks. There's a particular odor from those stoves, and I thought, I'll smell this for the rest of my life. It was really something. Then, they always gave the most recently married instructors to the WASPs. My instructor—well, I'd never seen anything so gorgeous in my life, but he'd been married only about three weeks so he didn't see any of us."

Madeline told me that they also had French students on the base at the same time as the WASPs. The WASPs were liked better than the French because the French often didn't want to finish. They would then have to go back into the fighting, so they would pretend not to "understand."

Madeline ended up rooming with Sadie Hawkins and they were dating two fellows who were great friends. "The four of us did a lot of things together," she said, "including horseback riding. Sadie was the only one who had ever ridden before, so she was getting a big bang out of it!" Madeline went on to tell me that if the saddle hadn't had a pommel on it, she never would have made it back.

Sadie Hawkins, by all accounts I have heard, was an excellent pilot, but she was not too much on talking about it. She did tell me a few things about B-26 school. "When we went to B-26 transition school," she told me, "it was great. I loved that airplane! We just took the same course that all the lieutenants did, and I remember when they did roll call. They did all the men first; it was, 'here,' 'here,' in deep voices. Then they got to the WASPs and it was, 'here,' 'here' in falsetto. Then, some lieutenant arrived late and they put his name at the end of the WASPs, and it became, 'here,' 'here,' falsetto, and then a deep 'here.' It was Lieutenant Hafkemyer, I still remember. We named him an honorary WASP, because he was always listed with us."

The seven WASPs who didn't complete B-26 school were not as upset over washing out as they would have been at Avenger Field. They were only "out" of B-26 school and were given other assignments flying other aircraft more suitable to their abilities. They were "reassigned," in other words. Clarice (Sid) Siddall said, "I don't think I was at B-26 school very long. It was just something I didn't want to do. I really didn't want twin-engine flying. I was more comfortable by myself, so it just didn't work out for me. They were telling me I didn't have the strength and that sort of thing. I don't know. It was something I just didn't do well. I was sent from there to Victoria, Texas, to tow targets in AT-6s."

Madeline Sullivan explained part of the reason why Sid had a hard time with the B-26. "I had kept pushing her to go to B-26 school," Madeline explained, "because we were such good friends, but it needed some strength to handle the B-26. You had to pull the nose wheel off the runway with the left hand, keeping the right hand on the throttle, and some of us were not strong enough with the left hand. We'd almost always take our right hand off the throttle and start to pull up—and they would whack you when you did that. Well, the fellow I was going out with had won a boxing scholarship to Syracuse University. We were complaining, and the next thing we knew, he was taking us over to the gym and teaching us how to do a routine they do with the left hand. Then we got those squeeze balls, and we'd go to breakfast, lunch, and everywhere with those little squeeze balls in our hands, trying to strengthen our left arms.''

Kay Herman resigned out of B-26 school. ''I got about twenty hours of pilot time,'' she said, ''and then twenty hours of copilot time. I don't think I'd ever have gotten through the thing, though. I really wasn't comfortable with the airplane. My husband stopped off at Dodge City to see me. He was in the Naval Air Transport Service. I had talked to the instructors and they were going to let him ride with us one day, but he wouldn't go in it! He said he would never fly in that airplane; it was a death trap. He could have, because we had permission for him, but he wouldn't do it. Then I got out on a medical from there. I was at a point where I couldn't handle it any longer. I was pregnant so I took a medical out, but I lost that baby.''

Anna Mae Petteys was another who did not care for the B-26. ''I was sent to B-26 school,'' she explained, ''and I didn't make it through. I was disappointed to fail, but I hated that plane. I'm sure it would have been very unpleasant for me to continue to fly it.''

Jean Moore was sent to B-26 school, and she wasn't too fond of multi-engine planes either. ''I'm a 'seat-of-the-pants' flier,'' she told me. ''I'm not an instrument flier, so I had a habit of getting the airspeed two miles an hour slower than I was supposed to, and my instructor would turn white because he felt it was dangerous to let the airspeed fall below designated levels in the B-26. He didn't like that, so I washed out. I wasn't really sorry about washing out because I didn't like multi-engines. Sid and I were sent to Victoria, Texas, to tow targets for simulated gunnery.''

Ruth Weller also did not graduate from B-26 school. She sent me a tape recording of her WASP days, but she had only this to say about B-26s: ''After graduation I went to B-26 school at Dodge City, Kansas. I then attended Officers Candidate School at Orlando, Florida. My last station was Aloe Field, Victoria, Texas, where I towed sleeve targets for the Aerial Gunnery School.''

Fran Laraway didn't make it through B-26 school, and she told me that most of her WASP experiences seem quite removed now. ''It almost seems as though it happened to someone else,'' she explained. ''When I graduated I went to Dodge City to B-26 school, but I didn't make that, and ended up in the Central Flying Command flying out of Goodfellow Field doing engineering testing after the students cracked up their Stearmans.''

Marge Needham was another who did not graduate from B-26s. She told me she had an instructor who was "out of this world he was so mean. If you were doing something he didn't like, instead of correcting you or telling you what not to do, he would hit your hands off the throttle. I don't remember his name. I don't ever want to hear about him again. I went into maintenance testing at Garden City, Kansas. There were four or five of us there, and I think Anna Mae [Petteys] was one of them."

The thirteen graduates had some hair-raising experiences both during and after their B-26 training. Mary Ellen Keil told me about her first solo in the B-26 and it sounded horrendous. "The first time I soloed a B-26 at night," she began, "I learned it was true that when you're really scared your knees knock together. My knees were just knocking. It was a terrible night. It was half fog and the fog would roll over the runway. Then they gave us a right-hand pattern to fly instead of a left. In the right-hand pattern, on the downwind leg, when you tried to turn onto the base leg, the whole runway was blocked out of your view. You had to just be sure you had started out right; everything was so critical on the B-26, because you were going so fast. You had to do a million things at once, and then to have your view blocked! Besides that, every once in a while the runway would be completely shut out by fog. That's the reason I love Rose Reese to this day, even though she doesn't write to me. She was my copilot on that ride and all the way around I'd ask, 'How am I doing?' because she could see the runway and I couldn't. She'd say, 'Oh, Mary Ellen, you're doing just great.' She was that cheerful Texan type and just cheered me up all the way around, or I never would have made it.

"It wasn't until I was up in the air that they told me I was going to have to fly that right-hand pattern. You see, if you flew a left-hand pattern, you, as pilot, sat on the left so it was all fine—you could see the runway and see when you turned onto your base leg and when you turned onto final approach. With a right-hand pattern, you couldn't see a darn thing because you were sitting on the left. Remember, we came in on our final approach at 180 miles per hour, and it would finally stall out at about 135. I'll never forget that!"

Mary Ellen and I were both sorry that Rose Reese didn't want to be tape-recorded or to participate in an oral history. Mary Ellen had been a friend of hers and was particularly disappointed that she didn't want to correspond with anyone.

Ruth Woods, on the other hand, said she had a lot of fun in B-26 school. "I enjoyed that. I had a little moment of heart-stoppage on a takeoff once and it was my own fault. I had failed to check my nose trim. In fact, I think my instructor had really pushed it forward on me because this was a test ride. I'm blasting down the runway in the B-26, and running out of runway, and it's not coming off. All of a sudden it hit me—that trim tab's wrong, and I just reached down there and flipped it. I didn't even look at it. I was using all the strength I had against that wheel. Well, we got off, and he gave me a lecture about that, but he passed me. I never did forget that again, never, never!''

Millie Grossman was also a B-26 graduate and she thought it was a difficult program. She also experienced a close call during training. "We went from AT-6s to a twin-engine plane without having had any twin-engine flying. It wasn't exactly easy. I had a lot of things happen to me, but I wouldn't say I was in any real danger, except maybe once. When we got to advanced training and were out practicing landings at a nearby field, I saw, on the ground, a plane that was pulling out to take off just after they had cleared me for landing. We just put on the power and shot up out of there because there definitely would have been a collision. I remember it was my instructor who was in the control tower, and he said afterward, 'Oh, Millie, I'm so glad that you realized what was going on, because it would have been my fault if anything had happened.' He was doing the control. But, you see, these things can happen to all of us—amazing!''

Esther Noffke told me she always wanted to fly the B-26. "I saw a B-26 come in there at Sweetwater when I was in Basic, and it was called the Martin Marauder. I thought, 'Gee, I'd like to fly that.' Then I saw them again down on the Texas-Mexico border, and I thought that I'd really like to fly those. I could never believe that I got that assignment! They had already made the selection of the twenty pilots who would go to Dodge City and I couldn't qualify because I was half an inch too short. We had the option of putting down three choices, and I put down B-26 school for all three so I finally got to go, but only because Joanne Wallace, who had been selected, decided not to go. I made it through and graduated, but, you know, it was tough. It was hard.''

Marge Gilbert and Mary Ellen Keil were discussing some of the B-26 stories when we met for a reunion at Dayton in September of 1989, and Mary Ellen said, ''Well, at Dodge City they said that we were better than the French pilots, because the French always landed on a bunch of cows when they made a forced landing. Then the Army had to pay for all the cows.'' They both thought that was pretty funny. I asked if they had any fatalities in the B-26 and Marge answered, ''No, that's written up in our official report.''

She went on to describe their training in plane recognition. "At first," she said, ''I couldn't even see the planes on the screen, and we were supposed to recognize them. I didn't even see the plane at all, they flashed it so fast. It was an interesting experience to see how your mind and eye could learn to pick up those planes when at first you couldn't even see them.''

Mary Ellen added, ''It was a fascinating learning experience for me, especially being a teacher—that you can learn to identify something that at first isn't even visible to you.

"Another thing—we outscored the men in B-26 ground school and they couldn't believe it. Here we were, supposedly uninformed women, and we got better scores than they did on the electrical system, the hydraulic system, the emergency system—the whole thing. We even had a higher score on the mechanical operation than the men did."

The WASP pilots received a commendation for their scoring on the ground school course. The following directive was sent to the WASP Class 44-2-C by Major John Todd. It stated:

"It is noted with great interest that on the B-26 Procedures Course (given by Captain Grandjean) the average grade of the WASPs was 77.8 percent while the average grade of the male students was 74.6 percent. All WASPs may well be proud of the high margin of superiority demonstrated in this, the most important ground school course.

"This showing would seem to indicate that the information required to pass the course can be obtained from the textbook by sufficient application, regardless of the background and prior training of the student. This thought is worthy of the serious consideration of all the male members of the class."

Marge Gilbert tells about a time when she thought she was washing out on B-26s. "I had been flying as first pilot with Captain Burton in the copilot seat and it was about time for me to solo. I came in for a landing and landed short, hitting some dirt just before the start of the runway, and I hit it a little hard. Captain Burton said, 'Take it on around. I don't think you'd better fly it any more today.' We went in for him to check out the airplane for damage. I was sure I had washed out, but when we went in for assignments, he said, 'You, Gilbert, will be doing so and so.' I said, 'You mean I'm not washed out?' He said, 'What made you think you were being washed out?' I said, 'You told me I shouldn't fly this airplane anymore.' 'No,' he said, 'it was because this plane might be damaged in some way and we shouldn't be practicing landings in it.' That was a horrible half hour. I soloed shortly after that. I liked Captain Burton. He was a nice guy."

Millie Grossman described a long B-26 cross-country flight she flew during B-26 training. "We went from Dodge City all the way to the East Coast and landed at Indianapolis on the way. That's where I'm from, so my mother, sisters, and great-great-aunt came to the airport. My aunt came because her son had flown in World War I and the day of the Armistice he was shot down. It was very sad, but she kept her interest in flying. She was quite old and could hardly see—she had cataracts—but she was there to greet me.

"On that flight we took off very late from Dodge City, and we ran into a big storm. Just over the Mississippi River we had St. Elmo's fire all around our props. It was exciting, and I didn't even know what it was. [St. Elmo's fire is an electric discharge that resembles a flame. It is more often seen on the mast of a ship at sea.] Then, in the B-26, there was this huge bubble where the bombardier would sit, where you could look out. I remember when it wasn't my turn to fly I went in there and just lay down and looked. We were going over the eastern Allegheny mountains and it was a sight I could never forget. I had a feeling of really flying, because there was nothing around me to detract from the view.''

Fran Smith and Joan Whelan both graduated from B-26 training. Fran was surprised that she made it because she was so short.

''They wanted girls five feet six,'' she explained. ''I was only five feet four. One time when I was talking to Deedie [Avenger Field Administrator Leoti Deaton], at one of the reunions, I asked her, 'Why did you send me to B-26 school?' She said, 'Well, you may not have been good in ground school, but you were a damn good pilot,' which made me feel good. At B-26 school I could fly it, but I still had trouble in ground school. I made it, though.''

All of the B-26 graduates were first sent to Boise, Idaho, where they towed targets for the gunners to shoot at. Then they would drop the targets at an auxiliary field where they would be picked up and returned to be evaluated. The base was also full of B-24s which were slow, slow planes. ''They were four-engine planes,'' Fran Smith explained, ''and of course the B-26 was two-engine. We would make a pass at the formation so the gunners could shoot at us to see how their aim was. None of us ever worried about it. We never realized there was any danger until we heard that one of the pilots at a field near us, Mountain Home, had his foot shot off because they didn't see the target he was towing and they shot at the airplane. When you're that age you don't think about the danger you're facing.''

One time Fran was flying as first pilot for a tow target mission. ''We had just dropped our target,'' she reported, ''and all of a sudden one engine quit on me. We discussed whether we should land there at the auxiliary field, or limp home. We finally did limp home to the base and I was able to land it with one engine and brought it in. It was a very strange situation. They congratulated me for bringing it home, but I got bawled out because there was no oil in the engine. Even though the check sheet said the oil had been put in the engine, no oil had been put in the engine. They reprimanded me because I hadn't looked to see that there was oil in the engine. I had burned up an engine which cost the government some money.''

Fran Smith and Joan Whelan were flying together one day, making passes at a B-24, and by the time the day was over Joan had walked into the propeller of their B-26, badly injuring her arm. Joan and Fran both gave me accounts of the episode. Joan said, ''At Gowen Field in Boise, Fran and I were flying a

B-26. When we landed, I wanted to get out of the plane before she parked it. She idled the engines, and I got out. I knew very well where to go, but I didn't. A jeep was just leaving and I wanted to catch it to get a ride to the flight line. I put my arm up to stop him and it swung right into the right propeller of the B-26. Three of the four blades nicked my arm and I have scars and a droopy little finger. I was fortunate that there was an orthopedic surgeon on the base. He worked on it very assiduously for many hours and put my arm back together, so I was very fortunate. It's fine now."

Fran Smith had a much more detailed description of the events as they happened that day. "The big episode that Joan Whelan was involved in," she told me, "was when we were pulling tow targets and I was pilot, Joan copilot. We dropped our targets and then we were making passes at the B-24s. Joan was flying as pilot by this time. (We often exchanged pilot and copilot positions in the air.) Joan got a little too close to the B-24, and we ended up with a big hole in our right wing, and the B-24 lost part of its tail section."

"You mean you ran into them—in the air?" I asked.

"Yes, we hit them!" she laughed. "Anyway, both of us were able to bring our planes in. The B-24 pilot brought his in, and we brought ours in. It felt as if we were bringing it in on one engine, but we landed safely and they told me where to park, which I proceeded to do. Then a jeep came up and the officer in it said, 'We've decided we don't want the plane here, we want you to put it somewhere else.' I had not cut my engines off, and for those of you who don't know it, the way you got out of the B-26 was to descend right behind the pilot and copilot seats, down between the wheels, and then you walked forward between the two engines.

"Joan said, 'Let me out here, you don't need me to go put the plane away. I want to explain what happened.' Joan got down, and completely forgot about the props still spinning! She was trying to wave to the jeep to stop for her, and her arm went into the spinning prop. Of course, I did not see this because she was below me. The next thing I knew was that somebody was telling me to cut the engines. I didn't know until I got out of the plane what had happened.

"I know why Joan wanted to go in such a hurry! As always, the pilot is captain and whatever goes wrong, she gets the blame. She wanted to tell everybody that she had been at the controls of the plane, doing the flying, when we had the collision. She didn't want me to get the blame. Joan was lucky there was a surgeon on the base who specialized in bone and ligament repair. She has never lost the use of her arm."

I can well imagine that Joan was upset enough to forget about the propellers spinning. After a midair collision, I'm amazed that they were able to land the plane safely, and I would expect that both of them must have been upset over such an unusual and near-disastrous occurrence. In addition, Joan was always such a conscientious person! Her primary concern at that moment was surely to see that the facts were presented so that Fran did not get the blame. Most midair collisions are fatal, with both planes crashing, so they were all very lucky to have landed safely.

Mary Ellen Keil gave me a little explanation about how the action went with the B-24s and the B-26s that towed the targets for them to shoot at. "First you'd fly by the B-24 and they'd practice shooting at you with cameras in their guns. That was at above ten thousand feet. The B-26 crew consisted of a pilot, copilot, and flight engineer. The engineer would release the target from the back of the bomb bay. The target was held on by means of a heavy steel cable which was towed about fifteen hundred feet behind the B-26. It was a tremendous load, which included the weight of the target and the long length of cable. I remember how it would snap the plane up into a stall position and you had to be so careful when you released the target."

Marge Gilbert added, "Sometimes they'd be shooting with live ammunition and there was always a funny guy who'd call up and say, 'I see the target out there but what's that in back of it?' "

Mary Ellen continued, "They did put some holes in some of the planes, though. It wasn't too close; they'd just hit the rear of the plane. The other flights we made were called 'pursuit interception.' We flew through the B-24 formation. We'd get up above them and fly down. We didn't just fly past them, we were diving through them, and that B-26 was so fast and so heavy that we had to watch out for the pull-out—because the plane would sink. There would be a tremendous drop when you'd pull out of your dive. That's what you'd have to watch for—that you wouldn't get too close to the planes you were coming down on.

"That's what happened to Joan Whelan. Also, those smart guys would say, 'You're too far away. Come in closer.' Of course, Joan was a good pilot and she'd take the dare and she kept coming in closer, but she came in a little too close. When she pulled out and got that high-speed stall, she just sank down with her wing on their tail. It was just a 'minor' midair, but when you know the chances of living through a midair collision are small, it was lucky that she lived through it and both planes got down all right!"

Marge then went on to describe a single-engine landing she had with Fran Smith. "I was copiloting for her," she explained, "when the plane lost the oil in one engine and she had to feather the prop and land with only one engine. She did an excellent job. I think it's the one that Mary Ellen was talking about that was just a real good landing. The one I had about a month later with Pat Patterson was not so good. We were flying tow-target and the accessory drive shaft in one engine broke, so we had to come in on a single engine. We feathered and called in from ten thousand feet and they said, 'You're number one to land.'

"We went on down and started to put the wheels down only to find the hydraulic system wasn't working either. The engineer had to pump them down by hand, so we had to go a little farther than we had estimated. We went to the next runway where there were some planes parked, but we came in and landed sort of in the dirt, but landed all right. Talk about shaky. My knees were shaking so I didn't even get out of the plane. I just let them haul us in. I couldn't even walk."

Mary Ellen added, "You don't know what an experience it was to have a single-engine landing in a B-26. Marge and Pat didn't even blow a tire! They didn't even get off the runway—just held that thing straight. They did a marvelous job. That really impressed the men, because very few of the men there had had a single-engine landing with the B-26."

Esther Noffke witnessed that landing and said that it was a spectacular event because the word went all through Gowen Field that two WASPs were up there in trouble. "Here comes this B-26, limping across the airport," she explained, "with one engine out, and they made a turn into the good engine and landed on a closed runway. There were airplanes parked on each side. They landed and didn't damage a thing! I'll tell you, the WASPs were 'in' after that time. Before that, the men were always a little skeptical about what women could do and what they couldn't. In this particular case, the whole Gowen field was out. They were standing on the ramp area watching. The cheer that went up after they landed! It was something to see and we were so proud of them!"

Sadie Hawkins was also at Boise, often teamed up with Madeline Sullivan. When I asked her if they used real bullets, she answered, "They did when we towed targets in the B-26. We had to tow the target and then drop it and count the number of holes in it. Unfortunately, there were not usually very many. I always hoped they'd get better.

"For a while they put cameras on the B-26 and decided they would let us fly a pursuit-intercept mission with B-24 crews, and we were supposed to do all sorts of things with our cameras and try to shoot the B-24 down with the camera. I have no idea how that worked out. Nobody ever told us, but it was certainly zippy, I must say that. The towing targets got to be zippy sometimes, too. We would fly along one side of the B-24 formation and they would shoot at the target we were towing. Then we would cross under to the other side. I remember getting a few shells in the nose of the plane one time as we crossed under, because the tail gunner was just getting rid of his ammunition.

"Another time we were presented with a tow target which had been dropped through some farmer's barn and he sued the government. We were asked by the base commander to come over for a presentation. We got all dressed up and we were presented with this tow target which had been used as evidence. I have no idea what happened to that tow target. I think the farmer did get some compensation from the government for his barn, or maybe a horse or a cow."

Another time, Sadie told me, she and Madeline were stuck out in eastern Oregon. They dropped the tow targets at an auxiliary field and had to land to pick them up. Nothing was there but the landing strip. "This time," she related, "the engineer had dropped the target quite a distance from the runway, so we turned the engines off. When we got back we couldn't start them up. We sat and sat, and the radio we had was only good close to the base. They couldn't hear us calling. Finally they realized we were long overdue and they came looking for us. They couldn't start the engine either, so it had to be replaced."

Madeline Sullivan added her version of their tow-target flying. "Half the time," she said, "when you'd be flying with the tow target, you pulled out and up behind them to let that whole formation turn to the right. Then you'd call the squadron leader to cease firing, but you'd see these puffs coming at you, and half of them wouldn't cease firing. Once, at least once that I remember, when Sadie was flying this seat, we had an engine shot out and had to make an emergency landing, because they were still shooting at us when they were not supposed to be. This was live ammunition, of course, because it was their last staging area before going overseas.

"That camera pursuit was a lot of fun, though. Those planes had a Plexiglas nose, and we had some yellow, rubbery cushions, so at the end of the mission, flying back from southeastern Oregon, I'd always take those pillows when I was copilot, and go lie up in the front and just look out that Plexiglas. It was really fascinating, because you'd be maybe fifty feet off the ground, and then all of a sudden you'd hit a big canyon and the ground would just drop away from you. It turns your stomach over just like the first hill on a roller coaster. It's the most incredible sensation when you're not expecting it."

Ruth Woods was another B-26 pilot sent to Boise who really liked the plane. "In B-26s in Boise," she told me, "those airplanes had been stripped down. Everything in them that could be stripped out was taken out, to lighten them. We flew those little darlin's like pursuit interception aircraft with cameras in our noses. We'd go out and then we'd be sitting there waiting for them up in the sun. We shot more of our own airplanes out of the air than they ever did. We'd come back in and they'd play the tapes back to us and we always got our plane, on our camera guns.

Other WASP pilots at Boise disagreed about the statements of women who said they flew B-26s with cameras in the noses trying to shoot down the B-24s. Three WASPS from the Boise group assured me that did happen, but others said they never flew such "pursuit-intercept" missions as they were called.

I noted that Sadie Hawkins had said "for a while" they tried that, so I can only assume that the attempt may have been experimental and was stopped before all of the WASPs had a chance to participate. That could explain the discrepancy in recollections of various WASPs from the same field.

"We could do a lot of things in those B-26s that you wouldn't dare try to do normally, because they were so stripped down. That sort of temptation resulted in the death of at least one person. They rolled it! I wouldn't roll a B-26. I knew good and well it wouldn't stress it. Well, it ripped and fouled the wings and that thing went in! It wasn't one of our girls. It was down at Del Rio, Texas."

Ruth told of another exciting B-26 experience. "We used to have to go over into Oregon to drop our tow-target sleeves. We had a fenced-off area—originally it wasn't fenced, but the wild animals would pull carcasses up on the hot pavement at night and we couldn't land the next day until somebody went out and cleared the runway—so we had to fence it. We went over there and we had dropped our target and were ready to take off when the right engine wouldn't rev up. We kept fooling with it and messing with it, and couldn't get heard by radio because of the mountains.

"I said to my copilot and engineer, 'You-all want to take a chance?' They said, 'You can't take a B-26 off with a single engine,' but then they said, 'Let's try it.' We started down the runway—I hit the mixture control and the engine caught, just about the time I was going to have to kill it, and we took off. The engineer said, 'Man, those women know how to fly! She took that plane off with a single engine.' Well, we didn't take it off on a single engine—we just thought about doing it, but we wouldn't have tried it!' "

Another funny incident that happened back in Dodge City was told by Madeline Sullivan. It involved an instructor named McKinster and his friend, who was Sadie's instructor. "They took a few students, including Sadie and me, on a long cross-country trip to New York. We landed at Mitchell Field and the instructor decided to give these people a surprise, so they put me in the pilot's seat (because it's my hometown), and Sadie in the right seat, and we brought it in. Then out comes the little jeep with a second lieutenant in it—you know, 'Follow me.' We follow him and he pulls around to where we're going to park. Then Sadie looks out one side and I look out the other side, and he looks up, takes his hat off, drops it on the ground and stomps on it. 'I can't believe it, two girls!'

"That really was so funny, we laughed like crazy. Then we didn't get out. We had a little engine problem. We were supposed to stay two nights, but with the engine problem we stayed for the third. When we were leaving to go back to Dodge City, I figured that, if we had the right wind, I would fly over my younger brother's school. I told him, if I figure it right, it will be somewhere between 9:00 and 9:30. You listen, and I'll run the engine up to say good-bye to you.

"Well, we barely take off, it seems to me, and I'm looking for the school, when all of a sudden—a big yaw. I'm thinking, come on, fellows, you don't have to practice a single engine now! [Sometimes an instructor would shut down an engine on purpose to test the student.] I hit the trim tab and I looked around, and the instructor's saying, 'Get out of here, get out of here.' We really did lose an engine. We had to limp back, and then we had another two days before we managed to get back to the base. That was pretty exciting."

Mary Ellen remembered one delightful experience she had with the B-26, she told me. "Ruth Woods and I were to fly some officers to Salt Lake City. It was in the wintertime and that was the most beautiful flight I ever had. The men didn't get finished—they had to go up there on business—and they were supposed to be through before dark. Even though we'd had night flying, we weren't supposed to fly at night, but they didn't get through until after dark and we had to fly home. That night it was just heavenly because there was snow all around and it was a perfectly clear night, and the power of those engines! What was it? Twenty-two hundred horsepower in each engine, and to hear those powerful engines flying over that beautiful, almost uninhabited, landscape! Of course, it was always fun to fly at night looking out at the airplane wings and all the lights. It was just a wonderful experience. We both remembered it as one of the highlights of our lives because it was so beautiful."

Almost all of the pilots I talked to remembered at least one flying incident that was so spectacular that it made a lasting impression and remained a highlight in their lives. It strengthened my feeling that many pilots watch for these encounters and are always looking for more of such unusual or dazzling occurrences. Even on commercial flights today, I ask for a window seat and spend most of the flight peering outside, watching for some unexpected, but magnificent, sight.

Fran Smith told me about one of the nice things that happened to her while she was flying B-26s. "It was when my brother flew in just to see me," she recalled, "in a P-47. He was there for a couple of hours. I was able to take him up in the B-26 and there were two or three of us who went up and we started flying formation to show him the B-26. He kept saying, 'Fran, you're getting too close. Fran, you're getting too close!' He was not used to the type of formation we used because the P-47 is different. I was thrilled that I got to take my brother up with me and that we had that time together, because he was killed overseas about three months later. He was shot down only about a week after he got over there. It's strange, I have a brother buried in Germany and a father buried in China.''

B-24 Liberators, such as those the men were flying at Boise and using for gunnery practice, were in the news that April. Five islands in the Truk region were bombed by Liberators and only a week later, on April 8, twenty-eight Japanese ships were sunk and the U.S. Navy smashed 214 Japanese planes. Meanwhile, six hundred B-26 Marauders from the Ninth Air Force pounded targets in France and Belgium, dropping more than a thousand tons of bombs—a record weight for those medium bombers.

American soldiers in England were preparing for D-Day and the question of when D-Day would occur was on everyone's mind. WACs were still being recruited, while the U.S. Navy was forced to take over the twenty-four-story Manhattan Towers in order to house hundreds of WAVES who were unable to find housing. The railroads were campaigning for women workers, claiming 100,000 jobs, formerly held by men, needed filling. The postwar economy was in the news often, portending a bright outlook for jobs for women.

Action on the European front was in constant turmoil. Plants in Nuremberg were battered by U.S. bombers, and the city was described as a ''blazing ruin.'' Planes also bombed Poland and Budapest. Russians were closing in on Odessa, where German troops were said to be cut off, and in less than a week the city was captured. P-47 Thunderbolt pursuits were converted into dive bombers so they could be used at the front, and a U.S. flier had invented a better bombsight, which incorporated an automatic deflection sight. In the midst of all the action, Mount Vesuvius erupted again!

In the Pacific, one returning B-17 Flying Fortress had flown 109 missions against the Japs, downing seventeen planes, seven ships, and two submarines. Seven crew members were injured during the missions. U.S. forces seized ten more atolls and airmen pounded New Guinea bases. Pilot Don Gentile surpassed Rickenbacker's total of planes shot down when he claimed a record twenty-seven planes destroyed.

Much of the news at that time revolved around flying—planes bombing cities, planes being shot down, flight records being set—so that the war seemed, indeed, an air war as Churchill had proclaimed. The bulk of the fighting, however, was still on the ground, and it seemed strange to realize that those fighting men seemed to get less publicity than the men in the air. Flying was glamorous then, of course, and nobody was more enthralled with it than the women pilots.

The WASPs at Dodge City, Kansas, and Boise, Idaho, had enjoyed their work immensely, they told me. They loved the flying, the excitement of towing targets, and the comradeship of their group. In addition, they relieved many of the men who had been flying tow-targets to serve overseas. There were no fatalities during B-26 training, or the subsequent flying at Boise, and the program certainly proved that women could handle the B-26 with as much ease as the men. The work was often difficult, and sometimes dangerous, but I think that all the women who served in this capacity felt that the job they performed was productive as well as helpful to the war effort.

B-26

CHAPTER SEVEN

Other Bases, Other Planes

"Neither of us had ever jumped and the dog hadn't either." —Mary Ellen Keil.

The WASPs who graduated from B-26 school had an unusual opportunity to prove that women were capable of handling a fast, powerful, and demanding aircraft. Their success with this airplane provided many exciting adventures and also proved to the Air Force that women, as well as men, could provide the country with an abundant supply of well-trained, competent, and resourceful pilots. When the war started winding down, however, the needs of the Air Force shifted. These WASP B-26 pilots were then transferred from Boise, Idaho, to other bases where they flew a wide variety of airplanes and engaged in many other kinds of flying.

Four WASPs were sent to Dyersburg, Tennessee, where they flew mostly L-5s, small, single-engine planes. "There were four of us," Fran Smith explained. "Sadie Hawkins, Marge Gilbert, Esther Noffke, and I. We ended up flying the little L-5s and L-7s, a big comedown from a B-26. Sadie and I both met our husbands there. Her husband and mine were the best of friends, and we were both married right after Dyersburg. Marge Gilbert went home and met her husband there, and Esther went on up to an airport outside of Chicago, Pal Waukee, where she's been ever since."

Esther Noffke said she had been sent to Mountain Home, Idaho, first, and then down to Dyersburg. "At Dyersburg, we flew L-5s and I got just a few hours in the B-17 there as copilot. Then they needed some of our group to go back to Texas to take the advanced instrument course before deactivation. Nobody else wanted to go, but I was glad to get the course because I ended up with a Green Card (instrument rating). You automatically received both a commercial rating and an instrument rating when you came out, which was very helpful."

Marge Gilbert told me about some of her adventures flying the little L-5s. "The guns on the ground would just train on us," she explained. "They had to be camera guns, though, because they were pointed right at us as we did Lazy-8s and other maneuvers—down fairly close to the ground. Just before we left, on December 20, one of the officers from Dyersburg wanted me to take him to Memphis. He had something official to deliver down there, but the trip was really for him to Christmas shop. We had lunch down there and I headed back in the L-5 by myself. I went up, flying just from Memphis to Dyersburg, and I didn't realize there was so much crosswind. I was flying along a railroad track and there was another track going off at an angle. I was being blown off on an angle and I thought I was going straight. I got lost. When it started getting dark I started looking for a place to land. I had no idea where I was. I found a deserted Army field, but when I landed, the ground was mushy and I went right up on the nose. It stopped the engine immediately and broke the propeller. Somebody came along and I asked them to call the Air Force base at Dyersburg.

"They drove out and got me and said, 'We'll cart that in.' I still have the broken propeller at home, but they fixed the plane up. Then, Sadie stayed around there at Dyersburg after we all went home. She told me that a lieutenant colonel took out the same airplane and stood it up on the end of the runway and broke its prop again! That thing was jinxed.''

Mary Ellen Keil was sent to Salina, Kansas, where she flew as first pilot on C-47s. The C-47, or DC-3 commercially, was a twin-engine cargo plane and was reputed to be easy to fly—just like a Cub.

"We didn't fly much as first pilots,'' Mary Ellen said. "Mostly we flew the most horrendous flying we ever went through.'' She explained to me about flying as copilot for some of the Eighth Air Force men who had returned from the fighting with battle fatigue. They all had Distinguished Flying Crosses, but she said she came closer to getting killed then than she ever did flying anything else, except when instructing after the war. "They were nice men,'' she asserted, "but they just had battle fatigue. There was no doubt about it. I took one flight with them and two of them were along for the ride and were big, hotshot Air Force pilots and they didn't want us women to fly.

"We sat in the back seat. They got lost near Kingman, Arizona, and they were so completely lost that the two WASPs—this is the truth—had to go up front and find where we were. It was wild country, hard to navigate, and we didn't have the navigation instruments that they have today.

"Then, we took another trip with them, and, as I said, they were all nice men, but we decided they got the Distinguished Flying Crosses because they never got to the target. We were flying from Salina to Seattle with a whole load of men—twenty-four fully equipped ground troops. They were to take off for overseas from Seattle, and we were on instruments. This pilot was scared, and

94

he learned that Seattle was on instrument conditions. That just panicked him. He didn't want to have to make an instrument landing in Seattle, so first he would go clear down through all of these clouds—and we had no altimeters that were that exact—we were supposedly flying on top. He'd go right through the clouds without any clearance to be in the clouds. Then he'd get scared because the mountains were getting higher and the valleys were getting slimmer, and then he'd pull up through the overcast and this was the way we went from Phoenix to Seattle.

"When we got to Seattle and went to land, it was completely camouflaged. None of us (I was flying copilot at that time) could see the runway. He started landing on the taxi strip instead of the runway. Finally he pulled up and saw he was heading for the strip and we went around. You couldn't say much to him. After all, he was the pilot. I was just scared to death all the way. Finally we got down, and he bounced all the way down the runway, and I mean all the way! He hit the ground and we'd go clear up in the air, and he'd gun it and then he'd put the nose down, hit the ground again and go clear up in the air. He did that all the way down the runway. I was so mad! I said, 'Now, you're going to go back there and you're going to tell those men that I did not make that landing.' I knew darn well that he would say that WASPs can't land these things for sour apples.

"He went back and said, 'I have to admit that I made the landing and it wasn't the WASP.' "

Another remarkable event that occurred during a C-47 flight was described by Mary Ellen. "Two of us were flying a C-47 from Seattle to Lincoln, Nebraska," she informed me, "and we were flying in rather bad weather. It was a long flight, and we'd call ahead and give them our ETAs [estimated time of arrival] at various ground stations. Every time we'd give an ETA it would change because our ground speed kept creeping up. Pretty soon we were flying that old C-47 at about 250 or 260 miles an hour. Its cruising speed was about 130 and we would be recording that our ground speed was 250 miles an hour. We just got hysterical about it—what were those people on the ground going to think? But it was true. We were hitting all our ETAs [estimated time of arrival] right on the button, and we kept going faster and faster. *We actually were one of the flights that helped them recognize a jet stream!* What we'd done was to get in the jet stream, and that's the reason our ETAs were accurate, even though they seemed just ridiculous when we were flying a low, slow C-47 at a 260-mile-an-hour ground speed. It was flights such as this one that first proved to weathermen that there was a jet stream."

Mary Ellen was also fortunate enough to get some flights in a B-17. She told me this story about a flight she and Eleanor Patterson made together in Salina. Eleanor is now deceased, so unfortunately we don't have her personal account of the adventure. "Eleanor," Mary Ellen said, "got acquainted with an engineering-pilot major who was performing engineering testing on the B-17 that morning. She had talked to him the night before (we both wanted to fly a B-17) and he took us up with him that morning."

She interrupted her story to explain to me about Eleanor and her dog. "She took that dog everyplace, in every base, and she was so sweet and cute that she'd get the engineers to build a dog pen for it and a doghouse. Can you imagine? The parachute people even made a parachute especially for the dog, so she just took it flying with her everyplace she went. Eleanor was nice enough and young enough to get away with it. The dog was a golden retriever.

"Anyway, we were all up flying around in this B-17 with the dog, and I was in the copilot seat at the time and the major said, 'Well, I'm supposed to be up here to test the props, and anyhow, I want to show you how well this plane flies if you lose an engine.' He pulled back one of the props and cut off the engine, and it did handle just as easy as pie. Then he said, 'It even flies very well with two engines off on the same side.' He pulled off another engine and then said, 'You know, it will even hold altitude and fly quite well with just one engine.' He pulled off the third prop, and sure enough it handled just lovely. Then he says, 'You know, it really glides just like a Cub. I'll show you'—and he told us what the glide ratio would be without any power. Then he reached over to pull off the fourth engine, but then he said, 'Well, maybe I'd better wait a minute. I'm supposed to be up here to test the props after they've been repaired.'

"He tried to bring back the first prop—no luck. [To "bring back" the prop meant to restart the engine that would spin the propeller.] He tried to bring back the second one—no luck. The third one—well, he couldn't get it to come back on either. Then he said, 'Well, you know, the regulations say that if you have to make a one-engine landing, you have to have the crew jump.'

"We said, 'Jump?' Neither of us had ever jumped and the dog hadn't either. He could see that we weren't eager to jump, and that's when his real heroism came forward. He said, 'Well, I'm risking my majority if they catch me landing with one engine and you're still in here, but I'll take a chance that I won't be demoted,' so he came in, and I hope the dear man wasn't demoted. He came in and landed on one engine. No problem. The dog didn't have to jump, and I don't know whether it was the major's concern for our jumping or for the dog's."

It seems that lots happened at Salina, where Mary Ellen was sent from Boise. She had agreed, with several others, that one of the reasons the women were put into B-26 school was because the men were refusing to fly the B-26, and with the women flying it they could hardly refuse to fly it anymore. She went on to say, "The same thing happened to the B-29 pilots. The men were refusing to fly the B-29. That was when Colonel, now Brigadier General, Paul Tibbets was somehow chosen to teach these two women to fly it and to prove that it could be flown without its catching on fire. It had that propensity.

"Salina was one of the training transition spots for the B-29 and we were sent down there on a cargo run to fly B-29 parts for the Second Air Force. They needed these parts badly; they were just putting these planes into production, so we had a regular cargo run, with the C-47, that covered all the airports that were having B-29 transition training—Second Air Force. We'd seen the B-29 takeoffs—the most ghastly looking takeoffs you ever saw! Apparently the cowling flaps were not correctly designed and by the time they taxied out, checked the engines, and took off, the engines would start to overheat as soon as they were airborne. They would overheat to the extent that the plane would often catch fire.

"Sally Keil [in her book *Those Wonderful Women in Their Flying Machines* (New York: Rawson Associates, 1979)] tells how then-Colonel Tibbets showed these two women from a class at Eglin Field, Florida, how to fly it without doing a run-up before takeoff. They would check everything in the plane, then start up the engine, taxi out, and take off. That way, the engines didn't have time to overheat and catch fire. At Salina, they were trying to just take it off as gradually as they could so they wouldn't be taxing the engine. You'd think they would never get off the runway, and then as far as you could see, they were about fifty feet off the ground. They never had enough speed to gain altitude. I guess when they modified the B-29 and got the cowl flaps to cool the engines better, it was satisfactory.

"Before that, however, by taking off without an engine run-up, the girls could fly it off without it catching fire. They had the two women flying around to the various B-29 bases and the men would see them land the plane and get out. That would give them second thoughts, when they saw a woman flying the plane! The two WASPs flew it around just a short time, when some commander got word of it and said, 'Take those women off my airplane. Don't let them fly it anymore,' so it was all over, but the women surely proved a point."

Ruth Woods had a bit more to say about Salina and the B-29. "They moved us down to Salina," she said, "and this was kind of exciting, now that I think about it. At that time, Salina was a highly secret B-29 base. We were Second Air Force Interstation Transport Command. Our job was to fly men and materials to the B-29 bases in the Second Air Force training stations. It was all very secretive. That's what we did there, flying C-47s. They were just like an old Cub after the B-26s."

Millie Grossman was separated from the rest of the girls when they were sent out of Boise. She went to Pocatello, Idaho. When the WASP were disbanded, she was there, but her last flight was from Pocatello to Dalhart, Texas, in a BT-13. Millie felt sad about this being her last flight, she told me. "I thought I should really have some fun on this flight since it would be my last flight and I was alone. On the way to Texas I thought, 'Gee, I want to see the Grand Canyon.' You know, you were not supposed to fly over the Grand Canyon, but I flew over it. Well, you know the BT-13 has two gas tanks, one in each wing, and I guess the trim tabs weren't just right, so one wing always weighed heavy. I thought, heck, I'll just use the gas out of that wing tank so it will fly a little straighter. Right over the Grand Canyon the little red light comes on, so I'm out of gas in that tank. It was scary for a minute because the engine died for a few seconds after the switch to the other gas tank, but then it restarted and went okay. That canyon was a beautiful sight!

"Then I buzzed a train and I buzzed a road, which of course one shouldn't do, and I thought I was really smart because I was staying above the telephone poles. But every so often there's a bigger pole. In the BT-13, also, the wheels are down; you can't retract them. All of a sudden I felt a bump and I thought, boy, what have I done now? I landed at Amarillo and wondered if my wheels were still there—or have I left the WASP in disgrace? There was a big air show there, anyway, with a lot of people, so no one was watching me. I parked the plane and went in to check the weather, but I looked out the window and saw one of the mechanics looking at the landing gear and he picked something off it and put it in his pocket, but he didn't say anything. Then I went back and found a piece of wire on one wheel, and I thought maybe I could have picked up an electrical wire with the wheel and blown out all the electricity some place."

Madeline Sullivan was the only WASP at Boise to be transferred to Colorado Springs. This was because she had met a colonel once when she was trying to catch a ride back east. He had given her a ride in a B-25 he was flying. On the trip, they found out that they had many mutual friends, and he told her that he knew the tow-target program was going to be closed soon and that Colorado Springs was a good place to be and he would see that she got there. "I was the only one sent to Colorado Springs," she told me, "and I stayed for a couple of weeks, but it didn't take long to figure out that at Colorado Springs all we were going to do, basically, was to pull up the gears for some four-hour desk jockey who had to get his flight time in for the month. They were always looking for WASPs for copilots. When I got there and realized what was going on, I heard about an advanced instrument course back at Sweetwater. I got myself transferred back there. I thought I might as well be learning something as staying there playing gear lift for these characters, so I got sent back there and took the advanced instrument course."

All of the B-26 WASP pilots I talked to, with the exception of Joan Whelan, were sent off to other bases before the WASP program was disbanded. Joan told me she stayed at Boise when the others were sent off. She was still recovering from the accident in which her arm was hit by a B-26 propeller following her midair collision. "I was in the nurse's quarters and I stayed there the whole time." Joan also said that the B-26 and a few other smaller planes were the only ones she flew during her service. Many of the other WASPs who were sent to other bases flew quite a variety of planes.

Two of the twenty WASPs assigned to B-26 school were unavailable for interviewing. Jane Rutherford is classified as a "lost graduate." No one knows where she is, or what has happened to her. Mary Saunders did not want to be interviewed. She told me she was too busy working on her farm and did not want to be involved.

The seven WASPs who did not graduate from B-26 school were sent to different bases: two went to Garden City, Kansas; two to Victoria, Texas; one to Goodfellow Field, San Angelo, Texas; and one to Officer Candidate School at Orlando, Florida. Kay Herman resigned straight out of B-26 school when she became pregnant.

At Garden City, Marge Needham was doing maintenance testing. After the mechanics repaired the airplanes, they had to take them up and see if they were safe for the students to fly. "Of course, the students just loved that!" she laughed. "The planes were BT-13s and we had a few AT-6s. No primary trainers. Then they closed the base and we were moved to Independence, Kansas. I flew instruments the whole time, so when I got out I was able to get my instrument rating and my instructor's rating."

Anna Mae Petteys, the other WASP at Garden City, said that the WASPs there were called engineering test pilots. She said, "My family laughed at this assignment because they thought I couldn't be that practical. When the squadron turned a plane in with something wrong, we flew it to determine what was required. Then we flew it again before it was returned to the squadron. We also slow-timed engines."

I asked her if she flew any other airplanes.

"There were some Cessnas there," she answered. "The war was winding down and they had assigned us to move out some BTs to be mothballed, so we did have some fun ferrying those.

"They would give us planes to use for the weekend, too. That was one of the nice things. It was good for me because I could go to Denver a few times. You know, Kansas is a dry state, and they used to laugh about all the good landings that were made on Sunday evenings when people came in with their 'cargo.'

"I hoped we had achieved something for the Air Force, but I was not unhappy about whether or not we were veterans. I liked the flying part; I disliked the military part of our job. I never would have got to fly that kind of equipment as a private pilot, so the flying part was a great experience.''

Clarice Siddall and Jean Moore were both sent to Victoria, Texas. Clarice (Sid) told me that their job was to tow targets in AT-6s. I asked if they were using live ammunition and she answered, ''No—cameras anytime I did it. Then Jean and I were transferred out of there. I went up to Waco, Texas. That was BT-13s. I can't remember where Jean went. I always felt that was being put down, you know, but at that time, everybody was being kind of shifted around. At Waco we were doing testing and also, when anyone had to go to other fields, we flew them—nonflying personnel. Sort of a chauffeur thing. The CO there was so nice! There were quite a few of us there, at least seven of us, I think. I remember Zillner came in. I have a photo of the WASPs that were there.

''At Waco, where they treated us so nicely, I remember I got permission to go back to Advanced Instruments and they let me do that. I also had permission to take one of the planes on a weekend so that I could go up and see friends, like Mad Sullivan at Denver. I remember I had a BT-13 and I thought I'd never get off that runway, but there was one neat thing that happened. I came back through Dallas. At one of the bases on the way in, there was a young sergeant who wanted a ride. I forget where I picked him up—at a gas stop someplace. It was night because I had taken as much time as I could so I was flying back at night. He didn't know whether he wanted to go with me or not, but he thought he'd take a chance—with this woman pilot. He was in the back of this BT-13 and it was just so neat, that flight! You know when you follow the light line at night? It was such a beautiful night and I just hoped this fellow was enjoying what he was seeing, but I guess he was just glad he made it.''

When Sid was sent to Waco, Jean Moore went to Enid, Oklahoma, to do engineering testing on BT-13s. ''That was kind of fun,'' she said, ''because you could go up and wring them out and bring them back. We had to fly them before the cadets could fly them. One cadet wrote one of them up, saying, 'Tail vibrates violently during third turn of spin.' Well, it did! But they all did! I wrote it up, 'Doesn't vibrate any more than any of the rest of them.'

''I'd go up (I had a routine), do two steep turns, a snap roll, and spin down, and come back in, and that was testing. If it held together, it was all right.

''Then they sent me to OCS [Officer Candidate School] in Florida. When I got back to Enid I was just turned around and went back out on the same train going to Sweetwater for the second instrument course. That's when we heard that we were going to be disbanded. Then, when I finished that course, I went back to Enid, and stayed there until we were sent home.''

Ruth Weller also attended Officer Candidate School at Orlando. ''Then my last station," she told me, "was Aloe Field, Victoria, Texas, where I towed sleeve targets for the Aerial Gunnery School."

When Fran Laraway left B-26 school, she was sent to Goodfellow Field at San Angelo, Texas. Her main job was to test the aircraft after the students had accidents. "The planes were repaired," she told me, "and before they could be put back on the flight line for the students, we had to give the planes a test flight. If there had been fuselage or wing repair, we checked them out with aerobatics. Whatever the damage was, you checked it out, whatever was needed. We were assigned to engineering. I did a little ferrying, even ending up in New York at one time. I remember sitting in the (then) Pennsylvania Hotel with my parachute on my back, in full uniform. That was a weird thing—being met by my family for a few hours before I had to go back. Of course, I made the most of it. It was really fun. I was the only one there at that time.

"I can remember standing with a certain feeling of awe in Pittsburgh at the airport where they actually had the word WASP on the restroom door, so I assumed that there had been some of us there before.

"Another interesting assignment I had was spending a month at survival school in Orlando, Florida, where we learned to eat snake and palm root and whatever. The only sad thing about it was that they did not parachute us into the Everglades and make us find our way out as they had planned to do for the men. At least we had a sample of the experience, and it was a nice change.

"I had a couple of interesting experiences at Goodfellow Field. One time I had to fly a sergeant up to Fruita, Colorado, which was west of the mountains and in a little valley. I had an awfully hard time finding the airport until, luckily, the sergeant spotted it for me. It turned out that it was nearly dark and I still had my sunglasses on and everything looked just about the same. That was a good experience, not because of the poor sergeant, who had to go home on funeral leave, but because I got a lovely break there—three or four days where we had wonderful weather for riding horseback and going hunting with the manager of the hotel where I stayed. We couldn't get back to Sweetwater because of the intervening weather in the pass; we couldn't fly over it.

"The WASPs, of course, had a lot of other adventures, but my most memorable one was when we were disbanded and were flown home, three or four of us, by one of the men pilots and he was making several pilot errors. For one thing, we stopped for gas at a very small base in the middle of Missouri in a snowstorm and he forgot to set the prop control, damaging it. We ended up having to stay there so they could keep the plane overnight in a hangar. We stayed in the BOQ [Bachelor Officers' Quarters] and they thawed the plane out and got him going again the next day. When we got to New York, it was dark and the lights were all on and he couldn't pick out which airport to land us on. They had to do a triangle fix to get us in so we were all going, 'Ha, Ha, Ha.'

"I remember one of the girls, Joan Goff, who lived in New York on Long Island, took us to her house and we had champagne and corn fritters. I always thought that was a wonderful feast. Her mother was a good cook in the middle of the night!''

Several 44-W-2 classmates who were not sent to B-26 school told me that they had been sent to Officer Candidate School. They had been assigned to serve at other bases first and later called to OCS. I never heard, however, of any others who were sent to survival school, except Fran Laraway. Interestingly enough, I think both schools were located in Orlando, Florida. The reason for the Officer Candidate training was because it was anticipated that the WASPs would be accepted into the Air Force, so the officer training was a step in that direction.

Nellie Henderson and Minkie Heckman had both been sent directly from Sweetwater to Aloe Field, Victoria, Texas. Nellie was later sent from Aloe Field to Officer Candidate School at Orlando. She told me that what happened there was one of her favorite stories. ''We were going for officer's training and intelligence. It was such a fascinating base. It was the hub of all international training. There was a big meteorology department and a big intelligence department. People came from all over the world. We had English, French, Russians—everybody was down there. I was just carried away with myself. I was so thrilled. I was going to be with all these fabulous foreign people. Here I was with my wings on and I was going to impress everybody.

"There were a bunch of WASP pilots coming in from back east, but I got in early and it was time to go to supper. I thought I'd go over to the officers' mess and just introduce myself to everybody. They would be so impressed with me in my cute little outfit wth my cute little wings on.

"I went in and the first person I met going through the door was a British major who was there in the Intelligence. He said, 'Well, come on over and join our table.' I went over and sat down, and right across from me was undoubtedly the biggest, slobbiest woman I've ever seen. She had a butch haircut, no makeup, and she was eating like this (scooping her hands to her face). She was just sitting there in this awful looking uniform, and I looked so cute and I kind of exaggerated what I did. I said that I towed targets and it was a very dangerous occupation. I think I sort of hinted that it was live ammunition, and, in my case, it wasn't. This guy I was sitting next to kept hitting me in the side, and I just kept on running off at the mouth. Finally she got up and left—this slob. Well, now I was really going to sparkle! I turned to the person next to me and said, 'Who was that awful looking thing over there?' He answered, 'That's Olga something or other. She's the Russian war ace with seventeen planes to her credit.' All I could say was, 'I hope to God she doesn't speak English.' (She was over here for some kind of advanced training.)

"We even had the Turks. They were always bragging about how good the Messerschmitts were, because they had German training. [Turks were neutral.] They had training at Aloe, and they had diplomatic immunity, and I hated them because they weren't loyal to us. They thought the Messerschmitts were better than our planes. It was all fascinating. We were there about two or three weeks. Then we went back to Aloe. It was shortly after that that we were disbanded. I think that was my most embarrassing moment. Sitting across from a Russian war ace and shooting my mouth off about my flying."

Nellie did tell me a few other things about her service at Aloe Field, which was at Victoria, Texas. She said that Minkie Heckman was sent there too. Minkie had asked for it, as well as Nellie. "I asked for it," Nellie said, "because most all the people from the base at Lake Charles, my hometown, had been transferred to Victoria, Texas. I knew half of the officers there and their wives. I thought, 'That'd be a nice place to go.' Minkie and I were the first two WASPs there, in the Southern Training Command. We were attached to a gunnery squadron. We towed targets, four- and four-and-a-half-hour shifts.

"We flew AT-6s, but no live ammo. Students went to Matagorda Island for the live ammo training. For us they used cameras, and it was so dull. They said they didn't think men would do it. It would take women to have that much patience. We had to fly at a certain altitude, at a set airspeed, over a set pattern, and not deviate from it, so the gunnery students could practice. We had an enlisted man in the back who put the tow targets in and out, and we had some close calls. We lost a lot of targets.

"Also, you'd have to make a wheel landing; you couldn't let the target down because it would wrap around the tail wheel, and you'd spin out right there. You had to make a wheel landing, and then very gingerly put the tail down. About ninety times out of a hundred you'd have a tow line wrapped around it.

"We also did some ferrying of nonflying personnel. There was a doctor who often had to go to San Antonio and I'd take him. We did things like that— aerial dishwashing jobs, which towing targets was—but we had a good time at Aloe! I have a picture of all the WASPs there. They were there for my wedding to Russ. We were married on the base at the Officers' Club.' "

Minkie Heckman told me a bit more about what went on at Aloe Field. "When we got there we were the first two women there and they were not prepared for us at all. There were no facilities for us. The men rigged the lockers around so they made a little dressing room for us. When we opened the doors they would cross and we could change from our dress uniforms into our zoot suits for flying. They gave us old fatigues which were too big, and they told us to go to the parachute department to be fitted, so we had fitted zoot suits!

"Aloe Field was just a temporary field, during the war. There was a permanent station on the other side of Victoria called Foster Field. They had a swimming place and all, but we had just tarpaper shacks and every time there was warning of a hurricane, or anything like that, the cables came out from under the eaves to tie the buildings down. The sidewalks were under the cables, though, so if you weren't careful, you'd either fall over them or they'd smack you in the face. They had more people in the infirmary from those cables than they had from anything else.

"For a while just Nellie and I were there, but later I think we had about a dozen WASPs before I left. I was sent back to Sweetwater and was retrained on instruments. Then, when I came back to Aloe Field they assigned me to the instrument squadron. I taught instruments there for a while and that was great. I really enjoyed that, and boy, did I get sharp! It helps when you can listen and see the stations all at the same time.

"We made one cross-country flight from Sweetwater to Wichita Falls under the hood. At Wichita Falls the weather shut in on us. It was so bad we were not allowed to fly out, even though we were on an instrument flight. We had to stay overnight. All we had on was our zoot suits and it was so cold that night we had to go into the PX and buy sweatshirts.

"Another time I had to do an administrative flight. I was assigned to take an officer up to Amarillo and deliver him there and fly back to Victoria, which of course, is on the Gulf coast. It was a beautiful, clear, gorgeous day. Flying along in such smooth air, with the oil rigs burning off the gas down below—that was one of the nicest flights I ever had."

Nellie and Minkie were more fortunate than some of the graduates in that they were able to go to their new assignment together. They shared some happy times and, today, still remain good friends, seeing each other at reunions. Many of our class members, however, were sent alone to a base where they did not know anybody. In Ann Craft's case, she was the only WASP sent to Randolph Field and she was not really welcome. "Randolph was a very difficult assignment," she explained. "They didn't want any girls there. I think I was sent there because I was a very easygoing person. I was a smooth pilot and had never had an accident. My job was to fly officers around. They were older men—I mean, really older men, like World War One, and they didn't fly. Most of them, at least, were officers. I went up to Dallas a lot, and to all the flight schools in Texas. I also went to New Orleans a couple of times.

"I couldn't live on the base because WASPs were considered civilians. I lived with two gals who were also civilians, but not pilots. At one time they sent two more WASPs, who had flunked out of B-26 school, down to Randolph, but they didn't stay. I never did see them again.

"When I look back on it all, I feel that Randolph Field was probably one of the most difficult places. When you gals all go back to reunions, you're going back to see friends that you flew with after training. My association with WASPs was all when we were at Avenger Field. I think Anne Berry flew in to see me one time, because she knew where I was, but I didn't see or live with the others. The tow-target girls, however, all lived together."

Ann Craft was not the only one to be assigned alone. At most bases other WASPs were there, even if they were not the old classmates. Lourette Puett told me, "I was assigned to Douglas, Arizona, where I was with some charming girls. We were flying advanced trainers, and got a little time in B-25s and B-17s as copilots, when they brought them down to serve as training planes. I also went to Army Air Force Strategic Air Training in Orlando, Florida. That was very interesting, but the weather was horrible. It was hot; I've never been so hot in my life! The training was excellent, however. When I came back, I was stationed at Bakersfield for about two weeks and then we were deactivated, so we didn't do anything at Bakersfield at all."

"What other planes did you fly?" I asked.

"I was never checked out in the B-17. They brought B-17s in when the B-29s went out, and I made a couple of flights in them. I really can't remember much about that, but B-25s and B-26s were there. Mostly we flew the little training planes, the Cessnas ('Bamboo Bombers') and the AT-9, a very hot little plane. You had to bring it in very, very fast. It killed a lot of people, too, that plane. Then, at Bakersfield, had I done any flying it would have been just basic training planes. It was fairly unexciting.

"It's funny. I was in Florida from six weeks to two months, and I never saw any of my classmates. I never reinforced any of the memories I had from training, until I went to San Diego for the convention and there I met Madeline Sullivan. It was a delight, and Mary Ellen Keil was there, of course, being secretary of the class. I think there were about seven or eight of us.

"Madeline and Joanne Wallace were very close friends and they were probably the leaders of our class, in our flight. They were the most popular girls, along with Kit MacKethan and Marie Michell. That couple always paired off and they were very popular."

In those days we called Lourette "Rose," so that is how she is listed in our yearbook. It's too bad that she was one of the ones to be sent off alone. Today she is an attractive, friendly, and very successful businesswoman.

Verda-Mae Lowe was sent alone to Williams Field Air Force Base in

Arizona. Verda-Mae was a bit different from a lot of the other girls who were stationed there. She explained it to me this way. ''I was assigned to Williams Field and they weren't happy with me. I never went to their parties, I never went with the men they went out with. I just kept my nose clean. I'd been brought up that way, and I was older than the rest, too. They apparently had asked Jackie Cochran to come and talk to me. I didn't know it at the time. She told me I was not fitting in and that I had to learn how to. I told her that I was not going to sleep with them and I was not going to go to parties with them. I did not drink, and that was that.

''Well, then she brought up the fact that I was dating a GI (not an officer). I said, 'Yes, I intend to marry him as soon as this is all over.' She said, 'You can't do that. You've got to associate with the officers and you've got to be an officer all the way through and live in the officers' barracks.' I said, 'No, I'm not living in the officers' barracks, I'm in the nurses' quarters. That's my upbringing, and I can't change.' ''

'''Well,' she said, 'I think it's to your advantage if you try harder to get along with everybody.' I didn't know I wasn't getting along. I had no idea I wasn't getting along.''

''What were you flying out there?'' I asked.

''We had AT-6s, AT-7s and 11s, and B-17s. We had a beautiful title: 'engineering test pilots.' I did some slow flight and gunnery, and some tow-targets. I even had an airplane with my name on it—Skippy Lowe—an AT-6. I stayed on there until the last when they disbanded, just before Christmas. Then I got married on Christmas Day right there at the base, in the chapel.''

The WASPs who were sent off alone perhaps had a more difficult time, especially Ann Craft, who had no other WASPs to share her flying duties. Still, they were highly productive and performed an admirable job serving the Air Force and relieving men for overseas duty. They were fortunate in one respect: their flying seemed to be more uneventful than some of their fellow WASPs. They reported no cases of airplane crashes or sabotage attempts. Such events did occur, and other WASPs provided me with some frightening tales.

UC-78

CHAPTER EIGHT

Test Pilots and Ferry Pilots

"You hated to say the plane's okay, and then some cadet gets killed because it's not okay." —Gini Dulaney

Twenty-nine WASPs, the ones not sent to B-26 school, had widely varied experiences and flew many planes—grasshoppers, pursuits, and bombers. They were sent in small groups, or singly, to many of the air bases across the country. At each place their reception was different. At some bases they were not welcome, but they persevered and did their job, whether or not it was appreciated. Often the men they came to replace resented being moved out of a safe job and forced overseas to join the fighting. Who can blame them? It was a long and deadly war. In addition to such prejudice, WASPs often faced problems with poor maintenance and even sabotage, making their flying more dangerous than it should have been. All the women I talked to, nevertheless, loved the work and were extremely sorry to see the program close. One big plus was the comradeship of the women; to this day classmates remain friends.

Twila Edwards, Gini Dulaney, and Doris Elkington had been good friends at Sweetwater and they wanted to stay together, if they could. Doris told me, "We couldn't, however, unless we went to B-26 school or to the ferry command. We didn't want to do either, so we picked California. That was where both Twila and Gini wanted to go. We looked to see what the openings were and there was one at Stockton, one at Merced, and one at Bakersfield. I selected Stockton, Gini took Merced, and Twila, Bakersfield.

"I was the only one in Stockton, and I'd been told to sign up with the adjutant. I went into the main office building and it was a big, wide-open building with all kinds of desks. I walked in the door and all the heads came up. They all just looked at me. I went to the reception desk and said, 'I'd like to see the adjutant, please.' They said, 'Just a minute.'

"I stood there with all my bags and this lieutenant colonel came out of his office. He welcomed me, shook my hand, and said, 'Come on in, come on in.' I thought, well, the adjutant is a lieutenant colonel, and I walked into his office, and here he was the executive officer. Then he took me in to see the colonel and the colonel sat me down and gave me a ten-minute lecture on wartime marriages. He said he didn't believe in them. Then he said, 'You're not married, are you?'

"I said, 'Yes.' I'd been married just before, in February, and this was March, so he laughed and said he had a daughter about my age and she was coming out soon. I checked in and they put me in the nurses' quarters. I had been there for about two or three weeks, flying as test pilot, when I was told I had a visitor in the operations office. I went up and there was Dulaney, sitting on the corner of the operations officer's desk, swinging her leg and having a big old time. I took her over to meet the colonel and she said, 'Colonel, do you have a place here for me?' He laughed and kind of let it go by, but the next week he got her transferred up to Stockton.''

"What were you doing there?'' I asked.

"As the planes came off the production-line maintenance, we would test them before the cadets could fly them. These were going through maintenance, not new planes. There were three men and the two of us, and we'd test all the planes. They were AT-17s. Gini and I had a regular routine. Since these were two-seaters, we would usually do them together. It was quicker that way. She'd do one thing and I'd do another.

"Gini was there with me until I was sent to Orlando for the officer training program. There were a whole bunch of WASPs there. They gave us all kinds of courses on identification, and we were there about a month. It was OCS—no flying. It was all ground school and indoctrination. Then I went back to Stockton and I had orders to Victorville, where Marie Michell was killed, when I had a telegram from Bill that he was coming home. I resigned and then went back to Detroit.''

I asked Doris about Twila Edwards. Twila died of cancer long before I decided to write this book, so I had no input from her at all. "I don't know what I can tell you about Twila,'' Doris said. "She was a swell gal. We really liked her, but she never came up to Stockton. When Gini appeared at Merced, they told her, 'We didn't ask for you and we don't want you and just stay out of our way.' That was her reception, and mine was so different. I was glad she came to Stockton. Colonel Hicks was the commander of the Stockton Air Force Base. Before I left, his daughter moved out there. He introduced us and told us to take care of her, which I thought was wonderful. We knew people around the base and he wanted us to introduce her to people. I thought that was a very high compliment he paid to both of us. I remember there was a Fighting Lady film in town, one time, and he invited Gini and me to go with him.''

Gini's reception at Merced was indeed different from Doris's at Stockton. She told me that some other WASPs were there, and their behavior had not been the best, according to what she heard. When she reported for duty, the officer in charge said, "Another one of you. Look, Miss Dulaney, just don't bug me. If you want to fly, get an airplane and go fly, but we don't have a job for you. Just go and have fun."

She said she warmed the bench in the operations room day after day, but he never gave her a job. Meanwhile, she made a lot of friends, and she hadn't made any trouble, and he was beginning to realize that she was a dedicated flier and really wanted to work. "I think he was beginning to feel a little bit sheepish about the whole thing," Gini went on, "because all the guys liked me. I was like the 'girl next door.' Finally, one day when I was sitting in the operations office, a General came in who wanted to be ferried from Merced to San Francisco. Now, I didn't know the country. I hadn't been away from Merced and had never been to San Francisco. It's a big city. Well, this general said, 'I've always wanted to fly with a woman. You're a pilot, aren't you?' I said, 'Yes.' He looked over to this officer and he said, 'Why don't you let her take me to San Francisco?' This officer said, 'I think that's a great idea.' I could have killed him. I hadn't even been checked out in the damned airplane. The only rides I'd had were with someone else. He says, 'Okay, fill out your flight plan, Dulaney!'

"I had to take this general to San Francisco, land, and fly back to Merced. I was nervous as a cat on a griddle. This was my one assignment at Merced. I've forgotten how many weeks I was there with nothing to do. This was my one big job. Well, the general was a talker. From the time we took off, he talked all the way to San Francisco, and I was trying to concentrate on landing at San Francisco. As far as I could see, you landed on the water. I've never been so scared in my life. I finally found where to land, made a perfect landing, and headed back to Merced. You should have seen the look on the officer's face. He said, 'You made it!' Like it was a big surprise. Then immediately thereafter, I went to Stockton.

"Did Doris ever tell you about the time we took the major up?" she asked. When I said no, she went on. "This major was grounded because he had bailed out of a plane and had broken his back. They wouldn't let him fly anymore because they said another parachute jump would kill him. He was doing some ground job at Stockton and no one would take him up because it would have been grounds for a court-martial. We didn't think we could get court-martialed because we weren't military. He said, 'All I want to do is to get up in the air. Just get up in the air. I'll sit in the back and mind my own business. I'll be real quiet. Just take me along.' "

Finally, Doris and Gini relented and one day they sneaked him into the plane and took off. "The first thing that happened," Gini began, "was that the flaps got stuck in the full down position. The major said, 'Oh, my God.' I said, 'Relax, Major, this happens to us all the time. No big sweat.' The next thing that happened was, an engine went out. I forget whether the right or the left. Now we were in big trouble. We had full flaps, one engine, and were over a heavily congested area. I called in for an emergency landing. The tower, for some reason, became excited and instead of saying 'Clear the pattern,' said, 'Clear the area.'"

By this time, Gini told me, the major had already traded places with Doris in the copilot seat, but he said he wouldn't interfere. It was a scary situation and the tower called for air silence. "It was dead quiet," Ginny said, "and then this voice came over the microphone, 'A woman's place is in the home.' I kid you not. It was hilarious! Well, really it wasn't so funny! We were coming in— we had to anyway because the major didn't have a parachute. The next thing was, the major said to me, 'Just let me land it.' I said, 'One thing I can do well, is land this thing.' 'I'm sure you can,' he says, 'but just let me do it.' I said, 'If you goof this landing, I'll never forgive you.' He said, 'All right.' Then he proceeded to make a perfect landing. What happened then was, in all the confusion, he hopped out and no one knew he was aboard. For weeks, I got compliments on my perfect landing. I hadn't made the damn thing and I couldn't say I hadn't!"

The plane they were flying was the UC-78, the "Bamboo Bomber." "These were old planes," Gini told me, "just hanging on by a thread. We had to sign the paper to say whether or not they could go on for a few more hours. You hated to say okay, it'll be all right, and then some cadet gets killed because it's not okay. Not a very happy task."

One other time, Gini told me, she and Doris were testing another UC-78. Just as they were taking off, a big, black cloud of smoke came out. That was pretty scary, she said. "We were too far over the field to land," she commented, "and we had to keep going. I heard yelling over the intercom, 'You're on fire, you're on fire.' I said, 'Yes, I can see the smoke.' I was just circling to come in and land, and I knew the mechanic had not fixed the oil line as he was supposed to do! When I pulled back the throttle, the smoke stopped. We landed and the crew chief came up kind of white, and he said, 'What happened?' I answered, 'I'll tell you what happened. You didn't fix the damned oil line!' He said, 'I did.' I reached across the wing and it was just slick with oil. I wiped up a whole handful of oil and smeared it across his face, I was so mad! 'What's that?' I asked. He hadn't fixed the oil line."

I made a comment that it was as bad as sabotage.

"Well," Gini replied, "it was just that they were overworked, underpaid, and underappreciated. These guys were in the military and they couldn't keep up with it, but they had no right to put it back on the flight line!

"We had some harrowing experiences, though. More often than not, the crew chiefs hadn't fixed things. They loved to fly as copilots, though, so when they wouldn't go up with you, you *knew* damned well that you didn't want to take that airplane up!"

Two other WASPs, Leona Golbinec and Kate Lee Harris, did not receive a very warm welcome when they arrived at their base in Dothan, Alabama. Leona told me, "Two WASPs from an earlier class, Buzz Stavrum and Donna Spellick, were already there. When Kate Lee and I came in, adding two more WASPs, the fellows were really upset about it. They already resented Buzz and the other girl flying. We were flight engineers. Dothan was an advanced school training base, so after the one-hundred-hour checks, or when the cadets would wreck a plane, we would take it up and test it.

"Some of the fellows resented it because that was what they had been doing and we took their jobs. Then they had to go into the fighting and they didn't want to go, any more than our instructors wanted to go into the fighting war when we disbanded. One pilot was checking me out and he was really giving me a hard time because he was going to have to give up his job. As we were taxiing along, I kept saying, 'Uh, uh,' and he said, 'I'm talking,' and he ran into another plane. This other plane was paying no attention, because we were in the wrong, definitely. I could see that propeller—it cut into our AT-6. It made quite a mess of our plane. They were both AT-6s. We were both on the ground, thankfully."

"What did he say about that?" I asked.

"Nothing. That was the last day he flew there. I never saw him again. We spent all our time at Dothan until we were deactivated. Later, two other WASPs came, Patty Pettit and Mary Ann Walker. Mary Ann started going with the Colonel, and after they got married everything changed. We were accepted then. We were treated very nicely. We lived in the nurses' quarters and had all our meals in the officers' mess. We had a nice time there. It was just like a country club."

Kate Lee and Leona were assigned to engineering testing. Kate Lee told me that one day she was out flying and saw a big storm approaching the field. "I called the tower," she said, "and asked if they were calling off flying. The male officer in the tower in a very nasty tone said, 'Why would we call off flying?' Sort of like, what's the matter, you female? This storm was getting closer and closer to the field so I thought I would go in whether they'd called off flying or not. By the time I got to the field this terrible dust storm hit (and in the meantime they had called off flying). Just as I came in, the wind hit the plane and tipped me up on my nose. It was just like instrument flying. You couldn't see a thing. I was afraid some of the student pilots coming in would land on top of me because they couldn't see. When the wind died down, a jeep came over and a little shavetail officer of the day stepped out and it was Bob Adams—who became my husband. That's how I met him. I was so mad—he said he's never seen me so mad since. I had two white spots for my eyes because my sunglasses had kept the dust off my eyes, and the rest of my face was dust.

"Then I learned that Bob had graduated one month after I had. We were able to have a cross-country trip once a month. I'd been there long enough to get a cross-country trip to Kansas City where his home was. I flew him to his home and later he flew me to my home, so we got to meet each other's parents.

"Another of the WASPs, Buzz Stavrum, and I flew over to Sea Island, Georgia, one weekend and landed at the St. Simon Naval Air Base. We taxied up and were getting out when we saw a jeep driving up with all this brass, and the commanding officer got out. We looked around to see what important person was coming whom he'd come out to meet, but he'd come out to meet the girls—us! Apparently when we called in and they heard a female voice on the radio they called the CO and he came down. They sent us over to Sea Island and picked us up when we were ready to come back. We got the royal treatment!

"By the end of the program I think they were just placing WASPs anyplace, but we kept plenty busy. We had P-40s on the field as well as the AT-6s. These were old, war-weary P-40s from the Orient. They had the Flying Tigers painted on them. Then we got in some P-51s also. We all got checked out in the P-40 and Buzz and Donna had checked out in the P-51. I was next up for the P-51 but we were disbanded. That was a great disappointment, that I didn't get to fly the P-51.

"The P-40 was easier than we thought it would be. It had about twice as much power as the AT-6, and with those spindly little landing gears, you'd have thought it would groundloop, but it was just a heavier plane. Of course, you had no one riding with you to check you out, as in a two-place plane. You were all alone up there.

"Once Mary Belle Ahlstrom, who came later to Dothan, was taking a plane up to check it out. Just as soon as she got off the ground she realized the controls were crossed—working backwards from the way they were supposed to. She was lucky enough to get it back down while she could still land it on the field. You never knew what you'd run into. Usually it would just be that one wing was heavier than the other and you'd bring it down and get them to correct it.

"We did a bit of ferrying. One time we ferried some Stearmans up to Geor-

112

gia, Warner-Robbins Field, arriving after sundown. This was the first time I had flown a Stearman and I thought, 'This really is sort of a strange landing.' After I got down I realized I had put my seat down to get out of the wind and had forgotten to raise it back up. Also I still had my dark glasses on—a real night landing.''

Leona Golbinec said they also instructed on instruments in AT-6s when they were short of pilots. They never did move them out, she explained, "because Mary Ann was married to the colonel and he wanted to keep the girls there. In fact, after we were disbanded, some of us went back and taught Link. We were hired as civilians and stayed for another year until they closed down the field.

"At one time some of the men who had been prisoners of war in Germany came back. We would take them up and check them out because they hadn't flown for a long time. We rode in the front seat and they rode in the back seat to get the feel of it again. Some of them had been in prison for a long time and they were scary to fly with. They had been instructed by men and they didn't like being checked out by a woman who was going to decide whether or not they could fly. Sometimes they would swear at us.

"We each had a mechanic who would check out the plane before we went up. My sergeant gave me a long monkey wrench to take with me in the plane. If I had to hit them on the head, he said, use it. This was because they would get on that stick and you couldn't get it away from them. One time I had to pound on the plane, 'Let go, let go.' They were bigger than we were, after all.

"One time, at Dothan, I had a crash. We were having a lot of sabotage on our field. In fact, they found a body in the swimming pool one time. I had taken off, and apparently there were some bolts that had been removed and they were rolling back and forth in the plane. I came down and I cracked up on the landing. I wound up in the hospital. I hit my head, and when I came to, it was Mother's Day. All I could think of was my mother getting this card saying I was dead.

"What happened was, I had no controls. All I could control was the throttle. I came in and just bounced and bounced and went over on one wing and then the other and tore one wing off. Finally it nosed over and when that happened I hit my head. They thought it was sabotage because base personnel found other items loose in the plane as well. They checked all the planes after that.''

"Did they ever find out who was doing it?''

"They had some civilians who were packing the parachutes and they thought some of them might have done it. They were working twenty-four hours, day and night. Our base personnel were kind of lax. No one really watched to see where you were walking, and the parachute place was right next to where we were testing. It was very easy to just walk over. We never thought anything about it until it starting happening to us.

"Not only that, but we had a lot of German prisoners of war working at our base. After that they watched them more carefully. They even had them in the kitchen cooking for the officers, and they stopped that. One of the other girls had the same kind of trouble. She tore off a wing too. I felt very lucky to get through it. I was lucky throughout my whole flying career."

The stories of sabotage seemed unlikely to many of us, but the possibility was taken very seriously by the girls who had encountered unexplained, serious damage to their aircraft. Albert Marrin, in his book *The Secret Armies* (New York: Atheneum, 1985, p. 37), said,

> Americans had a healthy respect for German saboteurs. During the First World War saboteurs had dynamited a railroad freight terminal at New York Harbor opposite the Statue of Liberty. Freight trains, warehouses, barges, and ships went up in a fiery tornado.
>
> The FBI wasn't taking chances in our second war with Germany. . . . They worried more about saboteurs than about spies, and with good reason. War industries were booming as factories worked around the clock. . . . Oil refineries stored millions of barrels of fuel, oil and gasoline. Saboteurs who knew their job or were lucky could paralyze large portions of the war effort with a few well-placed bombs.

In June 1942, eight Nazi saboteurs were apprehended by the FBI. Four of these Germans had landed on Long Island, and four others on a Florida beach a few days later. All were captured and six of them were executed in August of that year. The other two, who betrayed their comrades and turned them in, were sentenced to jail. After the war these two were released and deported to Germany.

In June of 1944, two years after the execution of the six saboteurs, Hans Haupt, the father of one of those who was killed, was convicted of treason for assisting his son back in 1942. Also in June of 1944, when the invasion of the European continent was imminent, the New York City Police Department was put on the alert to prevent sabotage of vital installations in the city, according to the *New York Times*. Extra vigilance was being called for to protect shipyards, bridges, piers, war plants, airfields, utilities, and transportation lines.

Acts of sabotage, therefore, could be considered a possibility. Some of the WASP problems with aircraft occurred during this time, but such small-scale damaging of individual airplanes seems unlikely. Nevertheless, poor maintenance does not seem to cover all of the strange accidents.

In other news, on June 5, 1944, Rome was captured intact by the Fifth

Army after fierce battles raged through the suburbs. It was the first of the three major Axis capitals to fall. On the following day, June 6, 1944, D-Day, the Allied armies landed in France in the Havre-Cherbourg area. The great invasion was under way! According to a communique issued by the Allied Expeditionary Force, "under the command of General Eisenhower, Allied naval forces, supported by strong air forces, began landing Allied armies this morning on the northern coast of France." By the seventh, the following day, the invaders were fighting their way inland. The climax of the war had been reached!

News articles in the following weeks offered proof that the war was winding down. One article spoke of fifteen thousand men discharged from the armed services who were finding jobs in aircraft manufacturing plants. Another article praised "negro" war aces whose outfit (segregated) had shot down seventeen enemy planes at the front. Two black captains had been awarded the Distinguished Flying Cross, Captain Curtis and Captain Charles B. Hall. Captain Hall dismissed his feat of shooting down two Nazi Focke-Wulf 190s and a Messerschmitt, saying he was more interested in what opportunities Negroes would have after the war. Captain Curtis stated, "I hope to stay in military aviation."

It would be nice to know what happened to these men. Very little has been heard about the black pilots of World War II, and perhaps their situation is somewhat akin to that of the women pilots. Now, at least, segregated armed forces are a thing of the past. Anne Berry commented on the segregated black pilots when I interviewed her at Martha's Vineyard in 1988.

"If you want to make sociological observations, after forty-odd years," she began, "I didn't think about it for probably thirty to thirty-five years, but there were no black women in the WASP. Maybe they didn't have the money. I don't know whether this was an economic thing. I tend to think it probably was, because at that time the armed forces were segregated and the black men were trained at Godman Field, Kentucky. Why they sent them south to train, I don't know, but they did. The black Army Air Corps pilots had a very good reputation." (Other black pilots were trained at Tuskegee Institute, Alabama, according to Dora Dougherty Strother.)

We probably will never know the answers to the causes of many of the WASP accidents. The death of Susan Clarke was another possible sabotage according to Joanne Wallace, a close friend of Susan. In a letter to WASP Kay Gott in May of 1989, Joanne said, "She [Susan] was taking off in a Douglas Dauntless in Greenville, South Carolina, when she crashed due to sabotage (sand in the carburetor)."

The Air Force version of Susan Clarke's death differed substantially. The official record states that she died in a BT-13 crash in Fairfax, Kansas. Carbon monoxide poisoning was suspected as the cause. There were rumors, unsubstantiated, that she had a GI passenger with her. I cannot explain the discrepancies between Joanne Wallace's statement and the official version obtained from Air Force records by Byrd Granger for her book *On Final Approach* (Scottsdale, Ariz.: Falconer Publishing, *in press*)—a complete history of the WASP program.

During my interviews with the members of Class 44-W-2, I had heard of three cases where the pilots were convinced that their aircraft had been damaged deliberately: Lorraine Zillner, who was forced to jump from her BT-13 because of a cut rudder cable; Mary Ellen Keil, who fortunately was able to bring in her AT-6 when the entire flight control unit had been unscrewed; and Leona Golbinec, who crashed after losing all of the controls except the throttle. Two of these cases occurred at Avenger Field where the training program took place.

Whatever the true reasons behind these accidents, many of the WASPs had some frightening and difficult emergencies. As Leona put it, she felt very lucky to have made it through alive. Many other classmates felt the same way, although none of them were happy to have been disbanded before the war was over. Right up until the December deactivation their flying contribution was needed, and they felt they were providing a service to the war effort. They loved their jobs flying, in spite of the hazards and in spite of the unfriendly receptions some of them encountered. All of these pilots were doing a "service" job, such as instructing on instruments, delivering parts or personnel, tow-target flying, and test piloting. The rest of Class 44-W-2, fifteen other women pilots, were sent to the Ferry Command.

When our class graduated from Avenger Field, three ferrying groups were accepting women pilots: the Fifth Ferrying Group, Love Field, Dallas; the Sixth Ferrying Group, Long Beach, California; and the Second Ferrying Group, New Castle AAB, Wilmington, Delaware. Ferry pilots had only one task—to deliver as many planes as fast as possible to where they were needed! Unfortunately, six of the ferry pilots are deceased—two killed in airplane crashes that year, 1944. Three others I have been unable to interview for various reasons. This leaves me with only six pilots who can give much information about ferrying, and the subsequent flying they did after being transferred from the Ferry Command.

Fortunately, Lorraine Zillner was a good source of information about what it was really like ferrying planes. Lorraine was assigned to the Fifth Ferrying Group at Love Field, Dallas. "That was really something," she exclaimed. "We never knew what we were going to be flying next until the night we got

116

back to the base. We would have to take off at sunrise and not land until sunset. If you went from the East Coast to the West Coast and kept gaining hours, believe me, by the time you landed, you were tired. Oh, were you tired! They wanted us to use every bit of daylight that was available to us.

"We started out ferrying Stearmans, and there was no radio, no nothing. It would take us three days to go from coast to coast in the Stearmans, because we'd have to land, refuel, and take off again, and then find a place to stay. That was something, too! All the wives would be traveling to meet their husbands. Hotels were full. We spent many a night in hotel lobbies. Most of us who traveled together would just be on the floor of the lobby with about umpteen other ferry pilots using parachutes as our pillows. Then up in the morning and out to operations. We'd have to leave the hotel when it was dark, and get out there and be at the runway ready for takeoff."

"What other kinds of airplanes did you fly?" I asked.

"Well, Stearmans, Sixes, and then once they closed some field, and a whole group of us got PTs that were going in to be mothballed. Now, those were in pretty bad shape. They were on their last legs. We flew them to Oklahoma City, and pieces would be falling off. We'd be flying along and little things would go by. We flew seven days a week. Someone commented on it and we were told, 'When the fellows are in the trenches they don't have Saturday and Sunday off. What do you think this is?' Well, that was enough of an answer. It was true. That was why we were there.

"In Dallas there were no planes. We would have to go to the factories and get the next planes that came off the line—factories all over. I went to New York, Wichita, and other places. Then we would take them up, test them, bring them down, and sign for them, for the Army, and then ferry them wherever they had to go. Most of the time it was just solo. You were alone.

"Our rules and regulations said that as soon as we delivered a plane, we had to get the fastest way back to Dallas. If we got in before 10:00 o'clock at night, we'd have to be on the line the next morning for orders. If we got in after 10:00 P.M., then we had a day off. On some of those grueling flights—and, believe me, some of them were really tough, with open cockpits, grease, oil, sand—we would try to work it so we'd get back after 10:00 P.M. so we'd get a day's sleep.

"Marie Michell was stationed at Dallas too. She was killed in a B-25, as I understood. I remember hearing about it, and she was married at the time, to a flight surgeon. She was only nineteen. Kit MacKethan, Shorty Stafford, and I made an awful lot of trips together. Somehow we'd come back at the same time and then get sent up to Wichita to pick up Stearmans and fly them to California. Maggie Chamberlain was there, too. Shorty would take her lipstick and write

117

on the outside of her plane, "MYRT," and on the side of my plane I'd put "GERT." We became known as Myrt and Gert as we'd go across country. Then we'd all end up together in California and then fly back. The next morning we'd get orders again together.

"I don't remember how long we were allowed to be in the Ferry Command, but at the end of a certain time I guess they figured we were burned out. I was sent to Waco. That was a Basic Training school for the men. Any BTs that were in accidents would be repaired. Then before the cadets could fly them, we'd have to take them up and test them. We were called engineering test pilots, and that was our job. That was what I was doing until we were disbanded in December 1944. We were disbanded from Waco.

"We were sad when we were disbanded. We had been living flying all through our training and our assignments. It was all we talked about or thought about. Then suddenly, in a few days' time, here we were—nothing. It was such a difficult transition. To this day all I have to do is hear a plane go overhead and I'm right up there with that pilot."

Kit MacKethan also was sent to Dallas, and she told me about buying a dog in Mexico. "I ferried out of Dallas," she began, "and I have a map of all the places I went all over the United States. On one of my ferry trips to the West Coast, I stopped at El Paso and went across the border, where I saw a man with some little dogs. The man said, 'Them genuine Chihuahua, them six months old, ten dolla.' I gave him ten dollars, and I put the dog in the big black bag that we all had, with his little head sticking out. Then we flew back and forth across the country until I took him to North Carolina and gave him to my mother. I delivered a plane to a base in North Carolina; that's how I got to see my mother.

"From Dallas I went to Cochran Field near Macon, Georgia, and from there I requested a transfer and they sent me to Maxwell Field, Alabama."

Kit was a very close friend of Marie Michell, but she preferred not to talk about her. When Marie was killed, Kit wrote a poem for her, which was printed in a brochure with Marie's picture on the cover. She and Marie had made a pact that if either of them were killed, the other would go to visit her friend's grieving mother. It became Kit's task to visit and comfort Marie's mother, which she did, sharing the poem she had written for her friend.

Jo Wallace was assigned to the Ferry Command and she said she had served at all the ferry bases. "Once I was on temporary duty in Wichita flying the twin-engine Beechcraft, the most popular plane in the Air Corps. It was the CO's airplane, and every field in the United States put in an order for a twin-engine Beech—the C-45, which is cargo. It was a staff plane. Every CO wanted that plane to impress people and to take places. When I would deliver these planes, men would demand to see the pilot and then want me to stay over and go to a dance, or to a big game, or go to Canada with them—anyplace, because they were so excited to get that plane! They wanted to fly it someplace! What made us feel so good, though, was that the Navy sent two men to deliver that plane, and the Army sent one woman.

The ferry pilots I talked with did move around a lot. All of them were sent to different bases at different times. Phyllis Tobias was no exception. She ferried planes at Wilmington first, but later she was sent to several other bases. "I put in that I wanted to go to the Ferry Command at Wilmington, Delaware. At first only Kay Cleverly, Jo Wallace, and Madeline Sullivan were to go, but as it turned out, Sullivan didn't want to go—she went to B-26 school—so they let me fill in. I've always loved her for that because, to me, the Ferry Command was my dream. Remember the picture on the cover of the July 19, 1943, issue of *Life*? For me, that was the job I wanted out of the WASP.

"The first thing we did was to get on a train and go up to Hagerstown and pick up a PT-19—just what we'd flown in Sweetwater. We were to take it to Chickasaw, Oklahoma, and that was exciting. I was from Michigan and I'd really never seen many mountains. Those Blue Ridge Mountains looked awfully big to me. Our first stop was Roanoke. From Roanoke we flew to Birmingham and then went on to Chickasaw. A couple of times I was copilot on planes coming into Detroit. Then we'd take a bus down to the airport in Detroit and my parents would come down and meet me. My mother really gave me support. She said, 'Imagine Phyllis flying with all those handsome young men. When they come into the airport everybody else gets bumped off the planes because the ferry pilots have to go back to work.' Of course, that made me feel great.

"Then we were sent from Wilmington to Fairfax Field in Kansas City. That was a B-25 base and we had training on the B-25. There was a North American plant there and we flew the B-25s to Savannah. I had an accident at Fairfax Field, but all they did was ground me for two months."

"What did you do?" I queried.

"I tried to take off with the controls locked—just from being so excited. They let us take up a plane and fly any time we wanted to. I had already gone out two nights before, flying west, and I thought I just had to do that again. It was so wonderful just to get up there at night. This was in a UC-78. This night I got down there at the end of the runway, and I revved it up, and I didn't go through my checklist. I forgot the control lock. By the time I realized it, of course, I stopped the plane in time to just barely bump the fence, but I felt so dumb. I thought surely they were going to can me. Boy, I was scared.

"The last two weeks of the two months that I was grounded, they gave me special training. All the young men pilots who had to take me up and check me were very kind. They gave me forty hours of remedial training. Then I started being a copilot; I couldn't be a first pilot again.

"After that they took all the WASPs out of there because that base commander did not like women. That was for sure—it was pretty obvious, but I couldn't blame him for my troubles. He wasn't the one who took off with the controls locked."

"But he kept you down for two months," I added.

"Well, yes, but at least he didn't throw me out. We went to Santa Ana next and were there for about two weeks. Then some of us went to Training Command and Helen Porter and I went to Peterson Field in Colorado Springs. That was beautiful. That was my last station, and they were good to me. I could take an airplane and go anywhere I wanted to. They called me an administrative pilot but the funny thing was, the base commander needed a secretary. He said they were going to ship me out of there because some other training command needed somebody. I said, 'Oh, I can't stand it. I just love it so much here.'

"The commander said, 'Okay, if you give me two hours typing every so often when I need it, I'll keep you here.'

"I went in and typed sometimes, and he was just charming to me. He was such a nice man. I had an A-26 and that was fun. I would take mechanics down to where there were downed airplanes, and some of them would be these old dog-faced guys who had been in the Army for a thousand years. They didn't like it when they had to fly with a woman pilot. But, later, it was all right, because I'd wait on the ground until they were ready to go back, and we got to know one another. Sometimes I'd just take the plane by myself and go out to Ogden and pick up parts. That was fun too.

"We also had a bunch of P-40 pilots there just back from England, and they had to go up to Pierre, South Dakota, for gunnery practice. Helen Porter and I would be pilot and copilot on a C-76 and fly them up to Pierre. One time we had about ten of them in the back and those guys decided to play a trick on us. They started running back and forth in the plane, unbalancing it. Helen Porter, who was pilot then, was able to control it. She's still flying, by the way. She had been flying before she went into the WASP and she's still flying, in 1989!

"One time I was in a UC-78 and flew two Army colonels from Pierre to some other place. They made me feel like a million dollars. They just thought I was so wonderful, those two old goats. I guess I shouldn't say that when they gave me all those compliments, but it was fun. I think administrative flying at Peterson Field was the best I had. The program ended then while I was still at Peterson Field and I never flew after that. When I got home I found out how really scared everybody was—that I'd come home in a box. After my father died it seemed a little too much to put my mother through anymore. I just never did fly again.''

Many of the WASPs assigned to the Ferry Command were moved around and served at several bases. Ferrying work was exhausting, according to most of the pilots I talked with. They spent long hours in the air, often in small planes. They flew small, single-engine planes and co-piloted larger ones such as the B-l7s, B-24s, C-47s. Some WASPs were fortunate enough to fly as first pilot on those larger bombers and transports. Others took the opportunity to go to pursuit school. Although their time of service was short, they were able, finally, to fly everything the Air Force had, including all the pursuits. Some of their stories tell a lot about the airplanes that were flown during World War II as well as what conditions were like back then.

B-24

CHAPTER NINE

Pursuit Pilots and Bomber Pilots

"I felt a bump, heard a crack, and I saw the roof of a house flash past my wing." — Ruth Adams

In Dover, England, in October 1944, the continuous shelling of the coast ceased, following the capture of the last remaining guns at Cap Gris Nez. For four years, citizens in Dover had been living mostly in deep caves as bombs fell daily. Singing and dancing in the streets was the order of the day as Dover residents moved out of the depths into the first real freedom they had known for a long time. The RAF continued bombing targets in Germany, mainly oil plants. American B-24 Liberators also were sent against the Reich, but there was little hope for the early defeat of Hitler. Americans were warned to expect a winter and perhaps a spring campaign. The war was, however, moving into Germany, cutting off German bombing capabilities. Fears of a winter famine within Germany were expressed.

In a major U.S. drive along the Moselle, Calais was captured with five thousand German prisoners taken. American air power smashed Japanese ships during an attack on Manila in the Philippines. The American infantry was advancing into Germany and on October 4 the Americans cracked the Siegfried line near Aachen and were driving on to Cologne. Also on October 4, the *New York Times* ran an article on the WASP stating that they would be disbanded on December 20. One thousand WASP pilots were to get a "certificate of service." Such a certificate was also to be presented to families of the thirty-eight women who had been killed in the service of their country.

"I am proud of the WASPs and their record of skill, versatility, and loyalty," said General Arnold. "They have done outstanding work for the Army Air Force, even exceeding expectations."

Later news reports showed that nurses, however, were still badly needed, with a large shortage expected by 1946. Total U.S. casualties were quoted at 417,085, with the Army accounting for more than half, and the Navy, 25,963.

Also in October, ten thousand tons of bombs were dropped on key targets in the Reich with a loss of fifty-one U.S. Eighth Air Force bombers and fifteen fighters. A new U.S. drive opened on Cologne, and the Russians swept into Hungary. Allied invasion forces poured into Albania, Greece, and many of the Greek islands. Samos was captured. Other news told of the death of Al Smith at seventy years of age. Wendell Willkie's death followed shortly after. He was only fifty-two years old.

In early November, six American ships, including the USS *Princeton* aircraft carrier, were hit and sunk by Japanese in the Battle of the Philippines. The Army Air Force quoted their total of planes at 75,500, with 23,000 combat planes. Figures were listed for bombers, fighters, transports, and Naval planes. A new British reconnaissance plane, the "Firefly," was introduced and scored its first success over Germany. In the meantime, B-29s ripped Rangoon in a record strike. Germans were retreating from Holland, and Russian troops were welcomed in Belgrade, the capital of Yugoslavia. B-29s also bombed Singapore while the Russians shelled Budapest.

It was clear to see that the war was winding down, even though much fighting could still be expected. At this time, WASPs were flying all three major types of World War II airplanes: pursuits (fighters), bombers, and cargo planes. They flew a variety of bombers, mostly the B-25 and B-26. A few flew the larger bombers such as the B-24, B-17, and B-29. Many women flew pursuits: the P-39, P-40, P-47, and P-51. Some in our class who flew a wide variety of planes were sent to Brownsville, Texas, to pursuit school.

Ruth Adams was sent first to New Castle Army Air Base, at Wilmington, Delaware, along with Susan Clarke, Joanne Wallace, Kay Cleverly, and Phyllis Tobias. Ruth, Susan, and Joanne were sent from there to Kansas City, where they were not kept very busy. When the call came for volunteers to go to pursuit school in Brownsville, Texas, however, not many responded.

"Nobody wanted to go," Ruth commented, "because that was hard. It was a pretty tough experience and a little dangerous, with pursuit planes."

Ruth and Joanne Wallace both volunteered for Brownsville duty, however. "I wanted to go because I wanted to be stationed near New Castle Base, where graduates would be sent," Ruth said, "but I was always afraid I'd do something dumb and wash out. At Brownsville I was flying in the back seat of the AT-6 for the first two weeks, and then, for the next two weeks, in a variety of pursuit planes. First we flew the P-39 Aircobra, then the P-40 Flying Tiger, the P-47 Thunderbolt, and the P-51 Mustang—all of those. We never knew what we'd be assigned on the days we went to the flight line, and we never had an instructor on those airplanes. We simply had to read the manuals. I would sit in the different planes on the flight line and go through the checkout procedures so I would know where everything was. The locations of the controls were slightly different in each plane. We had a manual for each plane that included preparations for takeoff and landing; settings for manifold pressure, RPMs, oil pressure; and so on.

"One day in the AT-6, we came in and, after landing, my plane suddenly went up on its nose and spun around and came down. We were still right side up but the landing gear had collapsed. I thought, 'Oh, hell, I didn't correct for drift. How could that be? With all that crosswind training at Sweetwater!' I was so mad at myself. But really the landing gear had simply collapsed. I turned off the gas and the ignition.

"My instructor had jumped out long before. He flew out of that plane! He was afraid it would blow up. I got out and found my instructor standing on the ground. The fire engine was there and the ambulance. The fireman asked the instructor, 'Did you turn off the gas?' My instructor looked at me helplessly and I said, 'Yes, it's off, and the ignition's off.' Then the instructor and I walked back to the ready room together and he said, 'I would have expected it of the other two, but not you.' That's when I knew that he thought well of my flying."

"How soon did you know that it wasn't your fault?"

"They had an investigation. In the meantime I was grounded. Then they called me in for a hearing. These officers sat behind a table facing me and I stood in front. They said, in effect, that they had discovered it was a defective landing gear, and not pilot error. They smiled and said, 'Run along,' so I got back into business.

"I had another mishap. I finished at Brownsville, graduated, and was stationed briefly at New Castle Air Base. A week later we all went on detached duty. I went to Long Island where I flew P-47s—sometimes as many as three a day—delivering them to the Newark Airport. Each time we would be ferried back in a C-47 to pick up the next plane.

"One day I ran the engine up before takeoff as usual and the engine didn't develop enough power at the designated RPM setting. I called a mechanic over and told him the power was low, but not down very much. He said, 'Well, that's not anything. Go ahead.'

"I took off, but at the end of the runway, maybe twenty feet off the ground, I suddenly felt a bump and heard a crack, and I saw the roof of a house flash past my wing. I wasn't climbing fast enough. My only thought was, 'Well, this P-47, thank God, will go through a brick wall.' The P-47 had a lot of protection around the pilot. P-51s had none. Pilots died in the P-51 if they crashed on takeoff, and many of them did. I picked up a little airspeed, climbed up, and called the tower. I asked if I should come back to the field or go on to Newark. I didn't know how much damage I had sustained.

"They said to come back, so I did and I came in fast because I didn't want to lose airspeed. When I landed, the fire truck and the ambulance were there—again. I found that there was a big dent in my horizontal stabilizer. It was about four inches deep, a foot wide, enough so it could have cut off the stabilizer. I had gone through the trunk of a tree—a fairly tall tree.

"Again I was isolated for investigation and they sent in a test pilot to talk to me. I don't remember if I told them about the mechanic and what he said. The whole thing had me upset. I told them, 'I didn't see the tree. I don't sit up high enough in the plane.' They decided the solution was to have some blocks made for the pedals so that I could sit up higher and see more. I was saved again.

"The only other thing that happened to me was when I was copiloting for someone in a UC-78. As soon as we took off, I noticed there was smoke coming from under the pilot's seat. That 'Bamboo Bomber,' you know, was made of spit and tissue paper! I pulled out the fire extinguisher and the instructions said, 'Operate thirty feet from the fire,' so I couldn't use it. We weren't high enough up to jump, so the pilot landed straight ahead, very smoothly in a nice, flat field. When she switched the engine off, the fire went out. She went to get help and I stayed with the plane. Later she wrote me up in a very complimentary way."

The most dangerous thing that happened to Ruth was when she flew a P-51 out of a base in South Carolina. The pilots had all been told about some trouble with P-51 engines failing on takeoff.

"Lois Cutler, [a WASP trainee in our class], told me she had watched a P-51 take off when she was on Civil Air Patrol. About fifty feet off the ground the engine failed. The plane came down on the ground right in front of her, where she could see the pilot plainly as he burned to death. You know, that made me feel insecure.

"At South Carolina we had been told to put the throttle way up to the fire wall on the P-51 on takeoff. I guess they thought if the engine was going to fail, it would fail on the ground. I gave it absolutely full throttle, right up to the fire wall, and I was about twenty feet off the ground when the engine started to cough and fail. I just eased back on the throttle, but my heart stood still. It caught—almost stopped, and then caught. I gained altitude and went on to Newark. When I signed in at Newark I was with a flight of P-51 pilots. All the rest were men. I told the pilot next to me what had happened and he said, 'You know, the same thing happened to me. There must have been water in the gas or something. I was never so scared in my whole life.' He was an ex-combat pilot! That was the closest I came to dying.

"When we were deactivated, I was of two minds. Those damned planes could kill me, or I could kill myself by doing something dumb. About 60 percent of me was glad that it was over. I had made it and was still alive."

Joanne Wallace also graduated from pursuit school at Brownsville, Texas. Joanne was one of the few WASPs in our class to fly all types of airplanes, including bombers, cargo planes, and all of the pursuits. She told of a harrowing experience at Brownsville with a P-47. She was cleared by the tower for takeoff and was heading down the runway when a male pilot taxied across the runway in front of her.

"My tail wheel was up, I had ninety inches of mercury, and I sheared his whole engine off. They wanted to condemn the woman pilot but the tower had the recording that I was cleared for takeoff. My plane burst into flames and I could see these men running, but they wouldn't come near me. I had my earphones off but I couldn't open the hatch. It was getting bright orange in there and I was starting to cook. I fought and fought to open the hatch. Those men standing near me wouldn't come to help because they were afraid it was going to blow up. I finally got it open, got out on the wing, and fell onto the tarmac. My face was all blood and my teeth had been pushed in by the gunsight. I was terribly upset about my teeth, and I thought my nose was smashed. After I fell to the ground, those brave men came and picked me up and took me to the infirmary. I kept saying, 'Where is my nose?' I thought my nose was gone, but it was really just absolutely numb, and I had two huge black eyes.

Did they have an investigation?

"No. It was just dropped. They didn't do a thing to the male pilot who taxied in front of me.

"Another time, on my first ride in a P-40 Flying Tiger, I had a funny thing happen. The P-40 is the only airplane with a hydraulic system that runs only when you press the electronic toggle switch on the stick. You can 'up' the gear and flaps, but they don't move until you connect the circuit by pushing the electronic switch. The pursuits are a one-man airplane, of course. You do it alone, never having an instructor. Also, one thing they stressed in class was never, under any circumstances, have a forced landing in Mexico—because they'd put you in jail and not let you out. My very first flight in a pursuit was on a south runway.

"Well, I 'upped' the gear and flaps and nothing happened. The cylinder temperature is going up into orbit and I'm just clipping the tops of the trees and heading for Mexico. I pulled out the instructions which said that if the gear wouldn't come up I had to pump it up.

"Now, on the P-40 they had something called 'pop-ups' on the wings, that were colored. Like little sticks. They show the degree the gear is up or down. When the gear is up they are flush to the wing. I'm pumping, looking at the pop-ups, and the cylinder head temperature, and thinking, 'I'm going to crash in Mexico and go to jail.'

"Never did I think about the electronic switch! I was so upset about the cylinder head temperature and the pop-ups and the gear being down, that I'd forgotten about the switch.

"Now I'm over the Gulf of Mexico working like a dog on the pump, and finally the pop-ups are flush and the gear is up and the cylinder head temperature is down. I climb and reach an altitude of whatever I was supposed to attain, and I read the instructions. They said, 'For your first hour in the P-40, practice simulated approaches and landings.' I thought, 'Oh, my God, I'd never let that gear down and have to pump it up again.' I'm sitting there feeling the plane out, and suddenly it comes to me—the electronic switch!

"I reduce speed, get real slow, and put the gear down, and up come the pop-ups, and everything works, the gear comes up again. I'm sitting up there at eight thousand feet feeling just like a Cheshire cat. What a close call! I could have crashed, but I was strong enough to be able to pump that gear up manually. I felt like crying. It was really dramatic."

You never told anybody about that?

"Never! Never!"

Did you have other close calls?

"Yes—I was such a cowboy! We had a group in Independence, Missouri, and they had a whole bunch of planes that they wanted to ground and put into mothballs in a field in the middle of Kansas. Our group of six women would fly the planes down to this field. It was so boring! Then a truck would come to get us, put us into another plane, and fly us back. Then we'd take another load of planes. I think we did about four or five planes a day. Fly one down, get into the truck, fly back. We were so bored we decided to fly under some high tension wires. I misjudged on this—I think another plane came too close to me. I moved away, and a wire wrapped around my wing. It didn't make me crash; the wire was severed instead. I was able to go ahead and land at the field. The event went unnoticed. These were old clunkers that they were putting to bed.

"Another time I buzzed my house in Longmeadow, Massachusetts. I had to deliver a plane in that area—I think at Westover Field. It was a Sunday, and all the golfers were out. Our house was on the golf course, so I had to buzz over the golf course to reach our house. I saw a whole bunch of people around the pool. I was told later that one man playing golf said, 'That must be Jo Wallace. I'm going to report her.' The three men playing with him said, 'If you do—' They were going to wipe him out. Since I had grown up there, everyone was my friend.

"One other funny thing happened to me. I was delivering a plane to Dorval Field near Montreal. I had had a long day and I was tired so I brought my papers inside and the man in charge handed me this thing—I didn't know what it was—

and I went to my hotel. When I got there I looked at it and it was a prophylactic kit; I'd never seen one before. Well, about a week later I delivered another plane to the same field and the same guy was there. He looked up and said, 'Weren't you in here last week?' I said, 'Yes.' He turned bright red and he said, 'I'm so apologetic. We've never had a woman in here before. It never occurred to me we'd have a woman. Next time, would you please speak? Or clear your throat?'

" 'I thought it was very interesting.' I answered. 'I never had anything like that happen before.'

" 'I hope you won't again,' he said."

Five ferry pilots from our class (44-W-2) were assigned to Long Beach, California: Anne Berry, Margaret Ehlers, Muriel Lindstrom, Mary McCrea, and Alice Montgomery. Both McCrea and Montgomery are deceased and Muriel Lindstrom did not care to talk about her WASP days. Margaret Ehlers told me that, in addition to the planes at Avenger Field, she flew the B-17, the UC-78, the B-24, the C-47, and the B-25.

"My best experience, I think, was copiloting with a major on a B-17 to Carney, Nebraska, from Long Beach. We left on Easter Sunday and got as far as Las Vegas. The next morning everyone was sitting around the pool and I asked why we weren't leaving. They said there was a snowstorm in Denver and we couldn't go in. We spent the day in Las Vegas. By the next day the weather had cleared and we got to Denver and then to Carney where we delivered our planes."

On one trip from Washington, D.C., to La Junta, Colorado, Margaret stopped at Columbus, Ohio, and was grounded for three days because the plane quit on final approach, so she had to make a dead-stick landing. From there she flew into St. Louis and then on to Topeka, Kansas. "When I tried to leave Topeka, there was a fire in the engine on takeoff. When I called the tower and said I was coming in for a landing, they asked, 'What's the problem?' I said, 'Take a look.' I came in, landed safely, and stayed there because again the plane was grounded. Anne Berry came from La Junta to pick me up so I got back okay."

Anne Berry is the only other WASP for whom I have information about the ferry work done at Long Beach, although quite a number of WASPs were stationed there. "The commanding officer was B. J. Erickson. I was impressed with BJ. She was a good administrator and a very good pilot. She has stayed with flying over the years and now has a daughter who is an airline pilot.

"I flew a lot of single engines, BTs and PTs, and I did copilot work on the B-17, the B-24, and the C-47. I liked the B-17 much better than the B-24. One of the male pilots was a Hell's Angels pilot, a much older man. [Hell's Angels were an old-time flight group, not to be confused with today's bikers.] We were nineteen or twenty years old, of course, and he was probably around forty, which put him right up there with Methuselah as far as I was concerned. I liked flying with him because he would let me sit in the left seat and do the flying.

"The trim tabs on those planes made flying much easier. When you land a B-17, it's heavy trying to hold the nose off with the wheel. You could reach down and flip the trim tab, right in the middle of the aircraft, and it would trim up quickly and take all the weight off.

"At one point I made a delivery trip with a C-47 with some guy who couldn't fly for sour apples. (Administrators had to fly four hours a month in order to qualify for flight pay; I figured this was what he was doing.) *The Caine Mutiny* had just come out then and I kept thinking, 'Shall I just take over this aircraft because this guy may kill us both?' But I didn't and he didn't."

Anne talked with me about our inexperience and naiveté at that time when we were all so young. Flying out of Long Beach, she learned that California is a really big state. She had a friend at the naval base at San Francisco whom she wanted to visit. "At that time we had something called 'Army Airlines.' These planes returned ferry pilots and others back to their bases. This particular plane was referred to as SNAFU and I thought this was its name. [SNAFU, in the Army, stood for 'Situation normal, all fouled up.' A second Army Airlines plane was called TARFU, meaning 'Things are really fouled up!'] I phoned and asked in all innocence if SNAFU had any trips up to San Francisco. A very frosty voice replied, 'The Army Airlines is going to San Francisco.' I went down and got a ride, having learned not to say SNAFU except in the right circles.

"Anyhow, we flew and we flew and by the time we got to San Francisco I realized that I was not going to get back to Long Beach that night. I had to call back and explain that I was not AWOL. I didn't realize that it's a four-hundred-mile trip from Long Beach to San Francisco.

"Another time I was flying copilot on a B-17 to Denver and we had been cautioned to fly around the enormous anvil clouds that lay in our path. I was thinking, 'My life is in this pilot's hands. What if he decides to fly through them?' Fortunately, he flew around them, because when we got to Denver we heard that a B-24 pilot flying ahead of us had tried to fly through one of the clouds. They had all gone down.''

This same B-17 pilot, she told me, had been rotated home after flying in Europe and he told her about a mission when three of his B-17 engines were shot out. "He praised the British organization called Air-Sea Rescue. Pilots could radio ahead and tell this Air-Sea Rescue that they expected to ditch in the English Channel, and about where and when. The rescue group would try to have a boat there to meet them. This was what he did. He had just one engine pulling him forward, but all the time he was losing altitude. He made it to the Channel; they ditched, and the rescue boat was waiting and took his crew off. They were all saved!

"Once I became lost ferrying a BT-13. I had picked up a Navy strip map which was smaller and easier to handle, but not as complete as the Army maps. I ran into weather and had to dodge some thunderheads, which took me off my map. I was running low on gasoline. Finally, I ran over a little airport and on the roof was painted, 'Wheeling, West Virginia.' That gave me orientation and I headed for Pittsburgh and made it! I read somewhere later that during the 1930s, one of the WPA projects was to paint city names on airport roofs, and I guess that saved my skin.

"When I finally brought the BT-13 to Bradley Field, however, the officer of the day said, 'I don't want it!' I thought, 'God, this is ludicrous!' I said, 'What do you mean you don't want it? It says right here I'm bringing BT Army number such and such'—and he gave me an argument! He didn't want that plane! I don't know how to account for it. Finally he signed the paper that said it was no longer my responsibility."

Anne also told me about flying a nonpilot officer from La Junta to Albuquerque in an AT-6. She was landing behind a B-24 and thought the B-24 was far enough ahead of her so she wouldn't hit any of his prop wash. "Wrong! I got in about fifteen feet off the ground, one wing went down, the other up—Holy Mackerel! I gave it full throttle, went around, and by then the prop wash was dissipated. I kept wondering what that guy in the back seat was thinking. 'This crazy female is going to kill me'? He didn't let out a peep. I keep thinking of him with great affection. He either had confidence in me or thought he couldn't do anything about it anyway. Later I thought, 'I'm glad he didn't grab the stick.' "

"My last post was La Junta, Colorado. At La Junta they were teaching the Chinese how to fly B-25s. Imagine the improbable setup—an American pilot instructor who spoke no Chinese, an interpreter who spoke Chinese and some English you hoped, and a third, the trainee, who spoke only Chinese. That Chinese trainee was trained by the one who could speak a little English—translating what he was supposed to do. How they learned to fly that way, I do not know. But they did! The instructors would laugh about it!

"Well, we were disbanded. When I went in to the CO to make my courtesy visit, he said, 'Well, you didn't mess up too much.' I didn't say anything, but I thought later, what did he think we would do? Crash his airplanes, or create general havoc? He seemed agreeably surprised to think we could fly there for three months without causing any trouble."

WASPs Mary Strok and Ruth Petry both were engaged in ferry work, yet

131

were not assigned to the Ferry Command. Both were assigned to Courtland AAF Base at Courtland, Alabama, for testing, but they seemed to get into all kinds of flying, including ferry work.

"I was assigned to PLM [production line maintenance] testing," Ruth explained. "I did that more than anything else. In testing, we would rev it up and then take off at as low a speed as possible. We'd use minimal throttle setting until it looked as if it wouldn't get off the ground. Then we'd give it a little more power. When it became airborne, we'd stagger to the nearest auxiliary field. If the engine went above a certain temperature, we'd land and call the tower. They'd send somebody out. I never had one go over the limit, but I had one or two that sat right on it.

"Mostly we would test after a plane had been in an accident, or had had a wing change. Then we would run stall tests on it, but the big thing was running the engines. When Mary and I went to Courtland, we were quite an oddity. They wanted to know how we got in the WASP. We said that we had to have two hundred flying hours to get in and that really amazed them.

"Flying military personnel could be boring at times. You'd take them somewhere and then sit around and wait. When they had to stay for two or three days, however, they would always pick the WASP whose home was the nearest their destination. If it were a two-day conference, she'd be free to go home for a day or two. They were very nice about that, and our six girls came from all parts of the country.

"Once I went down to Biloxi, Mississippi, where they had a big depot. Any large airplane with a landing problem was sent there because that's where the parts were. When we arrived, a DC-3 was having problems, so we were told to circle. The DC-3 was making bouncing landings trying to loosen the landing gear. Finally they told him to come in. People were gathered near the end of the runway watching this airplane. A fire truck and a jeep were waiting. At the last minute the landing gear started to crumple and the plane started to turn. That jeep just went up on two wheels and got out of there. Very funny! We did see some excitement occasionally!

"Once I was flying home at night with an engineering officer aboard. He wasn't a pilot; he sat in back. In BTs there was a red test light that would go on if there was an engine problem. We used to take the red cover off and use it for a map-reading light. I took the cover off and pushed the button and I heard the hatch in back open. I yelled, 'What's going on?' He replied, 'We have an engine failure.'

" 'No, we don't,' I said. Then I explained to him about using the light as a map-reading light. I guess he nearly had heart failure. He was about to bail out.

"In Courtland they really used us. Once we went out to test a BT and the prop pitch was set differently. It didn't climb worth a darn, but it went like mad in level flight. It seems this was a target-towing BT and they didn't want to re-rig it because it would soon go back to its base. Hence, it had real power in level flight, but was slow climbing.

"A wing change was another thing to watch for. Sometimes these planes would spin rather peculiarly. I had one do oscillating spins. Instead of spinning nose-down, this plane's nose would keep swinging up. We always worried about the possibility of mismatched wings.

"One time, Mary, two lieutenants and I were sent to pick up a couple of PT-19s, but when we got there we found they were Stearmans. Mary and I had never flown a Stearman, and one of the lieutenants hadn't flown a Stearman either. The other lieutenant hadn't flown one in years. They said, 'Don't worry. They're easy to fly.' I flew one, and the lieutenant who had flown them before flew the other. We took them to Decatur, Alabama—no problem at all. When we got to the ramp, we saw all these cadets with their mouths hanging open to see a woman getting out. It was so funny. They were so flabbergasted. I didn't realize how little they knew about women flying these airplanes.

"After that, I flew Stearmans several times and really enjoyed them. They're so maneuverable with all those ailerons. Once I had to ferry one in the middle of winter. There were a group of us and we all wore big heavy boots. When we got to our destination, we all wanted to 'wring them out' [fly them through some aerobatics], but we had these damned boots on! We talked about dropping the boots in the middle of the field and taking off again, but we figured the military wouldn't care for that. Stearmans were terrible groundloopers, though, because of narrow wheelbases."

Mary Strok, who had been with Ruth Petry most of the time, had more to tell about their flying in Courtland, Alabama. "It was mostly BT-13s and 15s. We used to do an awful lot of extremely unglamorous, unexciting slow-timing of aircraft. New and overhauled engines had been popped into these aircraft, and in those days, just as one did with cars, we had to fly them at reduced RPM to break them in. God, that was boring work—on a cold morning to get up for two hours and just do a pattern criss-cross for several hours—better than sitting on the ground, however!

"We ferried airplanes a lot, too—into the Training Command and into the Courtland AAF Base. We also ferried airplanes, mostly trainers from Dothan, Alabama, to Florida or Texas. It was singularly unglamorous. People said it must have been so exciting. It really wasn't, and yet I loved it.

"When a pilot crashed a plane in some field where it could be repaired, we'd fly it back out and have it patched. We did a lot of that. We also ferried non-pilots, and sometimes we'd ferry spare parts.

"I left the WASP shortly before they were disbanded, on maternity leave. It was a relatively short period of my life, but it was one of the most important and dramatic, as well as the most significant, I've ever had. It was an experience that I would never have parted with in any way."

My own assignment was also to the ferry command—to Love Field, Dallas. Unfortunately, I have little personal experience to relate about ferrying planes. Jerry and I were married in Sweetwater, Texas, right after the graduation ceremony at Avenger Field. When I arrived in Dallas, I was desolate at leaving my new husband, especially after learning that he was not expected to be sent overseas because of his "limited service" category. I recall the single-room quarters where we were assigned in a large, barracks-like building. Marie Michell and Kit MacKethan were roomed at the end of the hall. I flew as copilot on a twin-engine AT-10 and also, I believe, on an AT-11, delivering them to California and returning by way of SNAFU.

Mostly I remember being more lonesome than I had ever been in my life. I was beginning to rethink what military life was like. Much as I loved flying, the regimentation and loneliness overcame my better judgment. At that point, I resigned. It was not a good decision, I soon realized, because when I rejoined my husband (in an unlikely place called Vermont, Illinois), it was for a short time only. The Army decided, in Army fashion, that he was needed overseas, "limited service" or not, and I was left with neither a husband nor my ferrying job. I should have stayed with the WASP and served my term of duty even though the Congress deactivated the WASP not many months later. I did continue flying, however, and earned a commercial license as well as both instrument and instructor's ratings.

Many of the WASPs were, I am sure, even more unhappy than I when their flying careers were ended in December 1944. They had served the Air Force diligently, some losing their lives, only to have their efforts unrecognized. What most of the WASPs feel about the "deactivation," I believe, is that the resulting waste of all those trained women pilots was nothing less than a wartime blunder. Looking back from the year 1990, however, it is hard to see how all those pilots (both men and women) could have been used, except for those accepted by the airlines. Perhaps the waste must simply be counted as one of the costs of war.

P-40

Chapter Ten

Deactivation and Beyond

"The girls who went to the airlines, trying to fly, were not allowed in. It was men only." —Leona Golbinec

On December 20, 1944, the WASP program was deactivated. It was a sad time for the women who had served the Army Air Force all over the country. It was also unfortunate because it created a great deal of unfriendliness and friction between men and women pilots. The Army Air Force did not require so many pilots at this time, although the war was still going on. The women were chosen to be deactivated first, and perhaps that was logical, except that many male pilots were not interested in doing the kind of flying that the WASPs were doing.

"It would have kept on," Jean Moore commented, "if politics hadn't got mixed up in it. When we were going to be sent home, the pilots who had flown their missions and returned didn't want to do what we'd been doing. They wanted to fly their four hours a month to get their flight pay. They didn't want to take a BT up and test it. The day we were to leave, the twentieth of December, some depot called and said, 'We've got five airplanes to be tested.' We said, 'Sorry, you'll have to get your little boys to do them.' We did what we were supposed to do—like the Ferry Command. We worked hard. We were necessary—we were useful."

Leona Golbinec, on her way home after being deactivated, met with some serious prejudice. "I got to Montgomery, and I was at the desk filling out my flight form when an officer came up to me. He started berating me about 'women pilots,' just really reading me out. The enlisted man behind the desk called the colonel on the base. The colonel came out and reprimanded this fellow and asked if I wanted to press charges. I thought, 'We're already disbanded, and I don't want to do that.' I felt bad enough about not flying anymore. They took this fellow away, and the colonel apologized. I was really surprised by that incident.

"I was sorry we were disbanded, because I thought they should have kept us—I think they could have used us. Many men resented us, however. The women who applied to the airlines, trying to fly, were not allowed in. It was men only. I don't think they ever really accepted us—until now that women are flying in the Air Force—but maybe we broke the ground for them."

Although there were men who were resentful, and some who were against the WASP because they felt we usurped their places, many other men were supportive. Clarice Siddall commented that although there was prejudice at some bases, it was not everyplace. "In fact, at many places, and when flying into other fields, we found just awe, really, from the guys, and admiration."

I have to agree with her on that. I remember, while in training, a group of male pilots came to Avenger Field, although I can't remember the occasion. I do remember them as being highly supportive of our program, and they were having great fun learning some of our songs, such as "Rugged but Right." I think I copied down the words for them.

One of the reasons men were angry about women flying was explained by Phyllis Tobias. She had a friend who resigned from the WASP because of her husband. "They were both pilots, but when he enlisted they made him go into navigator school because they said they didn't need any more pilots. That really burned him up—that there were many men who couldn't be pilots because of the women's program."

Phyllis went on to say that she thought our service was very useful. "The fact remained that it was an experimental program and it certainly proved that, if they needed to, women could perform the job. When they didn't need us, they sent us home. I wasn't even bitter about that. I thought it was all such a great deal, and I thought it was all a lucky break anyhow."

Ruth Woods, who continued flying long after the close of the WASP, thought it was important that we did what we did "because we opened the door for the present women in the Air Force and other women in aviation. We opened that door so that they would be accepted and not sneered at. We laid the groundwork. We followed behind people like Amelia Earhart, who were loners. We came in as a body, a group—any group can exert a lot more pressure than a single individual. I personally feel that was our greatest accomplishment."

Mary Strok said she often wondered about whether the program was really worthwhile. "I don't know if it was worth the expense; my guess, in retrospect, is 'yes.' Because it set the pattern, it showed that women could do the same flying job that men could do, and at the same rate of casualty loss and production. I really think that in the long run, this would have had to be effective. I think the pluses outweigh the minuses. It was useful. Also I like to think that it did help relieve men from the kind of drudgery that they had to engage in on the home front."

Ruth Adams related an experience that pointed up some of the difficulties for women who wanted to continue their flying careers back in 1944. The WASP program, she thought, gave her confidence. Flying was something that she could do well, but the opportunities just were not there! "I wanted to continue flying as a commercial pilot; we all had commercial ratings. I had a classmate whose father was acting president of Republic Steel at the time, so she arranged for us to have lunch together and I knew that they had company planes. I thought maybe I could get a job as a company pilot, because I didn't think any airline company would hire me. Anyway, we had lunch, and I remember he was looking me up and down like a piece of meat. I thought I was pretty passable, but he told me that he didn't think the officers of the company would be comfortable with a woman pilot, and that was that. Was I mad? Well, I'm mad at the whole damn setup. I don't like the whole social structure! They pay women something like fifty-nine cents on the dollar. I'm very resentful."

While she is not happy with the social structure, Ruth did agree that the experience at Avenger Field was worthwhile. Esther Noffke was also of that opinion. "I thought it was a tremendous program. As I look back, I'm amazed at the efficiency with which it was carried out. It was well done. I didn't know enough about aviation back then to criticize, but now I think to myself, 'How great that was!' If I have any regrets, it probably is the fact that we weren't able to utilize our training. I was delighted when the WASPs got the recognition that they did. Women still have problems being advanced the way they should be. It seems that, even if you're a woman on flying status in the military, you have to progress a certain way, or you become ineligible. Several women have left the military to go into the legislature to try to change things, because that's the only way they will get changed."

Marge Gilbert also had some opinions about the program, and why we were disbanded. "The men had a big lobby against us, and that's why were disbanded. A lot of instructors thought they would have to go into the walking Army, and there was resentment over that, but I think it was a lot of politics, too.

"In looking back, I enjoyed it when I was going through it. My feelings about war have changed completely since then, but I know I enjoyed the flying and the feeling that you were doing something to help. We could have done more if the people who were in charge had let us go ahead and do the flying and to heck with the politics."

Lourette Puett said, "I think, perhaps, if the WASP had continued, we could have done more good. At the time I thought we were making a tremendous effort—better than Rosie the Riveter. The mood of America at that time was that everyone had to do something, so I felt I was contributing, but, in retrospect, I don't know that we really did contribute that much.''

Talking about sexism, Phyllis Tobias said, ''I guess there was some, honey, but I'll tell you I wanted the flying so bad that I wasn't going to let anything stop me. As far as I was concerned, it was 'all the luck I ever hoped to have.' I just thought it was wonderful.''

The majority of WASPs I talked with were highly enthusiastic about the value of the program as well as the benefits they derived from it. Jo Wallace declared, ''We were extremely lucky—just the luckiest people in the world—that we were able to take advantage of such a wonderful program. It was so educational. It gave us such skill that even if we didn't continue flying, I feel that the discipline was good for everyone. When the program was disbanded, some WASPs were just devastated, but that was understandable. It was so absolutely consuming. Your whole body and mind were wrapped up in the program!''

Fran Laraway, also, was depressed by the sudden dismissal. ''It certainly was helpful to the war effort—the actual jobs we did that released men to fight combat. The whole story of which way the war was going to go, and how long it was going to last, was scarcely predictable, so getting the women involved may have been important. All of us felt bad, however, that they thought we should be the first to go.

''I always felt strange about one or two girls who took the training and then scurried back to their husbands and didn't do any of the work. That was one funny little memory that I have. It used to break my heart because I was terribly patriotic about it. It was months after the deactivation before I could think of going out to work. I was just in quite a lull, where I watched the sky and missed it very much.

''Then there were interesting conversations about the different opportunities. Some women went to fly in South America, or wherever they could find a little war going on. One girl I knew of went to China and was never heard from again. Some went into barnstorming, and like the men, they had accidents. People who had learned to live on the high edge of things couldn't bring themselves down. It was too bad.''

Marge Needham was not really sure that we accomplished much, but she did think the training at Avenger Field was excellent. ''Some people have said that, by doing what we did, we were a help to the women now in the Air Force, but I wonder about that. I would have to reserve judgment. I have a feeling that they don't have the latitude that we had when we were students, but I think our training in the WASP was superior. A couple of people I didn't care for, but there are always a few people you don't care for. You have to put up with some of that. I took my commercial written exam and received my commercial license. Then I got my instrument and flight instructor ratings. It was very good to do it that way."

Millie Grossman and Kate Lee Harris both thought the program was useful and that we were fortunate. Millie said, "Yes, we definitely did accomplish something. We did help them relieve the men—although the men didn't really want to be relieved in some cases. Then, also, it pointed up the fact that women really could do this flying, and there was no reason why they shouldn't."

Kate Lee agreed with Millie. "Well, it was great, and of course the whole experience was priceless. We were in the right place at the right time. You know, it took something like a war to bring it about. Eventually it would have happened, but not back in the forties. We just were a privileged group, lucky to be there and to get through it all alive."

Doris Elkington thought the experience was valuable. "If not to my country, at least to me. I felt that I had done something to contribute. The disbanding was kind of abrupt, I think. I was delighted to see the Veteran status finally. I don't know how much practical difference it will mean to any of us, but symbolically I was glad to see it happen."

"We were something unusual," Mary Strok remarked. "We were the first. I have much respect for the women nowadays in the Air Force Academy. I think it is splendid that they are able to do it, but I think in a sense we paved the way. I'm so glad we did. It was a wonderful experience."

I think Fran Smith summed it up for most of us. "I believe history is going to prove that we did a tremendous service. First, because we did step in and help the country when it was necessary. Just as a bunch of the women did who went into the other services, and into factory work and so on. We did our part for the war effort. Also, I think we opened the eyes of a lot of people to the fact that women were capable of doing things! I feel we were the forerunners for the women who are in the Air Force today. One Air Force woman, who flew us in a C-131 when we were at meetings in South Carolina, told us that the women pilots in the military give us credit for opening the doors for them. I'm not sure I could do what they have to do these days, but maybe we did open some doors—and, selfishly, I had a great time. To me it was one of the best times of my life. It's strange, but my kids are so proud of me. I meet their friends, and they say, 'Oh, you're the pilot.' What a feeling!"

With their flying careers abruptly cut off, and the war still in progress, many WASPs chose to enter other military services, or went into the reserves. Their choices included the U.S. Navy, the U.S. Army Air Force, the U.S.

Marine Corps, and the Royal Air Force. In our class, 44-W-2, Velma Baumann (a trainee who did not graduate) joined the Army as a second lieutenant. Mary Ellen Keil joined the Army Air Force reserves and rose to the rank of captain. So did Marjorie Gilbert. Ruth Weller became a second lieutenant, and Lorraine Zillner rose to first lieutenant in the Army Air Force.

Ann Craft joined the Red Cross and served in Puerto Rico. Quite a few WASPs served in the Red Cross, she told me. ''I wanted to go to South America, but Puerto Rico was just a delight. We were on a permanent air base and it was beautiful, with golf courses, swimming pools, and so on. We served coffee and cake in a hangar on the airstrip. Soldiers were coming back from Europe; they would stop at Trinidad to refuel, then stop at Puerto Rico and then on to Miami. It was the end of the war. I have never flown since.'' Ann is too busy, I think, to miss her flying. She has an active family and lives with her husband in Colorado.

Phyllis Tobias never flew again, either. She married and later went into a business of her own, where she is still working. Kit MacKethan doesn't fly anymore. She lives in Winter Park, Florida, with her husband.

Anne Berry never flew after the WASP disbandment. ''I went to New York City and worked on a magazine. At that time flying time was still twelve dollars an hour, and I never had enough money to fly. Then I married and had children, and it just never seemed to work, but I was very glad for the experience and feel really quite privileged to have been part of it.'' Anne and her husband still live on Martha's Vineyard, where they have been for many years.

''What have I done since the WASPs?'' Sadie Hawkins responded, ''My husband was an Air Force pilot and he had an Air Force career, so I stayed fairly close to flying, enjoying it vicariously by listening to the men. I never did fly again, except for a few times.'' Sadie and her husband raised three children; they now live a very busy life in Fair Oaks, California.

Although she doesn't fly herself, Verda-Mae Lowe has a son who flies out of Falcon Field, Mesa, Arizona, and she sometimes flies with him. She is a painter and an organist, and these activities occupy a great deal of her time.

Anna Mae Petteys was a social worker before she became a WASP, so she had a career to return to. ''I went right back into my social work. I went to New York. I had a friend, though, who was living in Connecticut and was flying, so I got to fly with her. I would have liked to fly more but it wasn't convenient there and it was too expensive. You really had to fly regularly or not at all.'' Anna Mae also married and lived in Canada for many years, but is now back in the United States.

Doris Elkington did not continue with her flying after she left the WASP, but she did get a few chances to fly. ''I didn't do any flying except when we were stationed in Italy, at Rome. My husband was assistant air attache there. The air attache had the use of the ambassador's airplane. Bill, my husband, would fly for the ambassador at times, and when Bill went, I could go. I made a couple of flights and the colonel knew that I had flown, so he let me fly it. The plane was a DC-3, which was great. We made one flight to Florence with Mrs. Doolittle, and she didn't object to my flying. The colonel was one of Doolittle's pilots.'' Doris and her husband are now retired and live in Melbourne, Florida.

When Fran Smith ended her WASP career, she and her husband couldn't afford to fly. "After I started having a family, I wanted to get back into flying, but it was far too expensive then. I did go to ground school, because I never earned my private license. Not having kept up with flying, I found it hard to understand the new radio system, the Omni. I have flown since and found it is really no problem." Fran is now widowed and lives in Escondido, California.

Kay Herman was able to get in some flying after the WASP were disbanded. Her husband worked for the Lear company after the war in Santa Monica, California. She was able to fly some of the Lear planes, mostly Cessnas. Later they bought a Beech Bonanza and she flew it around California. She also tried some glider flying and loved it. She still lives in Santa Monica.

Kate Lee Harris was more fortunate than many WASPs. "Eventually, Bob and I bought a plane, so we flew all over the East. We didn't go beyond the Rockies, but we did fly from Canada to Mexico, mainly to visit friends and family, until just a few years ago." Now retired, Kate Lee and her husband live in Houston, Texas.

Marge Gilbert had a job waiting for her when the WASP disbanded. "I went back to my work at the Perfect Circle factory in Richmond, Indiana, and worked there until I married. I was doing as much good there as I was in the WASP." Marge and her husband are retired and live in Indianapolis.

No one in our class kept any diaries during our training or service. Millie Grossman, however, has some sketches that she drew during our time at Avenger Field. Millie did not continue flying after the WASP disbanded, but I'm sure she has kept up with her artwork. She and her husband live in Port Aransas, Texas.

What struck me most forcibly during my interviews with these women is how much they have done with their lives after their disappointing cutoff from their first-choice career, aviation. While only a few were able to continue with a flying career, others switched their talents to a variety of occupations and achieved some impressive results. Ruth Adams, who flew for the Ferry Command and checked out in most of the pursuit planes, went into medicine. Her first job after the WASP was as an electrical technician soldering wires and testing electrical equipment. Eventually she became uncomfortable with the job because she didn't know how much of her advancement in the company was due to her own talents or to a vice president who had taken a liking to her.

She decided to get professional training, so she became an M.D. and then a psychiatrist. She worked in psychiatric emergency and also as a psychiatrist in a juvenile hall. During this time, Ruth also took helicopter lessons. "I'm fascinated by the scene that you see in the movies or TV of helicopters that go up a precipice and practically pick someone off the cliff. They're so flexible. They do wonderful things. The trick is hovering. But then I began to get an appreciation for just how dangerous helicopters are, and I thought, 'Why am I doing this after all I've invested in terms of the blood, sweat, and tears of medical school?'

"Really, though, I got into the wrong specialty. I haven't the temperament for psychiatry. Manipulating others strikes me, somehow, as wrong. I don't like to do it. Believe me, I'm a good doctor, but later I just worked with psychotics and that's a strain. It wore me out. Also, I felt I couldn't do the wheeling and dealing to get rich. There's an 'old boy' network—always.

"Well, I decided in adolescence that I wasn't going to marry for a living. My aim in life was to support myself in the style in which I was brought up. I can tell you, I almost made it—but not quite!" Ruth is now retired and busy studying sculpture and painting.

Fran Laraway developed quite a different life-style. She and her husband raised four children and for twenty-five years were involved in the local community theatre where they played leading roles. Now retired from this busy activity, they spend time in the adult literacy program. "One of my students, who is a grandmother at forty, is trying to keep her girls from ending up on welfare like herself. She is braver than I ever would have called myself during my flying days."

After her WASP days were over, Leona Golbinec married. Her husband worked for a business in South America. "I flew to South America, but as a copilot. The company had a Cessna 310 and we used to fly to the oil fields. My husband was the manager, so when I went along with him, I got to be copilot." Leona is now widowed and lives in Ohio.

Jo Wallace told me that just before the WASP disbanded, she married, and her husband's brother-in-law owned a B-25. "He got it from an airline in Texas. It had all new Pratt and Whitney engines and he let me fly it. We went up to Nova Scotia and out west to Vancouver. I flew that B-25 for about six winters. We also flew down to Naples, Florida, where they had a strip we could fly into. After that, I just lost interest."

Joanne is the wife of our present ambassador to Singapore, so she keeps extremely busy with diplomatic duties. Besides a son, she has twin daughters, one of whom is named for WASP Susan Clarke, Jo's friend who crashed back in 1944.

It seems everyone tried to keep into flying as much as possible, after that fateful December 20, 1944. Lorraine Zillner went right to work at the Naval Air Station at Glenview, near Chicago. "I started work the next week. I was back by the planes, and I was happy working in operations and filing clearances out of Chicago. That was where I met my husband. Everyone there knew I had been a WASP. I was able to fly with him a few times. He was a Navy fighter pilot who flew off carriers. When he was assigned to shore duty, he had to get in his flight time. I was not supposed to go, of course, but somehow or other he would find me a Navy flight suit, and the two of us would go up together. The Navy knew what was going on, but no one said anything. When we started a family, however, I quit flying." Lorraine is now widowed and living in Virginia, where she produces some very beautiful paintings.

Lourette Puett really wanted to continue flying after the WASP were deactivated, so she went back to Fort Worth, Texas, and found a job ferrying UC-78 "Bamboo Bombers" from Wichita Falls to Fort Worth. "Some men had bought the whole field up there, and the planes had been sitting out for many years. Mechanics were getting them ready to be flown out to Fort Worth, and they put just enough gas in them to get us there. We had all sorts of problems. I had to land in a wheat field once. I was alone and I had to get out and drain the sump to get the water out of the gas tank. It was terrible. Some of the others who were flying these planes had their flaps fall off in the air. They were just decrepit old planes. I got out of the wheat field okay but it was bumpy as all heck.

"Then I got a job with five other pilots to ferry planes to Los Angeles. We would get in a car in Los Angeles, drive to Oklahoma, and pick up Beechcraft Bonanzas to ferry back. We went several different places, but I can't remember too much about it. I think we were paid $100 a trip, plus our food. That's when I decided that there wasn't a living to be made in that. Our $100 would be gone very quickly if we got weathered in someplace." Lourette no longer flies, but later she became a very successful realtor.

"I was good at real estate and I liked it, except I did burn out. I put my daughter through college, put myself through law school, and all the while I was selling more than a million dollars' worth of real estate a year. Of course, that's very easy to do now with the price of houses, but at that time I was selling twenty-thousand-dollar houses, so it was difficult. I had sixty to sixty-five escrows every year, so that's a lot of real estate." She is now retired and living in one unit of her own lovely sixplex in Santa Monica.

After the WASPs disbanded, Ruth Woods stayed in the reserves for a while. "I probably would have stayed longer, but they wouldn't let us fly, and then they didn't have a unit in Dallas. I dropped out, but I kept flying at a little local airport that had a contract for Navy pilots—young Navy boys coming in. When I was teaching them I had two different occasions where they froze up on me, and I quit. On the second one, I wasn't sure I could regain control of the airplane! When I did, however, I went to the man who owned the school and said, 'That was my last one! Just figure my time and pay me.'

"After that I went to work for a man who was buying surplus planes and parts. He hired me to bid on surplus aircraft. It was fun for a while. Then I had to pick up an old Navy plywood amphibian, and I told the Lord, if he'd let me get that bucket of bolts back down to Dallas, I'd never make that mistake again. I told the boss what he could do with that airplane! This was a big amphib—I think a Grumman Goose. Finally he bought a PT-19 that had been sitting in the open for God knows how long. Its wings were full of holes and he wanted me to move it and I said I wouldn't. He asked, 'Why not?' 'Because I'm afraid the wings will fall off.' 'If you're going to work for me, you're going to move it.' I replied, 'Then I guess I'm not working for you anymore.' Well, he wouldn't fly it either! Later I moved a Ford Trimotor for a friend. We took it across town to Love Field. That was fun.

"After all that flying I just went to work in business. I retired as a vice president, facilities management, of my company, the Extrafair Title Company in Dallas. My sister was a vice president for Safeco Land Title. We were competitors. But, to be honest, I don't fly anymore; I can't afford the luxury." Ruth was in great spirits during our interview at her home on a lake in Mabank, Texas, and talking about buying a new boat. Only a few months later, however, she died of lung cancer. I hadn't even known she was ill.

Other WASPs were fortunate to continue, at least for a while, in flying jobs. Madeline Sullivan was lucky, she believes. "I went back to see my old buddies at United Airlines at La Guardia, and my old boss was a frustrated flier. He and the manager of the airport kept saying, 'We'll get you a job.' Sure enough, they got me a job with a Mr. Watts, who was looking for a copilot. This was for a feeder airline and he had one plane, a Lockheed Lodestar. The pilot's name was Lew Dates. They had a saying, 'If Dates is flying, get in the hangar, because something will fall down.' I took my first flight with him to Miami and we stopped at Atlanta. I noticed he was flying the railroads, in order to navigate. Well, coming back he starts to land, making a regular traffic pattern, but at the wrong airport. The tower keeps calling us—'632, will you flash your landing lights? We don't have you in sight.' (Of course they can't see us—we're at another airport.) He's so busy flying the plane he doesn't hear them. I'm trying to get his attention—we're on final approach, this is serious stuff!

Finally I give him a shove, he hears me and catches on. He pushes the throttle forward and we wobble across the field and finally gain altitude and find the 33rd Street airport, where we were supposed to land. That was just one of many episodes with Dave."

Madeline went on to say that she started keeping a spiral notebook recording all these near-tragedies with this pilot and finally discussed the problem with her brother, who had also been in the Air Force. Her brother's answer was this: "It's very simple, Mad, quit and live, or fly and die. You're not going to last much longer with this guy." She tried to resign, but her boss, Mr. Watts, said, "Don't, we've got so many complaints about this guy, he's going. There's nothing we'd like better than to give you the left seat (pilot), but I'm afraid it won't work."

"In those days," Madeline said, "it didn't even occur to me to try to push them. Because, too many times, when we'd stop and get out, somebody would say, 'There's a woman up there? I don't want a woman up there.' I just felt lucky to have the copilot's job. They did get another pilot, and he was nifty. I stayed with that job for a while until we started having a lot of trouble with maintenance. I finally quit. My husband was coming home and he kept writing me to quit flying. He had lost a brother flying. I really didn't fly after we started having children."

Madeline raised six children and later, when the Ninety-Nines (an organization of women pilots) arranged a trip to Moscow, in the late 1980s, she and Pat Pfister, another WASP, joined that group. Madeline and Pat were the only two WASPs to go to Moscow at that time. These women pilots met with a group of Russian World War II women pilots, who were dubbed "The Night Witches." [A book about them with this title, authored by Bruce Myles, has recently been reissued (Nonato, Calif.: Presidio Press, 1981).] Madeline had not heard about the book before and was "flabbergasted" to hear about it. These Russian women, the "night witches," had not only flown in World War II, but had flown combat, some without even the benefit of parachutes. Many of them were killed. I think it may have been Russia's best-kept secret. Madeline told me the American and Russian women pilots met in Moscow in a beautiful old home built in pre-Revolution days.

"I was impressed by how many of these women spoke English. Also, the meeting was very well organized, because those who did not speak English brought their own interpreters. Valentina, Russia's first woman in space, joined us and, at her suggestion, after the formal part of the meeting concluded, we broke up into small groups. I was able to meet one of the "night witches," Tanya, who had been a bombardier-navigator in World War II. Her interpreter was Wilsa, who was head of the magazine *Soviet Woman*, which is similar to our *Vogue*. She was very attractive, very nicely dressed, and very much in charge of all this. They had television cameras and reporters there.'' A group of WASPs also visited Russia during the summer of 1990. I hope this will become a regularly scheduled event so the women pilots of Russia and the United States can remain in touch.

Esther Noffke not only engaged in a lot of flying after the WASP, but she has remained in the aviation business right up to the present day. ''When I was at Kankakee, I saw the name Pal Waukee many times, and I liked the name. It's a contraction of Palatine Road and Milwaukee Avenue here in Chicago—Pal Waukee. I came up here but they had no openings for pilots at the time, so I started working in the shop. Then an instrument school was opened at Pal Waukee and we were the only ones giving instrument training in this area. We also had a Grumman Widgeon we used for multi-engine land and sea ratings. I taught all the ground school and did the Link training. I have been here ever since.'' Esther seems happy to still be around airplanes, and her life revolves around the airport business. Her only comment about this book on our class of WASPs—''I just don't want us to sound frivolous. We weren't frivolous; we were really serious.''

Other WASPs were able to keep up with flying even after December, 1944. Minkie Heckman was one. ''I joined a flying club at Westchester County Airport, New York, and they had a Cessna 140, a rag wing. That was a very nice airplane. I did some freelance instructing in the Civil Air Patrol. They also assigned me as a check pilot in the flying club and I was very pleased about that. I felt pretty important until one day I flew a man who wanted to be checked out. I was conducting this in a very businesslike manner and said, 'Okay, go ahead.' He took over and he flew that thing as I had never seen a Cessna flown before. [By then we had a Cessna 180.] Later I came to find out he was an Eastern Airlines pilot, but he didn't give me a hint beforehand.

''I did quite a bit of flying there. I put in about six hundred hours and had some wonderful times. When I moved to Massachusetts, however, I couldn't afford it anymore and had to drop it.'' Afterward, Minkie worked, for many years, as a laboratory technician and has now retired to Florida where she lives in close proximity to her sister in St. Petersburg.

Nellie Henderson was also fortunate in being able to keep up with her flying. ''Russ and I married and we lived in Cuero, Texas, which was just up from Aloe Field. He kept instructing there, so I went out to the little private airport in town where they were running a little air service. I flew nonflying personnel back and forth to San Antonio. I did a little instructing, also, which I wasn't qualified to do—but they weren't so fussy in those days.

''Then I heard about a little extra money I could pick up. Cuero was also the dumping grounds for old trainers. The Mexicans wanted these planes, so we were flying trainers down to them. These were discarded trainers, with no instruments, nothing: mainly single engines. You could get fifty bucks just for flying from Cuero down to the Mexican border at Brownsville. Then they'd have a bigger plane to bring us all back. Mexicans picked the planes up at Brownsville. Everyone who had a commercial license was flying planes to the Mexican border.

"These planes would smoke and shudder, but they would get up in the air and make it to the border. The ground was flat all the way down; if one conked out on you, you'd have a million places to land. It didn't worry me at all, but you should have seen the airplanes. Oh, my God! It was an easy morning's work. Then we moved to Lake Charles, Louisiana. I didn't do any more flying after that, and Russ didn't either." Nellie and Russ still live in Lake Charles.

Jean Moore came home from the WASP and earned her commercial license and then her instructor's rating. She worked for a man who owned a flight school and she instructed in Indianapolis for a couple of years. She taught on Aeroncas and Taylorcrafts. "They had about four or five hundred students and when I went to apply for the job, they were desperate for instructors. I instructed five years altogether and then married. Cliff, my husband, had two flight operations going and we had eight airplanes, but I wasn't instructing then. I was raising the kids. Then he had a heart attack and they took his license away. We sold the airplanes." Jean still flies occasionally with her son; she is retired and lives in Maitland, Florida.

Margaret Ehlers did not fly after the WASP, but she came back to it a bit later and for a strange reason. "People would ask me after I was out of the WASP, years later, whether I was still flying. I got quite impatient with telling them all the time that I wasn't flying, so in 1976 I decided to go to Gillespie Field, which is east of San Diego, to get my commercial license reinstated. Fred Breise, my instructor from Sweetwater days, was again my instructor. We started on a Monday and finished on Saturday. He signed my log book and said my commercial license was valid again!" Margaret and her husband live in Edina, Minnesota, and travel to Sierra Vista, Arizona, in the winter.

One WASP who has flown extensively since the deactivation is Ruth Petry. "When I returned home to Ithaca, New York, my brother had sold the Cub, so I bought another one and kept it for two or three years. Then I went to work in New York City and that's when I got into a soaring group. I belonged to a club there that had only eight members; two of the members owned Stearmans, and the club had two two-place sailplanes. Practically the whole membership could be in the air at the same time. I did quite a bit of towing with the Stearmans, and then I flew the sailplanes also.

"When I moved to Washington, D.C., I flew a little bit with a club there, but it was pretty far away. Then I went to Cleveland where I did practically no flying. At Ithaca, when I was back there for a short time, they asked Mary Strok, two other pilots, and me to ferry a bunch of planes from Oklahoma back to Ithaca. I needed a commercial license for that but I could just convert my military rating, which I did.

"Then I came out to Phoenix, Arizona, and the word had gone out that I had been towing back in New York. Phoenix pilots knew I was a tow pilot and they needed one. Soon they called. Joe Lincoln was the first. He came around and asked if I would like to check out in his airplane. I knew he wanted me to tow his sailplane. He was a wealthy guy. I would tow for him and, since I had a silver C badge in soaring, I could be his observer and could seal his barographs as well. This was a pretty good deal for us both. Then another guy, John Ryan, asked if I would like to check out in his Cessna. By that time, I had caught on to why they wanted me to fly their airplanes. When they wanted to fly in a contest, I'd take their airplane over for them and then crew for someone else. It worked out pretty well.

"We flew all different places—Turf Paradise, Deer Valley, Estrella. I got free flying. About seven years ago, though, I stopped." Ruth still lives in Phoenix, but she enjoyed many years of flying. She is still working as a technical editor for the Sperry Flight Systems group of Honeywell, Inc.

Mary Strok, who flew with Ruth in Ithaca, New York, engaged in no such extensive flying career. "As far as any flying experiences that I had after the WASP disbanded, precious few. By that time, I had been married, widowed, and had a small baby to care for. When my daughter was a few months old, I had a few ferry trips that turned out to be over a week long because of bad weather. We ferried PT-17s from Ponca City, Oklahoma, to Boston. The weather was atrocious. It was over the Easter holiday, and I was so homesick for my little girl! I was doing this for Herbert Peterson, the manager of our airport. Ruth Petry, Mary Peters, and I had a merry old time, though." Mary has done little flying since then, but she has recently renewed her interest in the WASP because of questions asked by her grandchildren. She now lives in Virginia.

Gini Dulaney attained her most successful achievements after her WASP adventures: she broke two records for women in gliding! When the war ended, Gini's husband, Clyde, was assigned to Hamburg, Germany. "In Germany, this gliding club was made up of Luftwaffe pilots and they were still under British rule. They didn't have their sovereignty and they weren't allowed to fly aircraft. They were only allowed gliders, and they were poor as church mice. They'd just lost the war. Clyde kept saying he was sorry I wasn't getting to fly, so he suggested, 'How about gliders?' I thought gliders were those open airplanes that went a few feet off the ground and landed. I had no idea they were like airplanes, but Clyde knew all about them.''

Gini took lessons from a friend of theirs who later became a world's champion glider pilot. Everyone at the glider field took turns trying to fly from Hamburg to Terlet, Holland, to set a distance record, but they hadn't been successful. Finally it became Gini's turn and the only glider available that day was a Spatz that was a small glider. It was new and hadn't been flown yet by anyone at the field. Since it was Gini's turn, however, she took it and headed for Terlet.

''I never did get up to the altitude I was supposed to. I knew my altimeter wasn't right because I was too low. I could practically see the mustache on the guy on the canal. I thought, 'This is too low.' I was fighting for thermals the whole time, but, I got there! I sweated that flight out for eight hours and thirteen minutes! When I finally called back to Clyde it was 8:30 at night. He got there around midnight. By that time the party had been going on. You can imagine. I didn't know it was a world's record at that point.'' Her second record was an altitude record. This record was actually the most renowned one. It broke one of Hannah Reich's records.

''Anything Hannah Reich did was news in Germany. She was their national heroine. I became headline news. American woman beats Hannah Reich's record! This was in 1957. It was really incredible. I was on Saturday-night television in Hamburg. It was the damnedest thing you ever saw. The house was full of flowers. Flowers and congratulations came from people we never heard of. At first it was kind of fun, but then it got boring, because we didn't have any privacy. The record I made was twenty-eight thousand feet gained altitude—gained over my release point which was about two thousand feet. We soared to about thirty thousand feet. My barograph was sealed before takeoff. Boy, do they control it. It records your altitude, you know!''

Gini put in a lot of time on gliders and told me that she'd never go back to airplanes again; gliders were such a challenge! She and husband Clyde now are retired and have homes in Hawaii and on an island off New Zealand.

After the WASP, Clarice Siddall earned her instructor's license. Then she instructed at her local airport in Alliance, Ohio. When she married and raised four children, flying was out for a while. ''Then I got back into it in 1975 when the children were grown. The Taylorcraft was built in Alliance, as you may know, and we have a club called the Taylorcraft Flying Club. Now we're flying Pipers, however. We have three: an Archer, a Warrior, and a Piper 140. The Archer has all the instruments. Actually, I am the only woman in the club, so they (naturally) made me secretary! I've enjoyed it, and I get free flying time because I do this job. We have about sixty people in the club: it's more recreation than anything else. Last year I flew up to Saranac Lake, New York, where I visited a friend at the lake. It's so much fun. Now we are required to have a transponder, a mode C, and map capability if you're going into controlled airports. The Archer has Loran, which is a computer; you put in your route and it gives you bearing, distance, altitude, and airspeed. You can't believe it!

"I never did get my instrument rating, though, because I was working. Now that I'm retired, it's another challenge. Maybe I will do that." Sid still lives in Alliance, Ohio, and still flies.

Marge Needham is another who managed to fly a lot after we disbanded. "I got a job right away, ferrying planes from the factory at Middleton, Ohio, to Lambert Field in St. Louis. This was for a company that was a distributor at Lambert Field. I guess they felt if I survived the WASP, I could do anything. Then I instructed at Embry-Riddle in Florida for eight years. We flew the Cessna 172, a four-place plane. I was a flight leader and I taught instruments as well. I've been instrument-rated since the WASP. Well, Embry-Riddle and I came to a parting of the ways. The man in charge and I did not get along.

"Then I flew some air shows around St. Louis, and I flew little gliders and sailplanes. It makes you a better pilot. You learn to pick up the thermals. In gliders, you are always descending. The secret is to find air that is going up faster than the glider is going down, in which case, of course, you gain altitude—but the glider is always descending. Also, my husband and I usually had a school someplace, called the Walker School of Aviation. He was an instructor too. We had schools in Louisiana, in Kansas, and here in Florida." Marge kept flying until not too long ago. Her health is not good now, but she remembers a lot about the old days, and it was nice to visit with her in Port Orange, Florida, where she has retired.

Another really active WASP was Joan Whelan. In spite of her arm injury from walking into the B-26 propeller back in Boise, she kept going. "Right after we got out, a cousin of my father's bought an airport up in North Dakota, on the Canadian border, that belonged to Northwest Airlines. It was an auxiliary field that they used for emergencies. He knew nothing about flying, but he wanted to start a flying school there, so he hired me to fly the airplanes, hire the staff, and start the school. It was very interesting.

"We had a Cessna and an Aeronca that we used for training. This was very good flying because all the boys were coming back from the war with money and there had never been an airport there. I was instructing from sunup to sundown, almost nonstop. We started in March and all through the summer we were flooded with students. It was fun, but in late October, it snowed, and the next morning snow was halfway up the hangar door. That was that; no more flying.

"That's when I came to California. I started instructing at Santa Monica airport and then went into instruments, working for an instrument school and instructing. I taught instrument flying to Claudette Colbert's husband. The wife of Edgar Bergen was one of my primary students at Santa Monica. I also taught Link. From there I went to a company that sold Beechcraft and Lear radio equipment. I demonstrated Bonanzas and Lear equipment. Then I was hired by a man who had a business in Chicago and lived in Beverly Hills, spending three weeks in Chicago and three weeks in Beverly Hills. He based his Bonanza in Santa Monica. I flew him from place to place; it was lots of cross-country flying and I loved it. We flew out of Chicago for three weeks, to New York or New Orleans. Then we'd come back to LA and fly out of here. I was still doing that after I was married. I quit, because we had seven children, and I didn't fly after that." Joan and her pilot husband have retired in Mission Viejo, California. Their home contains one room full of flying memorabilia, including some beautiful old photographs of their flying days.

Mary Ellen Keil, who was secretary for Class 44-W-2 for many years, now serves on the WASP Board as Director of Region I. Mary Ellen not only kept on with flying, but built up her own flying school in western Michigan with Marge Johnson, also from Class 44-W-2. Marge Johnson did not want to be interviewed, but Mary Ellen answered, "I think, in the first place, it—the WASP experience—changed almost everybody's life. I was going to go on and get my Ph.D. and become a college professor, but after the WASP all I wanted to do was to keep flying. Marge and I ran the school for six years. Both of us had business experience, so we were way ahead of the game. And because we were WASPs, we had a reputation and people came to fly with us once word spread. We also got a lot of GI trainees, because we started our school before the war was over. We both became ground school instructors in every subject. Engines was the toughest subject. We had a big operation—five airplanes of our own, and about sixty to seventy students at that time.

"There were just the two of us, and we worked sixteen hours a day, seven days a week. We made money; we just made it hand over fist. We started selling airplanes, and Marge was a natural saleswoman, and I guess I was too. We bought planes with money we saved during our WASP service. We started out with one airplane that had been wrecked, and about sixty or seventy students at a time. Soon we had an airport that was just over one hundred acres. By then we had five airplanes, but after six years Marge decided she had had enough of the hard work and long hours. We had to move airplanes in and out of hangars, change the planes from skis and back to wheels, keep the grounds up. At that time, I was afraid I would be called up in the reserves, whereas Marge wouldn't because she hadn't joined. Well, I bought Marge out and figured I should sell the inventory while I could. I sold all the planes, but I never did get called up.

"Then I read an ad about a company wanting aviation technical writers— someone with an English degree, so I applied. I was hired and they paid me a fabulous salary because of my good pay at the flight school. I wrote the pilot handbook for two of the Navy planes, the FJ-4 and the AJ-2P. That was an exciting experience, but I never saw the light of day, so I was unhappy with it. I went back to teaching school—elementary. What a struggle! Teaching elementary school was the only thing that was harder than flying the B-26. It took all my mental, physical, and moral strength to teach those kids. I taught the rest of my career, it was such a challenge! I taught fifth and sixth grades for twenty-five years.

"While I was teaching, I heard about a WASP who was instructing, and I went out and got recertified. Then this instructor, Marian Brown from class 42–2, and I started flying the races, which was a lot of fun. She asked me to fly with her in an international race to Managua, Nicaragua. We flew down—Marian had a Piper Comanche—and we had to wait a week to have the planes checked. This was at the time of Somosa, and all of the Ninety-Nines' women pilots who had entered the race were President Somosa's personal guests that whole week. He wanted us to come down there because the United States had just supplied Managua with their first large commercial airport. This was about 1967 or '68. Somosa was a very forward-looking man in many ways. He wanted to show Nicaraguans what the American women were doing. There were about sixty of us, and about forty planes. The race was from Managua to Panama City, Florida.

"Marian and I were in about fifth place and we were excited about it. She was a marvelous pilot. We started very early in the morning. Everything was fine until we got about fifty miles north of McAllen, Texas, near the border. Then, 'bang, bang, bang,' all eight cylinders went 'oof.' We were in mesquite country and we looked around, and right in front of us was a little landing strip— in the middle of nowhere! When we got out of the plane we saw a little path; I went down the path and ran across some Mexican cowboys. Their foreman spoke a little English and I spoke a little Spanish, so the foreman sent for a mechanic. They were cooking breakfast outdoors in huge iron skillets, so we had breakfast and found we were in the middle of the King Ranch! Well, we didn't win that race, but we had a marvelous time." Mary Ellen is now retired, living in Columbus, Ohio, and spends a lot of her time doing work for the WASP organization.

As for me, I earned my commercial license and my instructor and instrument ratings. I taught flying for a while at Rutland, Vermont, but it didn't pay

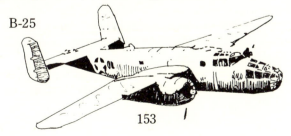

well, so I went back and worked in the payroll department of a plant that made airplane parts. When Jerry returned from overseas, we bought an Aeronca Champion and flew it around New England a while before heading for Minneapolis, where Jerry enrolled in a Ph.D. program in zoology. We raised five children, moving from there to Louisville, Kentucky, and eventually to Tempe, Arizona.

Our five children were born almost within five years and we were not wealthy. The task would have been formidable without super cooperation. Fortunately, I had married the right man for the job. Jerry changed diapers, washed dishes, and babysat. He encouraged me to go back to school and, with his help, I was able to earn both a B.A. and an M.A. degree in English. I returned to work and eventually became an editor of a publication at Arizona State University. I still get to fly because our daughter Wendy owns a Cessna and takes me up occasionally. Jerry and I are now retired and live in Flagstaff, Arizona.

For me, the greatest value from the WASP experience came from the opportunity to meet, and become friends with, my classmates—and later with other WASPs whom I meet at the biennial meetings. The interviews that I conducted for this book showed me some wonderful, exciting people. With each visit, I realized that I was privileged to look in on lives that seem to me extraordinary. As Mary Strok described them, "It was an enormous cross-section of women, and it was like nothing I had ever experienced before. It was a revelation. They came from all walks of life and were of all ages. They were terrific. There were women who flew on their own; women who flew professionally; women who were married and divorced; and those who hadn't gone to school. They were a marvelous group, all loving one single thing—flying."

I think that what we did back in 1943–44 was something that any woman could have done, given the ambition and drive that we had, but it was unusual for the time. I sincerely feel great respect for the accomplishments of these pilots, not only in 1944, but during the rest of their lives. Those I interviewed are still active, vital, and ready for new activities. All of them remember, with sorrow, our classmates killed in service, who did not live to complete the full lives that we have been fortunate enough to enjoy. We won't forget those friends, and perhaps history will not forget them either.

B-25

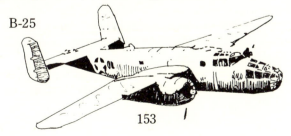

153

Epilogue

Young people of the 1990s, who have read this account, tell me they find it difficult to see how these WASPs could happily accept the adjustment from their flying careers back to their old roles as housewives and mothers. It was not an easy adjustment, as many have suggested, but it was accepted, and I suppose for many of us that was how it had to be! Our class does number two suicides, plus a few who do not want to talk about their WASP service, for whatever reason. It is true, also, that there were postwar propaganda posters saying, ''Thank you, women, for your war effort—we know you'll be happy to be home again.'' Not exactly what most of us had in mind.

My daughter Sally asked me, ''How can people go from living on the edge to cooking and sewing, without feeling mad or depressed? Some of the women seemed to think of the whole experience as almost illicit—off-limits to them but, because of the war, temporarily opened up to them. 'We were so lucky'— as though they had no legitimate right to fly! It was just a big joy ride. The keys were right there in the Porsche, and they took it for the spin of their lives, but of course it was only to be expected that they'd get caught and sent back to the station wagon!''

Well, back then things were really quite different from what they are now, in 1990. I can only report what really happened back in the forties, and how others viewed it, as well as myself. Arnold Toynbee tells us we are prisoners of our time and place. He said, in his essay ''Why I Dislike Western Civilization,'' that this is one of our human limitations. He adds, however, ''. . . It is characteristic of our human nature that we rebel against our human limitations and try to transcend them.'' We did rebel, I think, each in her own way, but perhaps it was a bit too much to expect that all of us would continue to rebel for the rest of our lives, although I think some 44-W-2 WASPs may still be considered rebels! I am glad, however, that I have children with whom I can discuss such topics as history, philosophy, and the changing times!

The WASPs, among their repertoire of songs, had one entitled ''Zoot Suits and Parachutes.'' One line of the song advised, ''If you have a daughter, teach her how to fly.'' I think we have taught our daughters how to fly, both in the literal and in the figurative sense, and they are flying higher than we ever could. Our granddaughters and our great-granddaughters, I can only assume, will fly ever higher—perhaps they will even reach the stars!

PT-19

Glossary

Aeronca

A small, high-winged fabric plane made by the Aeronca Company, similar to a Piper Cub. The earlier model was called a Champion and featured tandem seating. A later model was called a Chief and offered side-by-side seating.

Auxiliary Field

A field close by a large airport, usually with paved runway, used for practice flights.

B-4 Bag

Canvas luggage that converts to a hanger-type bag.

Barnstorming

Flying around the country, stopping at small air fields to present air shows or to give passengers rides.

Base Leg

Part of a flight's landing pattern; a short leg lying at right angles to, and downwind from, the landing strip. The base leg follows the downwind leg and precedes the final approach to landing.

Bays

Rooms within the barracks where WASPs were housed at Avenger Field. Each bay housed eight women.

Beam

A radio sound made up of a combined A (dot-dash) and N (dash-dot) Morse code sound, making a solid hum, which led a pilot to the airport runway.

Biplane

An airplane with double wings, one above the other.

Blackout	Unconscious state resulting from blood draining from the head to larger muscle groups in the lower body—caused by excessive "G" (gravity) forces experienced during some aerobatic maneuvers.
BOQ	Bachelor Officer Quarters
Buzzing	Flying aircraft fast, close to the ground, or close to some structure, a dangerous and illegal practice.
CAA	Civil Aeronautics Authority (Federal)
CAP	Civil Air Patrol. An organization formed in 1941 to help America during World War II. The CAP today is an all-volunteer civilian auxiliary of the Air Force.
"Cattle Wagon"	A large open-windowed van used, principally, to transport WASPs from the base to auxiliary fields.
"Cemetery"	In this book, a place where all the cracked-up aircraft were dumped.
Chandelle	An abrupt climbing turn of an airplane in which the momentum of the plane is used to attain a higher rate of climb. In this maneuver, the plane starts with a dive, gains speed, climbs, and turns to end in level flight facing 180 degrees in the opposite direction.
Commercial License	A federally issued certificate allowing a pilot to carry passengers for hire, or to haul freight.
Cone of Silence	The airspace above the intersection of four "beams" where no signal is heard. Usually this point lies at a beacon near an airport from which a pilot can find her way to the runway.
CPT Program	Civilian Pilot Training Program—a federal program to assist individuals in learning to fly.
Cross Controls	Rather than coordinating controls as in normal flying, a pilot can use opposing control surfaces to achieve a particular effect, such as a skid or a slip, or a crosswind landing.

Downwind Leg	Part of the traffic pattern, this first leg of the flight path parallels the runway opposite to the direction of landing.
Fence Hopping	A buzz maneuver where a pilot flies the plane so close to the ground she has to hop over any fences encountered—a dangerous and unauthorized maneuver.
Fifi	A logo designed by Walt Disney displaying an imaginary woman pilot named ''Fifinella.''
Final Approach	Last (third) leg of the flight pattern, where the pilot descends from pattern altitude to the runway, normally into the wind.
Flaps	A part of the aircraft control surface at the trailing edge of the wings which, when lowered, causes increased lift (and drag), thereby allowing the aircraft to fly more slowly. Flaps are used most commonly for landing.
Ford Trimotor	A unique old-time aircraft with three propeller-driven engines.
Grasshopper Pilots	Pilots of small aircraft during World War II who landed and took off from grass fields—hence, grasshoppers.
Ground Loops	A high-speed skidding turn of an aircraft on the ground after landing, usually caused by loss of control.
Horizontal Stabilizer	A fixed part of the tail section which helps stabilize the vertical axis, or pitch, of the plane.
Instructor's Rating	A federal rating requiring testing, that allows a pilot to instruct and sign for a student's flight time.
Instrument Conditions	When there is no visible horizon, or when the ceiling is lower than allowable for visual flying.
Instrument Rating	A federal rating allowing a pilot to fly legally in instrument weather conditions.

Lazy Eight	A maneuver requiring skillful coordination in which the airplane's nose patterns a figure eight sideways to the horizon.
Light Line	The line of lights on highways that is easily seen by pilots flying at night.
Link Trainer	A training device (now known as a "simulator") with actual aircraft instruments and controls that allow a pilot to practice instrument flying without leaving the ground.
Mixture Control	A control in the cockpit that allows the pilot to adjust the mixture of fuel and air in the engine.
Mothballed	A term used for old airplanes being put away for possible later use or sale.
Ninety-Nines	A very early organization of women pilots founded November 2, 1929 by Amelia Earhart and ninety-eight other women pilots at Curtis Field, Valley, Stream, Long Island. This prestigious organization is still in operation today and many WASPs belong to it.
"Pad" the Log	Adding flight hours not yet flown to one's log book (requiring collusion with flight instructor, to sign for the time).
Pattern	The three-sided pattern usually flown as an approach to landing at an airport: downwind leg; base leg; and final approach.
Piper Cub J-3	Best known of the old-time small, high-winged, single-engine aircraft, built by the Piper Aircraft Corporation.
Pitch	Up-and-down motion of the nose of the airplane over its lateral axis.
Pop-ups	Small sticks on the leading edge of the wings in some pursuit aircraft that showed the pilot the flap position.

Private License	A federal license given a pilot who has demonstrated sufficient skill to be allowed to carry passengers, but not for hire.
Prop Control	A control used in aircraft with variable-pitch propellers that regulates the pitch of the propeller blade.
Prop Wash	A wind caused by the spinning propeller of a plane, sometimes strong enough to be hazardous to aircraft taxiing or landing behind.
Ragwing	An airplane with wings covered with fabric instead of metal.
Redout	A state of semiconsciousness to unconsciousness caused by excessive negative ''G'' (gravity) forces experienced in some aerobatic maneuvers, sending too much blood to the head.
Slow Roll	A maneuver in which the aircraft is rolled about its longitudinal axis 360 degrees, returning to level flight, in a relatively slow and coordinated manner. This requires precise control if done properly.
Snap Roll	An abrupt rolling maneuver which is accomplished by pulling back the stick and rapidly applying full rudder in the direction of the desired roll. The result is a rapid horizontal spin called a snap roll.
SNAFU	Situation normal, all fouled up.
Spin	A maneuver where the aircraft descends vertically, spinning around the vertical axis of descent. If intentional, achieved by stalling the aircraft with stick full back and applying full rudder in the direction of the spin.
Stall	A condition of flight where the angle of attack exceeds the wings' capability to provide lift, thereby causing the nose to drop and the plane to lose flying speed—a function of nose attitude and airspeed which is also used in landing the plane.

161

Stick	A control device usually found in single-engine aircraft, which operates the ailerons and the elevators.
St. Elmo's Fire	A flaming phenomenon sometimes seen in stormy weather at prominent points on an airplane, a ship, or on land, that is in the nature of a brush discharge of electricity.
Student Pilot License	A federal license allowing a pilot to fly alone, but not to carry passengers.
Taylorcraft	Another brand of old-time, high-winged, fabric aircraft similar to the Piper Cub and the Aeronca, built by the Taylorcraft Company in Alliance, Ohio.
Vertical Stabilizer	The vertical section of the tail of an airplane to which the rudder is attached.
WAAC	Women's Auxiliary Army Corps
WAC	Women's Army Corps
WAFS	Women's Air Force Ferry Service
WASP	Women Air Force Service Pilots
WAVES	Women's Appointed Volunteer Emergency Service
Wind Tee	A large movable structure on the ground that indicates wind direction, also called a tetrahedron, and often shaped in the form of an airplane.
Wishing Well	At Avenger Field, large shallow water body where pilots were tossed after their first solo flight.
Yaw	An airplane's motion from side to side around its vertical axis.

Index